MW00560413

STORIED WATERS

35 FABLED FLY-FISHING DESTINATIONS AND THE WRITERS & ARTISTS WHO MADE THEM FAMOUS

DAVID A. VAN WIE

STACKPOLE BOOKS

Guilford, Connecticut

Published by Stackpole Books
An imprint of The Rowman & Littlefield Publishing Group, Inc.
4501 Forbes Blvd., Ste. 200
Lanham, MD 20706
www.rowman.com

Distributed by NATIONAL BOOK NETWORK
800-462-6420

Copyright © 2019 by David Van Wie

Photography by the author unless otherwise noted
Illustrations by Jill Osgood

All rights reserved. No part of this book may be reproduced in
any form or by any electronic or mechanical means, including
information storage and retrieval systems, without written
permission from the publisher, except by a reviewer who may
quote passages in a review.

British Library Cataloguing in Publication Information available

Library of Congress Cataloging-in-Publication Data available

ISBN 978-0-8117-3820-0 (paperback)
ISBN 978-0-8117-6821-4 (e-book)

∞™ The paper used in this publication meets the minimum
requirements of American National Standard for Information
Sciences—Permanence of Paper for Printed Library Materials,
ANSI/NISO Z39.48-1992.

To Cheryl, Rosa, and Garrett

Testament of a Fisherman

By Robert Traver, pen name for John Voelker

I fish because I love to;

because I love the environs where trout are found, which are invariably beautiful and I hate the environs where crowds of people are found, which are invariably ugly;

because of all the television commercials, cocktail parties, and assorted social posturing I thus escape;

because, in a world where most men seem to spend their lives doing things they hate, my fishing is at once an endless source of delight and an act of small rebellion;

because trout do not lie or cheat and cannot be bought or bribed or impressed by power, but respond only to quietude and humility and endless patience;

because I suspect that men are going along this way for the last time, and I for one don't want to waste the trip;

because only in the woods can I find solitude without loneliness;

because bourbon out of an old tin cup always tastes better out there;

because maybe one day I will catch a mermaid;

and, finally, not because I regard fishing as being so terribly important but because I suspect that so many of the other concerns of men are equally unimportant—and not nearly so much fun.

Permission granted by Kitchie Hill, Inc.

Contents

Preface

In my view, there is no clear line between literature and fly fishing.

Fly fishing is, by tradition, a literary sport. Fishing has long been synonymous with storytelling. After all, who hasn't heard a fish story?

And whether that storytelling is instructional, autobiographical, or purely fictional (some would argue that all fishing stories are fiction), writers have been entertaining readers for centuries with tales of rivers, streams, and ponds and the fish that inhabit them.

Fly fishing for trout is complex; it can take years to master the skills and tactics for catching fish. Most serious fly fishers rely, at some point, on books to help them learn a new technique, to understand the ecology of trout and their habitat, to glean tips about fishing in a new location, or to find encouragement and vicarious enjoyment during the winter months. Countless stories and articles have appeared in publications like *Field and Stream*, *Outdoor Life*, and *Sports Illustrated* during the golden age of magazines from the 1930s through the 1950s, and more recently in *American Angler*, *Gray's Sporting Journal*, and *MidCurrent*. Reading books and articles is a fundamental, or even unavoidable, part of fly fishing.

Of all the types of fishing literature, my favorites are the stories. Some tell of a singular conquest. Others are more about the characters and the place, or an unusual situation. The best stories transport readers in time and space so they can feel the water rushing around their legs, smell the ferns and cedars along the banks, feel the adrenaline rush when a trout takes the fly, or hear the good-natured ribbing from friends about the tribulations of this sport we all find so humbling.

The notion for this book started with a simple invitation: Come visit Uncles. It was no ordinary invitation. My heart raced when I read it. Uncles, I knew, was also called Frenchman's Pond, where John Voelker, one of my favorite writers, had built a camp on a famously secret, remote beaver pond on the Upper Peninsula of Michigan. Frenchman's Pond appears in a number of his beloved trout-fishing stories, written under the pen name Robert Traver in the 1960s and '70s.

Since Voelker's passing in 1991, the pond has remained in family ownership. When I contacted his daughter Grace V. Wood to get permission to reprint "Testament of a Fisherman," an immortal passage from her dad's book *Anatomy of a Fisherman*, she offered me the opportunity to visit and fish at Uncles with her husband, Woody.

As a longtime fly fisher and lover of great fishing stories, this was an offer I couldn't refuse. A chance of a lifetime. It was . . . about another dozen clichés and cringeworthy superlatives that have no place in a book

Spring arrives late on Michigan's Upper Peninsula, where blossoms frame John Voelker's Frenchman's Pond, also known as Uncles.

about fly-fishing literature. Bottomline: I realized I had to go, sooner than later.

"Take time by the forelock," Thoreau said, "Now or never! You must live in the present, launch yourself on every wave, find your eternity in each moment."

But the Upper Peninsula—the UP to the locals—is hard to get to, a long drive from Maine, where I lived at the time. My first thought was *Okay, Dave, you might as well fish your way there and back.* Then I started thinking about other fabled locations in fly-fishing literature between here and there: the Battenkill in Vermont, the Beaverkill in southern New York, the Poconos and spring creeks of Pennsylvania, the Ausable River in upstate New York, the Au Sable River in Michigan, and the Big Two Hearted River, also on the UP, in Hemingway's story of the same name. I realized that another one of my literary heroes, Aldo Leopold, had fly-fished on the

Alder Fork and the Flambeau River in Wisconsin in his classic book, *A Sand County Almanac.*

What if I were to go to all these places in one epic trip? I'd never get to see even half of them by visiting just one or two at a time. It would be the ultimate test of my fishing skills to try my hand in each spot, one after another.

Once this cockamamie idea took root in my head, it possessed me. What other writers and locations would I include? Friends willingly shared their favorite fly-fishing writers: Corey Ford, Louise Dickinson Rich, Edmund Ware Smith, Howard Frank Mosher, Charlie Fox, Jim Harrison, and many more. Each new suggestion created another possibility.

Before long, I'd mapped and scheduled an itinerary starting at Walden Pond—for obvious symbolic reasons—near Boston, across southern New England, New York, and Pennsylvania, up around the Great Lakes through

Wisconsin and the UP, back south through lower Michigan, east to the Adirondacks in New York, and across northern New England to the Maine Woods. Start with Thoreau and end with Thoreau. I hatched the plan for my wife one evening, and, bless her heart, she gave the all clear.

For practical reasons, I decided to stay east of the Mississippi. There are some fabulous locations and authors out west: Zane Grey celebrated the Rogue River in Oregon in the 1920s, Norman Maclean made Montana's Blackfoot River of the 1930s famous in his 1976 novella, *A River Runs Through It*, David James Duncan featured the Rogue and the fictional Tamanawis in his 1983 masterpiece *The River Why*. But those and other western

Fly-fishing literature is an impressive body of work. No matter how many books you read, there are always more to add to the pile.

locations and writers will have to wait for a future adventure.

My list of writers and candidate destinations got longer and longer. My stack of books to read grew to the ceiling like Jack's beanstalk. I reached out to friends and friends of friends along the route to ask for an afternoon or two of their time to help me out. Key dates over the six-week trip—during prime fishing time from mid-May to late June—fell into place.

An adventure like this required a balance between concrete plans and flexibility, so I left a few days blank on my calendar. Knowing I'd be posting stories, photos, and video to my blog and social media, I also built in blocks of time for writing and editing photos. And then there was all that driving: My initial estimate was about 3,300 miles, but that didn't include back roads, side trips, and late-night beer runs. I expected I'd stay one-third of the nights with friends, another third camping somewhere, and the rest in cheap motels.

As you might have guessed, the Storied Waters odyssey did actually happen, roughly according to plan, or you wouldn't have this book in your hands. Did it play out like I expected? Were the storied waters anything like I'd read in the stories? Did I catch any fish? Well, that's the very subject of this book: part travelogue, part literary history, part natural history, and part fishing porn.

I don't want to spoil the tale, so let's just say I had lots of fun and there was plenty to write about: dozens of very special places, some fine fishing, plenty of adventure, and interesting characters and new friends met along the way.

I hope you enjoy my Storied Waters adventure and that you learn as much as I did in making this remarkable odyssey.

Let's go.

- 1 -

Fishing for Inspiration at Walden Pond

Time is but the stream I go a-fishing in.
—Henry David Thoreau

Friday, May 12

Finally, the day of departure arrived.

I had packed and repacked the car, double-checking everything. Fly rods, waders, vest, wading staff. Check. Photography equipment. Check. Laptop, notebooks, small library of books. Check. Luggage packed with clothes for warm and cool temperatures. Check. Rain gear. Check. Cooler for snacks and cold beverages. Fly-tying kit. Check. Sleeping bag, tent, and fold-up cot. Yup. All set.

Confident finally that I hadn't forgotten anything important, I kissed Cheryl good-bye. 'Twas a long, lingering kiss and hug that would make our twentysomething children blush and groan had they been there to see me off. "Get a room!" our daughter Rosa would say.

One more squeeze and then I climbed behind the wheel and turned the key to start my journey.

Cheryl waved as I drove down the driveway, knowing it would be late June before I'd see our house again. Upon my return, our yard would be blooming with daylilies instead of daffodils. The afternoon was warm, so I opened the sunroof as I drove down our tree-lined road toward the sleepy village of Gray before turning south onto the Maine Turnpike. My first destination: Walden Pond in Concord, Massachusetts.

I had created a special playlist of songs for my six-week trip, each featuring a river or water or fishing reference, however tenuous the connection might be. "Nothing but Water" by Grace Potter and the Nocturnals. "The One That Got Away" by The Civil Wars. "Riverside Drive" by Ray Bonneville. "Waterfalls" by TLC. "Down Down the Deep River" by Okkervil River. "Many Rivers to Cross" by Jimmy Cliff. "Fisherman's Blues" by The Waterboys. And many more. As I reached cruising speed, I closed the sunroof and cranked the tunes. Two hours to Concord, estimated time of arrival: 5:15 p.m., just in time for a solid evening of fishing before dark.

After a slight delay in Friday afternoon traffic around Boston, I exited I-95 toward Minute Man National Historical Park. In under a mile, the road narrowed beneath the shade of tall trees. Apple blossoms were set off against a backdrop of subtle greens from the

1

The early evening sun reflects off Walden Pond in Concord, Massachusetts, on the first day of the Storied Waters adventure.

spring leaf-out. Historic buildings stood quietly, belying the fierce battle that occurred here during the American Revolution.

Two miles farther down the road, I turned left onto Walden Street and soon swung into the parking lot at the Walden Pond State Reservation, where lilacs were basking in the late afternoon sunshine, the first after several days of rain.

Norm Richter, a dear friend from college, met me at my car with a smile, a firm handshake, and an ice-cold Green Head IPA from a cooler in his car. Norm lives just minutes away in Lexington, and I would be staying

boy, he's come to love the outdoors and the mysteries of fly fishing.

"Welcome to Walden," he laughed, "and here's to a fabulous journey." We clunked cans. Now it was time to fish. Norm's rod was already rigged, so he cheerfully strung my rod for me while I put on my waders.

"You picked the right day to start your trip after all that rain. It's nice to see the sun again," he said. "And I'm excited to hear your plans. I hope to catch up with you next week in Pennsylvania on the way down to visit my dad."

"I hope so, too," I replied. "We'll have a few of our usual crew at Ed's place in the Poconos. And Lou [Zambello] will be joining us there, too." Our group of seven classmates had recently published a collection of "essays, art, and tall tales" about our annual fly-fishing adventures and our lifelong friendship in a joint memoir called *The Confluence*. The experience of writing that book had set off the chain of events that precipitated this unique journey I was just beginning.

Norm and I crossed the road and descended the long, steep stairs to the pond glimmering in the late day sun. Over a dozen fishermen dotted the sandy shoreline around its circumference like numerals on a clock. Two canoes and a small boat drifted languidly in the middle.

"Popular place!" Norm said. "I've ridden by here on my bike, but I've never been here to fish. They stock it with rainbows, browns, and brook trout, I hear. Let's see how it goes."

"Lou fished here once and said he hooked a couple rainbows on tiny midges, but it wasn't easy."

with him, his wife Pam, and younger daughter Annika for the night. Every June for over twenty years, Norm and I have been fly-fishing together with five other college classmates in northern New Hampshire at a place called the Second College Grant, which is owned by Dartmouth College. Wearing his trademark red ball cap, Norm is quick with a compliment or a wry remark. A self-proclaimed city

As Norm and I stepped onto the broad beach near the bathhouse, we saw several trout rising within casting distance of shore. We looked around, noticing that the beach near us was clear, and wondered aloud

Trout were rising steadily to midges on Walden Pond.

why no one was casting to the rises. Glancing around the shoreline, it appeared that everyone else was either bait fishing or spin fishing. We looked at each other, shrugged, and said, "Why not?" We'd have to watch our backcasts when the occasional walker ambled down the beach on their evening stroll. I waded out knee-deep, about fifty feet to Norm's right, and started making long, looping casts toward the rise rings ten to twenty yards out from shore, squinting—even with sunglasses—into the bright sun reflecting off the calm water.

Within minutes, Norm had a splashy strike on his dry fly, but his reaction was both too fast and too hard, and he missed the

cooperation from the picky trout, which had now moved out beyond our casting range, we decided to walk down the shore. We stopped here and there to chat with some of the bait fishermen waiting patiently for a strike. Soon we met a fellow fly fisher walking toward us on the beach, who said he'd had no luck fishing dry flies on the surface, which perhaps explained why we had the beach and rising fish to ourselves. He said he caught two brook trout beneath the surface on a Woolly Bugger, which looks like nothing in particular but seems to fool fish into thinking it's food. Not all fishermen tell the truth, of course, but this guy seemed trustworthy. Good to get some local knowledge.

In just over half an hour, Norm and I circumambulated the sixty-acre pond, stopping now and then for a few casts along the way, but still with no success. We passed the trail to Thoreau's cabin on the west end of the pond. There, just a few paces away, was the spot Thoreau had etched in history:

> I was seated by the shore of a small pond, about a mile and a half south of the village of Concord . . . but I was so low in the woods that the opposite shore, half a mile off, like the rest, covered with wood, was my distant horizon. (Chapter 2, "Where I Lived, and What I Lived For," *Walden; or, Life in the Woods*)

I told Norm that I planned to check out the cabin location the next morning when I had more time, as he and I had just a short time left to fish.

The sun was crouching behind the treetops when we returned to the swimming beach. Again, we both cast to rises, this time with Woolly Buggers beneath the surface. The fish continued to ignore our offerings. Such is the reality of fly fishing: Sometimes the fish

take. "You yanked it right out of its mouth!" I teased. *Easy for me to say*, I thought, given I hadn't yet had a strike.

Rise rings continued to appear one after another for over an hour as what appeared to be large fish sipped tiny midges from the surface. Neither of us could entice the trout to take our imitations of the hatching bugs. After a while, frustrated with the lack of are very picky, especially in clear, calm water, locking in on a particular bug. Sometimes they get spooked by our casting. And sometimes they're simply "not in the mood," as Robert Traver, the author whose secret pond I would be visiting in a few weeks, was fond of saying.

At 7:45 the park ranger walked down the stairs, bellowing through a bullhorn that the parking lot gate would close us in if we didn't leave by 8:00. Dusk is prime fishing time, but we didn't want to be locked in for the night. We were both hungry, so we headed to Lexington to grab dinner and a cold brew. Norm said that Pam and Annika had their own dinner plans, so we were on our own to catch up on life.

The restaurant seemed dark after an evening spent watching the sky change from blue to silver to gold. We sat at the bar and I told Norm I was making a point of sampling local or regional brews, so we ordered a couple 603 Brewery Winni Ales from nearby Londonderry, New Hampshire. As he munched his Cubano sandwich, Norm asked me how my spring semester had gone. I had been teaching environmental studies at the University of New England, and Norm was considering two prospective teaching positions at local universities, one a graduate class and the other for undergraduate students. "I love teaching," I said, "but the pay for adjunct faculty is pretty much minimum wage given the hours I put in."

"Yeah, teaching sure isn't the road to riches!" Norm said. "The schools get a bargain from those of us who want to give something back to the next generation."

The conversation shifted to my trip, which I had dubbed the Storied Waters Tour. Norm knew about my basic plan but was eager to hear more about the particulars—where specifically I would be going and who I planned to meet along the way. As an English major, an avid reader, and a writer himself, Norm appreciated my continuing obsession with authors from different eras, from Thoreau to Hemingway, Corey Ford, Howard Frank Mosher, and Edmund Ware Smith.

"I love that you're starting and ending with Thoreau," Norm said. "Those are proper bookends for a literary journey. But I'm curious to hear about your visit to Hemingway country in Michigan. Are you planning to fish on the Upper Peninsula, where Nick Adams went in 'Big Two-Hearted River'? I wrote a paper about that story in college."

"Yup," I replied. "Hemingway based the story on his own trip to the Fox River near Seney when he was just back from Italy, ya know. I think he was about twenty. I won't be the first to retrace Nick's journey, but I can't wait. Same with going to the Beaverkill, where Corey Ford and Sparse Grey Hackle fished. I think it'll be a kick to chase the spirits of all these writers and see what the rivers and ponds are like today."

"Man, I wish I could join you! But I'll settle for reading about it on your blog," Norm said as he pulled out his wallet and generously picked up the tab.

"I hope I'll have something worth writing about. Writing about great writers will be an interesting challenge. And I better catch some fish! Let's hope the weather cooperates. I sure don't want to hear six weeks of 'You should have been here last week!'" I laughed. Those are the seven words you hate to hear when you are fishing.

After dinner, we drove the several blocks to Norm's house. We entered to loud music playing as Annika and a friend were dancing in the living room to "Getaway" by Saint Motel. I got a hug from Pam (whom I call the Woman Who Never Ages). "I'll add that song to my playlist. 'Getaway' seems appropriate enough," I said, after the girls turned off the music and headed upstairs.

In a nod to John Voelker, Norm poured me a bit of bourbon, and again we toasted to a successful trip.

"Ha! As you guessed, one of my dreams—among others, I suppose—is to drink 'bourbon out of an old tin cup' when I get to Voelker's cabin at Frenchman's Pond. We'll see."

"Yeah, that's a great line," Norm replied. Voelker wrote under the pen name Robert Traver. He is revered by generations of anglers for his exemplary fishing stories and, of course, "The Testament of a Fisherman" is sort of the Lord's Prayer among the fly-fishing faithful. Voelker's most famous book was *Anatomy of a Murder*, which was made into a movie starring Jimmy Stewart, George C. Scott, and Lee Remick.

This extended fishing and literary adventure was sparked by an invitation from Voelker's daughter Gracie after I contacted her to ask permission to reprint "Testament" in our book, *The Confluence*. Her kind offer to show me her dad's "secret" spot got me thinking about other fabled fishing settings in literature. Soon I was daydreaming about other famous fly-fishing locations that I wanted to visit.

"You'll be going to the Northeast Kingdom in Vermont, right?" Norm asked. "It was so sad to hear that Howard Mosher had passed away. I just finished reading some of his stories."

"Yeah, I was heartbroken!" I replied. "I really wanted to meet him after he was nice enough to review our book. I wanted to hear how he created the Kingdom River as a blend of the real rivers around Irasburg. I'm heading up there anyway. I'm trying to connect with a friend of his who'll show me around and hopefully catch a few fish."

We raised our glasses to Howard, a fearless writer and devoted fly fisher. He was one of the best.

It had been a fun and memorable evening. Norm set up the coffeemaker and showed me to my room. I planned to be up early to seize the day by fishing Walden Pond at sunrise. I had one more shot at landing a fish on my first stop. With a full family schedule on Saturday, Norm elected not to join me on my predawn excursion. I slept soundly with visions of rising trout in my head and rose quietly before dawn to slip out of the house while everyone else was asleep.

I had read *Walden* at some point in college and more recently skimmed through sections of *The Maine Woods* when a friend brought a copy along on a fishing weekend. Both of those narratives elevated my opinion of Thoreau, but he remained a dense and often bewildering voice. Most people are more familiar with pithy Thoreau quotes than with his full-fledged writing. When I decided to start my trip at Walden Pond—considered by many to be the birthplace of American nature writing—I realized I needed to study up a bit about Thoreau and his time at Walden Pond. So, I kept reading, and in April, when I was traveling to Boston on other business, I visited the good folks at the Walden Woods Project/The Thoreau Institute to learn more about Walden Pond and Thoreau's body of work.

The Walden Woods Project (WWP) is a not-for-profit organization whose mission is to "preserve the land, literature, and legacy of Henry David Thoreau to foster an ethic of environmental stewardship and social responsibility." They own about 170 acres in Walden Woods, the unique sandy pine forest and hills surrounding the pond, where they maintain hiking trails and conduct educational programming. WWP does not manage

Henry David Thoreau. INK WASH AND CHARCOAL
DRAWING BY JILL OSGOOD

the actual pond, however, which is part of the Massachusetts state park system.

I was fortunate to meet with Matt Burns, the conservation director at WWP, who explained some of the ecological and water-quality challenges at Walden Pond, which is in a fairly developed suburban area and gets over 600,000 visitors per year who walk the shore and trails, and swim in the clean water. Thanks to the Walden Pond State Reservation and the Walden Woods Project, over 80 percent of the forested land around the pond is protected, so the water quality in the pond has remained very good. Perhaps the biggest water-quality issue is the thousands of swimmers who pee in the water, adding too much nitrogen to the natural water chemistry. I bet Thoreau would be surprised!

Walden Pond itself is a geological marvel: a sixty-acre kettle pond created when a huge chunk of glacial ice, half buried in deep deposits of sand and gravel, melted at the end of the last ice age, leaving a deep hole that filled with water. Only a few hundred yards in diameter, Walden Pond is over one hundred feet deep. Thoreau, being a surveyor among other things, created a detailed map of the pond, including depth soundings along eleven transects. He spent many days studying the pond's flora and fauna, documenting when leaves burst from their buds, flowers blossomed, and birds returned. His detailed observations and phenological data are now being used by scientists to study climate change; for example, we know that budding now occurs earlier than Thoreau's observations 175 years ago.

Matt Burns mentioned, however, that the pond was treated in 1968 with the pesticide rotenone to kill all the nongame species of fish because the state fish and game department wanted to stock the pond with rainbow trout and brown trout. This kind of bone-headed "let's improve on nature" attitude was prevalent in the 1960s and '70s—even at Walden Pond, of all places.

Fortunately, the perch, pickerel, pumpkin-seeds, and hornpout (bullhead) that were there in Thoreau's time have been reestablished and can still be caught along with rainbows, browns, and brook trout, plus smallmouth and largemouth bass that have been stocked over the years. Matt also noted that Walden Pond is now home to an invasive freshwater jellyfish, *Craspedacusta sowerbii*, originally from China, and reportedly an invasive softshell turtle. The pond still faces formidable challenges from invasive species and other threats but now supports a diverse aquatic community. And excellent fishing for a suburban pond, thanks to regular stocking.

I have found no clear evidence that Thoreau actually fly-fished. In *Walden*, he tells of going "a-fishing" at midnight and seems content to fish with worms. In *The Maine Woods*,

Thoreau seems as happy to catch and eat fallfish (he called them chivin; we derisively call them chubs today) as he does salmon. But most of his fishing on that trip was done with alder sticks cut streamside. Thoreau was no split-cane rod snob, that's for sure, but I suspect he must have at least tried fly fishing, which was practiced during his lifetime. Perhaps he cast a fly or two as a scientific inquiry, or watched someone casting and asked if he could give it a try. I've found nothing about it in his writing.

If Thoreau had been an avid fly fisher, we would all know it. He would have filled several volumes of his journal with commentary about how fly fishing is morally and spiritually superior to . . . well, you get the picture. We all know fly fishers who sport a massive superiority complex, so let's just say, "Why would Thoreau be any different than the rest of us?"

He certainly was fascinated with water and fish. In all his essays, he described the rivers, streams, and ponds that he visits in reverent detail. In his first book, *A Week on the Concord and Merrimack Rivers*, Thoreau devoted much of the early chapter titled "Saturday" to talking about the many species of fish that inhabit the rivers. He also lamented how humans have impacted sea-run fish, notably salmon, shad, and alewives, that were blocked from ascending the river, even in the 1840s, by a dam at Billerica.

"Poor shad! Where is thy redress? When Nature gave the instinct, gave she thee the heart to bear thy fate? . . . Who hears the fishes when they cry?"

Thoreau wrote the first draft of *A Week on the Concord and Merrimack Rivers* while living at Walden Pond from 1845 to 1847 (he wrote *Walden* a few years later and published it in 1854.) *A Week* was, among other things, a paean to Henry's dear brother, John, who paddled with him on that literal and metaphorical journey in 1839 (which actually took two weeks) before John tragically died in Henry's arms of tetanus only three years later. John's death deeply affected Henry, so his first book was very important to him, even though it didn't achieve the success of *Walden*.

The scholars at the Walden Woods Project also noted that one of the most famous Thoreau quotes about fishing is actually misattributed. Thoreau never said, "Many men go fishing all of their lives without knowing that it is not fish they are after." That passage was innocently penned by Michael Baughman in his 1995 book *A River Seen Right* apparently to paraphrase a passage from Thoreau's journal about ice fishing for pickerel. Baughman wrote:

"I think it was in Walden where he wrote that a lot of men fish all their lives without ever realizing that fish isn't really what they're after."

What Thoreau did say is this (in his journal on September 26, 1853):

It is remarkable that many men will go with eagerness to Walden Pond in the winter to fish for pickerel and yet not seem to care for the landscape. Of course it cannot be merely for the pickerel they may catch; there is some adventure in it; but any love of nature which they may feel is certainly very slight and indefinite. They call it going a-fishing, and so indeed it is, though perchance, their natures know better. Now I go a-fishing and a-hunting every day, but omit the fish and the game, which are the least important part. I have learned to do without them. They were indispensable only as long as I was a boy. I am encouraged when I see a dozen villagers drawn to Walden Pond to spend a day in fishing through the ice, and suspect that I have more fellows than I knew, but I am disappointed and surprised to find that they lay so much stress on the fish which they catch or fail to catch, and on nothing else, as if there were nothing else to be caught.

And thus, the famous (mis)quote has taken on a life of its own, particularly among fly fishers and especially on the internet. A key lesson learned from my visit is that much of what we "know" about Thoreau is as much folklore as it is scholarship. And that there is much more to fishing than catching fish.

Thoreau's writing influenced other environmental writers and thinkers, including John Muir (founder of the Sierra Club), Gifford Pinchot (founder of the US Forest Service and advisor to President Teddy Roosevelt), and Aldo Leopold (author, professor, and cofounder of the Wilderness Society). Muir even visited Walden Pond in 1893 and laid flowers on Thoreau's grave in Concord's Sleepy Hollow Cemetery. I made a mental note to ask about Thoreau's influence on Dr. Leopold when I visited the Aldo Leopold Foundation in Wisconsin later in my trip. After leaving Walden, I would not be leaving Thoreau behind.

Saturday morning, May 13

Saturday morning, I was up at 4:45, made coffee, ate a bowl of cereal, and snuck quietly out of Norm's house before the 5:30 sunrise. Matt Burns had suggested I get to the pond at first light, as that would be the quietest time. By 8:00 a.m., swimmers would arrive to do long laps across the pond, which would make fly fishing more of a challenge.

When I walked down the stairs to the pond shortly before 6:00 a.m., there were already a dozen fishermen around the perimeter and two boats sliding through the mist: a green canoe and a red fishing platform rig with an electric motor. Busy place at such an early hour!

The trout were rising sporadically in about the same place near the beach, but again I had no luck. I tried tiny midges on the surface, a few big attractor patterns with a midge on a short outrigger line as a separate option for the fish, and then a handful of streamers, including the touted Woolly Bugger. Nada. Zip. Zilch.

After forty minutes or so, I noticed that the area to my right looked shallow enough to wade farther out from shore. *Perhaps I can reach the rising fish from out there*, I thought. I moved down the shore. As I waded slowly and quietly in the calm, clear water, I noticed several large dark-colored fish cruising along a submerged sandbar. I quickly realized that these were male smallmouth bass building and defending their nests! The larger females would likely be prowling around, looking for a strong, industrious mate for an amorous hookup.

Now, the rising trout were the furthest thing from my mind. I was using a 4-weight rod with floating line, so I pulled a tiny bass popper out of my vest (yes, I had anticipated this possibility) and tied it on the leader. I cast the "fly"—a tiny frog imitation about the size of a pencil eraser with rubber-band legs—out ten yards, picked it up, and cast it again a little farther.

On the second cast, WHAM!—one of the bigger bass I've ever caught slammed it and quickly leaped into a tail walk, coming down with a flop. I realized the fish was well hooked, so I reached into my front wader pocket to pull out my iPhone, flicking on the camera with one hand, while playing the bass with the other. This was not easy but the result was worth it: a short video and a few good photos of my first fish caught on the Storied Waters adventure. Not a bad start!

My first fish of the trip was a smallmouth bass that slammed a surface popper on Walden Pond.

When the thrill of the catch had subsided, the chill of the morning permeated through my multiple layers of clothing, so to warm myself I walked down the trail toward the site of Thoreau's cabin, which Norm and I had passed the evening before. The location of the cabin is marked with granite monuments. The pond is visible from there through the tall trees. For some, this would be the end of a pilgrimage, but it marked the start of mine. Inspired by its place in our intellectual history and national mythology, I had to wonder how many others come to this celebrated sanctuary with a fly rod (or in my case, two fly rods) in their hands.

Thankfully, I had the moment there to myself. I recalled another favorite Thoreau quote—"I love to be alone. I never found the companion that was so companionable as solitude"—which is echoed in Voelker's "Testament of a Fisherman": "because only in the woods can I find solitude without loneliness." I soaked in the solitude for a few moments then followed the path originally worn by Thoreau's feet from his cabin door back down to the pondside.

In the cove near the cabin site, I caught another bass, smaller than the first. As I worked my way down the shore, the open-water swimmers were starting their laps in the pond in their wetsuits and bathing caps. Two were swimming close to shore, making it tough to cast. I didn't want to hook a human, so I decided it was time for coffee before moving on to my next stop in Vermont.

Back at the parking lot, I came across Peter Hoffman, the park supervisor, getting in his truck. We had traded emails, so he knew that I was starting my trip that day and had been keeping an eye out that morning for a fly fisher with Maine plates. Peter has been fishing at Walden since he was a kid. It was fun to hear his stories about how the park's visitor patterns had changed over the years, creating inevitable conflicts among users. More open-water swimmers and shore walkers today make it tougher for anglers, as I had experienced firsthand. Soon Peter had to go, so we shook hands and wished each other well. "Glad you caught something here at Walden!" he said as he drove off.

I didn't bother to break down my rods. In fact, I wouldn't do so for the entire six-week trip. The car warmed me up as I looped through Concord to get coffee and a pastry. I drove past Ralph Waldo Emerson's house (Thoreau lived with Emerson's family for a while), the Thoreau-Alcott house (Thoreau lived and died in the house; Louisa May Alcott purchased it in 1877), and the grassy park at the confluence of the Assabet and Sudbury Rivers, which join to become the

Where & How—Walden Pond

Access: Access is not a problem, but parking can be a challenge when it's crowded or when Walden Pond State Reservation is closed. There is paid parking at the visitor center near the main beach. Early in the morning or after dusk may require some creativity. I parked in the gift-store lot early in the morning and left before the store opened. The entire shore is walkable, depending on the water level.

What Works: Walden Pond is very deep. The water is clear and clean, and the pond is heavily stocked, mostly with rainbow trout. Most people fishing the shoreline for rainbows use bait and bobbers or spinning gear. I heard one fellow who caught a rainbow on a spinning lure say the fish's stomach was full of midges.

Canoes and pontoon boats with electric motors can be launched from a boat ramp. Gasoline motors are not allowed. According to the fly fishers I spoke with that evening and observed the next morning, the go-to gear is a sinking line or sinking-tip line and a Woolly Bugger or streamers, either trolled or cast from shore.

The rainbow trout rise to midges and small flies near shore during low light but are difficult to take on the surface, especially when the water is choppy. Lou Zambello, author of *Flyfisher's Guide to New England* had success with midge emerger patterns size 20-24 and a tiny Elk Hair Caddis size 20 on a long 6X leader.

Mid-May is spawning and nesting time for bass. Bass will rise through several feet of water to take small poppers on the surface with gusto. A crayfish fly pattern, such as Dave Whitlock's classic NearNuff Crayfish pattern or May's Clearwater Crayfish from Orvis, retrieved near the bottom is also a good choice with smallmouth or largemouth bass when the fish are in deeper water. ∎

Concord River. Here, just above the Concord battlefield and the Old North Bridge, Thoreau had launched his canoe for the two-week adventure with his brother, John.

No, I didn't cast a fly in the river. Maybe I might have hooked a pickerel or a chivin, but I was discouraged to see a sign warning of mercury contamination in fish in the Sudbury River. Not that I'd eat my catch either, but I preferred to stick with cleaner waters. I simply paid my respects to Henry's immortal spirit, and his brother's, before moving along.

Thirty minutes later I was motoring west on Route 2, leaving the Boston 'burbs behind.

My plan was to drive the three hours to Manchester, Vermont, before the heavy rain forecast for the evening arrived. I would be staying with Bill McLaughlin, president of Orvis and a fellow Dartmouth alum, and his wife Martha. Bill and I had fished together the previous June at the Dartmouth Grant in northern New Hampshire. I sent him a text message to let him know I was on my way.

As I crossed into Vermont, Thoreau's words again came to mind: "We need only travel enough to give our intellects an airing." On I went, seeking to air my intellect. With my first stop at Walden Pond, my grand excursion was off to a fine start.

- 2 -

Big Water on the Battenkill

Saturday afternoon, May 13

After leaving Walden Pond, where Thoreau "lived deliberately" for two years, two months, and two days, I traveled on to Manchester, Vermont, where Charles F. Orvis founded the Orvis Company about a decade later in 1856. Orvis and his brother Franklin, owner of the Equinox Hotel, were consummate promoters of tourism to the area. As the reputation for Orvis fishing tackle grew, the Battenkill, which flows through Manchester and Arlington, Vermont, into New York, became world-famous. Both Orvis and the Battenkill have been icons of American fly fishing ever since.

It's funny to think of Thoreau and Orvis as contemporaries. Who knows if Charles Orvis ever read *Walden*, which was published in 1854? Thoreau never trekked to Vermont. The closest he came was Mount Greylock in northwestern Massachusetts near Williamstown in 1844. I'm guessing Orvis, who lived until 1915, would have read *Walden* at some point, as the book was well-known in his lifetime. I also guess that Thoreau would have enjoyed fly fishing had he been given fly-casting lessons by Mr. Orvis himself on the Battenkill.

I had read a story about the Orvis company in *Forbes* magazine a few days before my departure. I was especially impressed to learn of Orvis's «50/50 by 2020» initiative, run by Jackie Kutzer, to get more women involved in fly fishing. I was looking forward to meeting Jackie and her husband, Pete Kutzer, the star of many Orvis fly-casting instructional videos. Bill McLaughlin, my host in Manchester, had arranged for Pete to be my guide Sunday while fishing on the Battenkill.

The Hudson River valley was settled by the Dutch West India Company in the 1600s, so they named streams in the area with the Middle Dutch word *kill*, meaning " stream" or "brook," such as Poesten Kill, Quacken Kill, and, of course, the other "kill" renowned among trout anglers, the Beaver Kill. Some maps say Batten Kill River, which is sort of redundant, and many writers combine the name and simply say Battenkill or Beaverkill, which is what I will call them.

I rolled into Manchester on Saturday afternoon just in time to fish for an hour before dinner with Bill on the upper Battenkill. A tall, soft-spoken man who came to Orvis in

Bill McLaughlin ties on a fly on the upper Battenkill near Manchester Center, Vermont.

2015 from Minnesota, he and Martha met when they both attended the Tuck School of Business at Dartmouth College in Hanover, New Hampshire, where Bill first learned to fly-fish. After several decades of fly fishing, he modestly commented, "I'm still learning." My response: "Aren't we all?"

Fortunately, the expected rain held off. Bill took me to an area called the Pig Farm less than a mile from their house, where the stream was narrow and meandering and fairly shallow with some deeper-cut banks that looked like they could hold bigger fish. The water was clear and cold, so we were both feeling optimistic. This section holds both native brook trout and wild brown trout. Brown trout, sometimes called German browns, were introduced in North America in the late 1800s. They reproduce in the wild here but aren't truly native. Browns can tolerate warmer water than brook trout, so they are especially desirable in waters that do not support brook trout. They can grow to be several pounds, and are more wary and challenging to catch. Browns are the predominant quarry in the lower part of the Battenkill and across much of southern New York, Pennsylvania, and Wisconsin.

We started by sneaking up on some deeper pools, making long casts with dry flies toward the overhanging willows that were just starting to leaf out. When that didn't yield any response, I tried swinging some wet flies and streamers in the current. Basically, I had no idea what to do in this section of the stream, so I tried a little bit of everything.

This part of the river is beautifully described in Margot Page's remarkable collection of twelve essays called *Little Rivers: Tales of a Woman Angler* (1995; new edition 2015), which will transport you right into the cold water at twilight in May as brown trout sip hefty Hendrickson mayflies. Bill and I enjoyed similar conditions, except for the Hendricksons and the sipping brown trout.

In her stories, Page tells how she fell in love with fly fishing and a particular fisherman with whom she shared the upper Battenkill (as a "fishermom") while she and her husband raised a young daughter, aptly name Brooke. It's worth pointing out that Margot Page may have inherited her writing skill from her grandfather, the late, great story-teller Alfred W. Miller, better known to many of us by his nom de plume, Sparse Grey Hackle, who wrote the 1971 classic *Fishless Days, Angling Nights*. Page has also earned a special place in fly-fishing history, working for six years as editor of *The American Fly Fisher*, the journal of the American Museum of Fly Fishing in Manchester. Her stories in *Little Rivers* add a depth and extra dimension to the experience of fishing the Battenkill. Here is a sample of her writing:

Margot Page. INK WASH AND CHARCOAL DRAWING BY *JILL OSGOOD*

A patient parade of cows backlit by the sun passed above me on the bank while I was midstream, the rust and yellow mountain ridge looming behind them. The light illuminated their whiskers so each hair was outlined and the drizzle hanging from their mouths glistened. They plodded gently past me, one by one in the afternoon light, slowly heading toward milking relief, occasionally glancing curiously at me, several stopping to stare and sniff the breeze with their huge moist noses.

Oh yes, then there was the light on the water. The twinkling prisms and diamonds that hypnotize and blind you, seducing you into believing for just an instant or two that the world is timeless.

Despite Bill's and my enthusiasm, no trout reciprocated our earnest efforts to connect on a more personal level, but we enjoyed being serenaded by a variety of warblers that were chirping while searching for bugs in the vegetation along the river banks. Before we knew it, it was time to return to the house for dinner. Bill and I drove past a few cows on the way home to dinner, and the evening light on the water had been muted with the oncoming weather. Yet, Page's pastoral scene is certainly indicative of what we witnessed on our first evening on the Battenkill.

Back at Bill's and Martha's place, we washed up, sat down for some appetizers, and were soon joined by Pete and Jackie Kutzer. Pete is literally a larger-than-life character. He is six feet eight inches tall and every bit as ebullient and knowledgeable about all things fly fishing as the Pete who appears in dozens of Orvis fishing videos. Jackie's star burns just as brightly. With long auburn hair and a sparkling smile, she matches Pete's presence and energy despite the fact that he seems to be about twice her size.

Pete entertained us before dinner by tying a couple of big streamer fly patterns we would use on Sunday morning: a weighted woven sculpin pattern and a rabbit-fur Zonker called the Battenkill Bastard. While downing a Long Trail Double Bag ale, he tantalized us with tales of the big browns he had caught the week before, all in the 20- to 24-inch range. I tried not to let my expectations get too high. This is fishing after all. You hope for the best but know that getting skunked, as we had been that evening, happens to the best. And, yes, it did feel already like "you should have been here last week" could well be an issue for me.

Dinner was a delightful affair with many a fish tale told, highlighted by Pete's and Jackie's stories about fishing for striped bass before and after their wedding the previous June on Cape Cod. All too soon it was time to say goodnight. Pete said he'd come by in the morning to take Bill and me out to the river.

Sunday morning, May 14

Rain drummed steadily on the roof overnight, but stopped while we were having breakfast, shortly before Pete arrived at 10:00 a.m. I climbed into Pete's truck while Bill followed behind in his Subaru as he was planning to head to the office after an hour on the river. Our first stop was a stretch of water near the Arlington Recreation Park, just below the confluence of the Battenkill and Roaring Brook. The water level in both streams had come up and was running fairly high, fast, and a little milky. Pete put a positive spin on the situation, noting that there was still enough visibility for the big browns we were stalking to see our fly from ten feet away.

Pete kindly provided me with a sweet 7-weight Orvis Helios 2 rod (bigger water, bigger fish, bigger rod) rigged with a sinking-tip line and the weighted sculpin fly that he

had tied the night before. My challenge was to roll cast that bad boy out into the current and swing the streamer back to the near bank. Pete then went downstream a piece with Bill to get him set up before coming back up to check on my casting, which felt and, I assumed, looked awkward because of the heavy fly.

Pete was patiently teaching me a circle roll cast and giving me pointers when I managed to hook a big brown as Pete looked on. I felt the rod bend as the fish gave my fly a few good shakes before I lost him. I had allowed the line to go slack for just a second while trying to take in the extra line on the water and put the fish on the reel. And in just a few seconds, the fish was gone. A rookie mistake with a big brown, I now know. "Let him put himself on the reel," Pete advised, after the fact. The expression on Pete's face told me that I had probably blown the only chance I'd get all day. Oh well. But a valuable lesson that I would remember later in the trip.

We continued to flog that pool for another thirty minutes, but no more strikes. As we walked back to the vehicles, Bill said he was heading to the office and left me in Pete's expert and patient care. He and I continued on to a place known locally as Hazardous Waste Pool because of some discarded trash visible on the far side. "It's not really hazardous," Pete assured me, "but the nickname is colorful and has stuck around."

Here, again, wading in high water up to my hips was, shall we say, exhilarating. Less so for Pete. He waded confidently into the current, the water barely at mid-thigh, and cast long, strong loops toward the far bank. I cautiously drifted my fly along the near bank, worried that I'd be swept away if I stumbled a few more feet into the river. When he returned, Pete reported that he'd felt a few taps on his streamer, but no solid takes. I had nary a

Pete Kutzer braved the deep, fast water to demonstrate his casting prowess on the Battenkill near Arlington, Vermont.

nibble, but was having a blast watching Pete casting skillfully in live action.

Finally, we ended the morning at the Keenan House pool in Arlington off Route 313, where the river turns right to head west into New York. This stretch is as picturesque as a Norman Rockwell painting. This is no coincidence, because Norman Rockwell lived nearby and painted in the area from 1939 to 1953, while casting flies himself on the Battenkill in his free hours. During the same period, illustrator and fly-tying artist Jack Atherton lived in West Arlington and often fished the Battenkill with Rockwell. Atherton wrote and illustrated *The Fly and the Fish* (1951), a mostly forgotten classic about fishing in Vermont. I'm sure Rockwell and Atherton fished the very pool where Pete had me casting streamers and hoping for a big strike.

Lee Wulff also lived downstream from Rockwell just across the New York border in Shushan. Wulff later became one of the most famous fly fisherman in 1960s America with his movies and TV shows featuring fly-in adventuress from Alaska to Newfoundland. One night in 1943, Rockwell went to hear Wulff speak at a local high school about one of his fishing adventures. Afterward, Wulff, Rockwell, and another friend returned to Rockwell's studio in Arlington to chat. Later that night, the studio caught fire, apparently from ashes carelessly dumped from his famous pipe. Rockwell lost a number of original paintings, costumes, and props. A few days later, he bought a historic house in West Arlington, which is now a quaint inn. Rockwell later moved his studio to Stockbridge, Massachusetts.

Where & How—Battenkill

The Battenkill is one of the world's most famous destinations for trophy-size brown trout. The New York portion is stocked, but the Vermont portion is all wild fish, with over twenty miles of water from Manchester to the New York border offering a wide variety of water conditions requiring different tactics. John Merwin's book *The Battenkill* is the ultimate reference. With all the pressure this river gets, the fish have become picky and well educated. But if you hook one, it is likely to be a memorable fish.

Upper Battenkill: The upper river is smaller meandering water with cutbanks, downed logs, and shallow glides between small but deeper pools. That section is more brook-trout water with a moderate number of decent wild brown trout. Because of the marble and limestone bedrock and slightly milky color, the upper river is classified as a spring creek with a wide variety of insect life.

What Works: The Battenkill is famous for its Hendrickson hatch, but a wide variety of mayflies, caddisflies, and stoneflies hatch throughout the season. There is a hatch chart in John Merwin's book. People come here for the classic dry-fly fishing experience. These are wild fish in catch-and-release water. Pete Kutzer of Orvis offers the following advice for the Hendrickson hatch in May:

It's best to fish the Battenkill in the afternoon. At midday, start with Hendrickson nymphs and then switch to wet flies, such as a pheasant tail softhackle, around 2:00 p.m. As the day progresses, you might see duns coming off around 3:00 p.m., but it's hard to predict where they will be hatching

John Merwin, the late editor of *Fly Fisherman* and founding publisher of *Fly Rod & Reel* magazine provided these and other interesting details about Wulff, Atherton, and Rockwell in his informative and insightful book, *The Battenkill* (1993). I had picked up a used copy of Merwin's book, thinking I'd just flip through it for some local insight, but found myself pulled in, reading it from cover to cover. I loved the combination of history, personal inspiration, scientific facts about ecology and geology, and good old-fashioned fishing wisdom. In the final chapter, Merwin spills the beans about how he fishes "the 'Kill":

This could be a suicide note or a love letter. I am not sure which.

The Battenkill is more crowded with fishermen now than it was in 1975 when I first began fishing it regularly, and my suggesting places and ways in which more and larger trout can be caught here will only increase the crowding. . . .

"Don't worry about it," [his friend Carl Navarre] finally said, smiling. "The kind of fishing you're describing is so demanding of patience that most people won't bother or be able to do it anyway. . . ."

The Battenkill is also among the most—if not *the* most—technically difficult fly-fishing stream in America. I say this not from some perverse hometown pride but from experience.

on any given day, so bounce around the river looking for healthy concentrations. By 5:00 p.m. there will be spinners falling while duns are still emerging until about 7:00 p.m. The locals like to stay out until dark, dark, dark during a good spinner fall.

Pete suggests slim and sparse Hendrickson patterns. "A good ol' Rusty Spinner usually does the trick, unless the fish have been pressured. At Orvis, we have a pattern called the Lexi's Tactical Get 'Er Dun mayfly and also a spinner version in sizes 16, 14, and maybe 12, but mostly 14s have been the go-to fly the past few seasons."

When the water is calm, extremely quiet wading and patience are critical. John Merwin noted that standing and waiting, sometimes for as much as an hour, may be necessary to allow the bigger trout to settle down and start feeding near the bank.

Proper presentation is important to avoid spooking the fish with false casts or dropping the line too hard.

Lower Battenkill: Near Arlington and downstream to the New York border, the Battenkill gains strength and width. This section holds more big but easily spooked browns, which may hold tight to the banks. The bigger fish will take big streamers, especially at dawn, but will also slurp Hendricksons at dusk or on cloudy days, or hoppers from the surface when warmer days arrive.

What Works: Merwin recommended it is best to sight fish to feeding trout with long casts and long, light leaders. Blind casting to rocks and seams is much less productive than on other rivers. At early dawn or dusk, the bigger fish will take big flies on sinking lines, such as Zonkers, Meat Whistles, and Woolly Buggers, as well as streamers such as a Mickey Finn, or even a mouse pattern on the surface. ■

Merwin went on to explain the problems of spooky, fussy, well-educated fish, as well as sloppy wading, careless casting, and curling currents that will drag a dry fly off line. He sums up his sentiment by comparing the Battenkill to rivers out in Montana:

Listen to the honky-tonk jukebox down by the Madison. It's a loose, fun, uninhibited kind of fishing. The Battenkill is more like Bach; with green hills, covered bridges, and white-clapboard villages forming the gently repeating steps of a sweetly insistent fugue in which rising trout play an occasional part. Perhaps you will develop a taste for it. As I have.

At about 2:00 p.m., I thanked Pete for his gracious guidance and casting instruction, and for giving me the better part of his Sunday. After several enjoyable hours, Pete, Bill, and I had proved that Merwin was right: The Battenkill is a difficult river to fish, but well worth a try. That one strike by a bruiser brown trout was enough to forever capture my fancy. I hope to get back there another time to try again. Maybe that will be when big browns are happily sipping mayflies from the surface on a picturesque Margot Page and Norman Rockwell day.

Sunday afternoon, May 14

When I returned to the house, Bill and Martha invited me to join them on a walk up the

We crossed over old stone walls on the flanks of Mount Equinox while searching for morel mushrooms.

trails behind their house on Mount Equinox to hunt for morel mushrooms. Their Labrador retriever, Bema, joyfully roamed the woods while we humans searched around the bases of ash trees on either side of the trail. Wouldn't it be great, I thought, if Bema could sniff them out, but he was more interested in squirrels and chipmunks. The understory was open, so we could holler when one of us spotted the oblong honeycomb dome of a morel. Classic New England stone walls deep in the woods marked the boundaries of former pastures. We managed to find a few of the delicious polypores along with a bunch of ramps, a type of wild onion that Martha cooked to perfection with the morels for dinner.

Yes, Sunday had been a "fishless day," to use a phrase from Sparse Grey Hackle. But in just twenty-four hours, I had been immersed in the history, the culture, and the ecology of the Battenkill, and came to fully appreciate the challenge this famous river has provided anglers for well over a century.

- 3 -

The Four Freedoms

Monday morning, May 15

Bill McLaughlin had invited me to give a talk on Monday morning about my nascent *Storied Waters* adventure to a group of Orvis associates at company headquarters in Sunderland, Vermont. Nearly everyone in the audience was a fly fisher and a reader of fly-fishing literature, so the question-and-answer session after my talk offered an exchange of ideas and experiences about the fishing along my route and about favorite authors. I picked up some names of people who might help me in Michigan and the Adirondacks, as well as a generous offer to stay at a camp on a lake in Maine at the end of my trip when I would fish near Mount Katahdin on the West Branch of the Penobscot River. "Nobody will be there the week you're coming through," Jim Lepage said. "I'll email you directions and instructions for where to find the key." Now there was an offer I couldn't turn down.

I was pleased to meet Tom Rosenbauer, who has written over a dozen of Orvis's "how-to" fly-fishing books and has been the longtime host of Orvis fly-fishing podcasts. I swapped a copy of *The Confluence* for Tom's hot-off-the-press book *The Orvis Guide to Hatch Strategies*. Tom happens to be the "particular fisherman" who had wooed Margot Page to Vermont and was married to her when she wrote about the Battenkill in *Little Rivers* in the mid-1990s.

After the Orvis event wound down, I zipped back into Manchester for an appointment to meet the staff at the American Museum of Fly Fishing (AMFF). Founded in 1968, the AMFF is located in a nineteenth-century farmhouse next door to the Orvis retail store. The seed for the museum's extensive collection was a set of wood panels created by Mary Orvis Marbury, Charles Orvis's daughter and the first manager of the fly-tying business at Orvis, for an exhibit at the 1893 Chicago World's Fair. She displayed flies and photographs of well-known nineteenth-century fly-fishing locations in the United States and Canada. The panels were rediscovered in 1963 in an attic above the Orvis rod factory. They were a sister project to Marbury's illustrated book *Favorite Flies and Their Histories*, which she published in 1892, that was based on correspondence with anglers from Maine to

Manchester, Vermont, is home of the venerable American Museum of Fly Fishing, founded in 1968.

California to Canada who had shared stories of their favorite flies with her fly-tying team at Orvis. The historic panels and original flies and photographs from her masterpiece book are now displayed at the museum.

The AMFF is closed on Mondays, but Bob Ruley, the director, and Kathleen Achor, the journal editor, were kind enough to give me a behind-the-scenes tour, including the museum's amazing collections of flies, fly rods, reels, books, and other exhibits that celebrate the rich history of fly fishing. And no fly-fishing museum would be complete without a few gigantic stuffed fish!

My wife, Cheryl, is oddly entranced by the TV show *Mysteries at the Museum* on the History Channel. Doing my best to indulge her obsession, I asked the AMFF folks if they knew of any mysteries that have stumped their experts. Bob thought for a moment, then walked into the next room to pull out some old bamboo fly rods. He showed me the metal ferrules that hold the sections together.

"Why," he asked, "do bamboo rods have female ferrules on the end of the handle and reel section with male connectors on the second section, but all modern rods have it the other way around?"

Hmm, well, it wasn't an unsolved murder or a tragic tale of mistaken identity or the famous case of Ernest Hemingway's missing trunkful of fly-fishing gear, but it was a mystery nonetheless. I had no idea why bamboo rods would be different, but I assured Bob I would inquire along the way on my trip to see if I could solve his mysterious mystery. And I surely couldn't disappoint my wife, who was thrilled to hear I was on such an important mission.

As we wrapped up the tour, I spent a few minutes browsing through the impressive library, which contains perhaps every book ever written about fly fishing. I could have spent a month in there, thumbing through book after book, but I had a big enough library in my car already, and it was time to push on.

In Arlington, I came across prints of Norman Rockwell's painting Freedom of Speech, *the first of the* Four Freedoms *featured in Franklin D. Roosevelt's State of the Union address during World War II.*

NATIONAL ARCHIVES AND RECORDS ADMINISTRATION #513536, WIKIMEDIA COMMONS, PUBLIC DOMAIN

I had a bit of driving to do to meet my friend Craig Sutton after dinner in southern New York, across the Catskill Mountains, where we planned to fish on the East Branch of the Delaware River and the storied Beaverkill.

On my way out of town, I passed the Sugar Shack in Arlington, a classic Vermont tourist trap on old Route 7 next to the Battenkill that makes maple syrup products and sells Norman Rockwell prints, books, and memorabilia. They have a gallery of prints and magazine covers that span Rockwell's career, especially when he lived in Arlington in the 1940s and '50s.

Maybe, I thought, *they have a Rockwell painting that shows a fishing scene on the Battenkill or someone with a fly rod in their hand.* I found nothing of the sort, unfortunately, only a few goofy pictures typical of Rockwell's lighthearted *Saturday Evening Post* covers, including one with a guy sitting on a stool fishing in a bucket.

But I did find a welcome surprise.

Rockwell's career spanned World War II and the postwar era, so the topics of his myriad illustrations and prints reflected the nation's mood and issues of the day. Front and center in the gallery was an exhibit of his most famous series of prints: *The Four Freedoms.*

In January 1941, President Franklin D. Roosevelt gave what became known as his Four Freedoms State of the Union Address. FDR argued that the United States could not and should not isolate itself from the war overseas, where much of Europe was under Nazi control and Great Britain was barely hanging on. Roosevelt saw the "Four Freedoms" as America's mission in the world and

as fundamental to a productive and peaceful global community. Rockwell honored that speech with four paintings: *Freedom of Speech, Freedom of Worship, Freedom from Want,* and *Freedom from Fear.* They appeared on four consecutive covers of the *Saturday Evening Post* with essays by famous writers and went on a popular national tour to sell war bonds. The originals are now on permanent exhibit at the Norman Rockwell Museum in Stockbridge, Massachusetts.

According to the FDR Presidential Library and Museum, "the ideas enunciated in Roosevelt's Four Freedoms were the foundational principles that evolved into the Atlantic Charter declared by Winston Churchill and FDR in August 1941" and ultimately the United Nations.

Another famous Rockwell print from 1961 honored the United Nations and the diversity of our global society. The inscription of the Golden Rule across portraits of people representing all races and religions is a stunning reminder that the Golden Rule is a bedrock of civil society. This is a timeless message that resonates as much today as in any prior era.

As I climbed into my car and headed toward my next destination, the Catskill Mountains, I looked out at the picturesque American landscape. Land of the free, home of the brave. The last thing I expected was that my fly-fishing adventure would wander down this path, but I guess it would be naive to think I could escape the polarized politics of the day for very long, even on an extended fishing adventure. It was good to be reminded that these important works capped Rockwell's remarkable career as a visual storyteller.

- 4 -

At Home on the Hudson River

Monday afternoon, May 15

The Battenkill flows through West Arlington under the red covered bridge that leads to Norman Rockwell's former home and studio, now an inn, and continues west into New York State. Soon after crossing the state line, my route intersected with my own personal story. I passed through Cambridge, New York, where I learned to downhill ski at Willard Mountain, and the Schaghticoke Fairgrounds, where, in eighth grade, I nearly lost my lunch atop the roller coaster while on a date with Mary Behan. Too much junk food and too many whirling rides got the best of me, as I recall.

Route 22 is the main drag through Speigletown, where I attended Cub Scout meetings. To my left, I looked up at Bald Mountain (aka Mount Rafinesque), where I grew up in a house that looked out over the Hudson River valley. We sold my childhood home years ago after my mother died, so there was no reason to stop. On I drove, down Oakwood Avenue in Troy, past Oakwood Cemetery where my parents are buried. I'm not much into visiting graves, so I just waved and said hello

as I passed. My sister and brother and several childhood friends still live in Troy, but I hadn't scheduled time to visit on this trip. Family gatherings would have to wait until later in the summer.

My immediate destination on this day was the Beaverkill and the Upper Delaware River on the far side of the Catskill Mountains. If I was lucky, I'd arrive just in time to make a few casts before dark.

Soon I could see the familiar Albany skyline with the Catskill Mountains rising tall some sixty miles in the distance. When I looked out at that same view from our house on the hill in the 1970s, a dark cloud of air pollution shrouded the Albany skyline and obscured the distant mountains. I also remember that the Hudson River was terribly polluted, virtually an open sewer. My dad's office overlooked the river from the second floor of a Victorian building on River Street. We would watch barges deliver oil to the tank farm across the river while fetid bilge water poured into the river. Nobody fished or swam in the river in those days, as it was nearly devoid of aquatic life and certainly dangerous to human health. My schoolmates claimed that if you fell in the river, you'd dissolve. Hyperbole, yes, but barely.

I was an impressionable twelve-year-old in 1970, when the first Earth Day focused public consciousness on the air and water pollution that were so obvious in my hometown and across America. Earth Day inspired me to do something about it by pursuing a career in environmental science and policy. Years later, as director of the Maine Bureau of Land and Water Quality, I worked to protect, maintain, and restore that state's incredible water resources.

I hadn't yet learned to fly-fish when I lived in Troy; however, my pals and I were pretty fond of throwing bass plugs and Rapalas with our spinning rod in the lakes and ponds nearby. I also did a little trout fishing in the Poesten Kill, Quacken Kill, and the Hoosic River, but mostly with worms and lures. I learned to fly-fish after college while living in Wyoming in 1980 and have been exclusively a fly fisher ever since, but I cherish the memories of spin fishing with my young buddies.

Fortunately, thanks to passage of the federal Clean Water Act in 1972, the Hudson River and many other polluted waterways have made quite a comeback. Today, municipal and industrial wastewater is treated before being discharged into the river. Pleasure boats now motor up and down the Hudson and dock at restaurants with decks overlooking the water. People waterski and fish from canoes, sights never seen in the 1970s or '80s. Today, the formidable Atlantic sturgeon, American shad, and striped bass have returned in solid numbers, along with over one hundred other species as far north as the head of tide at the Troy Dam (yes, the

This covered bridge over the Battenkill in West Arlington is located near Norman Rockwell's former home and studio, now an inn.

Where & How—
Hudson River for Stripers

Trout they ain't, but a Hudson River striper on a fly is now on my list. I'd love to catch a big striped bass in the river near my dad's old office, just to see the river come full circle.

Big stripers run up the river in April to spawn when the water reaches 40-something degrees, and, according to area guides, the "five weeks of craziness" often run into June from the George Washington Bridge up to the Troy dam. Smaller schoolies stay in the river all summer.

What Works: According to Rob Streeter, outdoor columnist of the *Times-Union* newspapers, stripers prefer bait when the water is below 56 degrees, but will take flies as the temperature gets into the mid-50s; try a Clouser Half and Half in chartreuse and white or a big herring pattern when the river herring are running. Fishing from a boat is best. A few charter boats offer fly-fishing trips, such as Reel Happy Charters out of Cairo, New York, but most people fish with bait or lures.

Locals say that the shallow flats where tributaries enter the Hudson warm up earlier, and stripers will stalk herring and other prey in these waters and take a streamer near the surface. There are places to access the river from shore near the dam in Troy, but it's a big river, so a boat is a preferred strategy to reach more water. ■

Hudson is tidal all the way to Troy.) There are now charter tours and guides who focus on stripers in the main stem of the Hudson, including the section near my father's family's ancestral homestead, settled in the 1600s, on Van Wie's Point south of Albany.

The lower part of the mighty Hudson still has its issues, including PCB contamination and pollution from urban stormwater runoff, but it's marvelous to see osprey and bald eagles soaring over the river again, and to know that sea-run and resident fish are again swimming beneath the waves, as they should

be. Maybe someday I'll try fishing for stripers in the Hudson near Van Wie's Point.

After crossing the Route 7 bridge over the Hudson, I turned south onto I-787 toward the New York State Thruway. With my eyes on the horizon, I was excited to see the Catskill ridgeline getting closer. I would finally traverse the mountains I'd been eyeing from afar since I was a boy. I'd be passing through Washington Irving country along the Rip Van Winkle Trail. Perhaps I'd see ol' Rip and my Dutch ancestors playing ninepins among the hills and clouds.

- 5 -

In the Catskills: The First American Fly-Fishing Story

When and where did all this writing about fly fishing begin?

Way back in 1496, Dame Juliana Berners wrote *A Treatyse of Fysshynge Wyth an Angle*, or at least that's the story we are supposed to believe. Whether the *Treatyse* was really written by a fifteenth-century English prioress may never be known, but the book launched a long tradition of writers combining wit and wisdom to share "how-to" information and captivating stories about fly fishing.

A century and a half later, Izaak Walton recorded his passion for piscatorial pursuits in *The Compleat Angler*, published in England in 1653, one of the most influential books ever written on fishing and nature. Walton not only promoted the "brotherhood" of our sport but also championed many of the fundamental concepts of conservation and environmental protection that are essential to providing clean water and habitat for fish and wildlife. According to the Izaak Walton League (one of the oldest conservation organizations in the United States, founded in Chicago in 1922), Walton encouraged his brethren to develop a detailed knowledge of natural history and ecology and to advocate for conservation.

At the time Walton was writing *The Compleat Angler*, my Dutch ancestors were settling along the Hudson River near Albany as part of New Netherlands. Another century and a half later, Washington Irving lampooned the early Dutch settlement of New Amsterdam on the island of Manhattan in his fictional *A History of New York* (1809), purportedly penned by an equally fictional Diedrich Knickerbocker, who Irving also used as the narrator of Irving's famous tale "Rip Van Winkle." Knickerbocker later morphed into a sort of mascot for New York City and served as inspiration for naming the New York Knicks basketball team, as well as a (now defunct) brand of beer and a historic hotel recently reincarnated on Times Square.

In 1820, Washington Irving published what is considered by many to be the first American fly-fishing story, "The Angler," released along with "Rip Van Winkle" as part of *The Sketch Book of Geoffrey Crayon, Gent.*, which was actually published in England, where Irving was living at the time.

Washington Irving set his 1820 short story "The Angler" in the Catskill Mountains somewhere near Kaaterskill Falls, the tallest waterfall in New York State.

Researchers doubt that Irving himself actually did much fishing (much of his writing, usually in the fictional first person, was pure fabrication). He once claimed that when he wrote "Rip Van Winkle" he had never stepped foot in the Catskills. Presumably, this would be true also of "The Angler." Irving reputedly based his descriptions on tales related to him by other residents and travelers of the Catskill region.

Nevertheless, "The Angler" opens with the narrator describing a believable yet frustratingly fishless excursion in the Catskills. One of his companions was "attired cap-à-pie for the enterprise. . . . He was as great a matter of stare and wonderment among the country folk, who had never seen a regular angler" in such a fancy getup. The mountain brook where they fished "would leap down rocky shelves, making small cascades, over which the trees threw their broad balancing. . . . Sometimes it would brawl and fret along a ravine . . . filling it with murmurs." The narrator then describes his own inexperience and the jaded result:

> For my part, I was always a bungler at all kinds of sport that required either patience or adroitness, and had not angled above half an hour before I had completely "satisfied the sentiment," and convinced myself of the truth of Izaak Walton's opinion, that angling is something like poetry—a man must be born to it. I hooked myself instead of the fish, tangled my line in every tree, lost my bait, broke my rod, until I gave up the attempt in despair, and passed the day under the trees reading old Izaak, satisfied that it was his fascinating vein of honest simplicity and rural feeling that had bewitched me, and not the passion for angling. My companions, however, were more persevering in their delusion.

The tale then leaps across the pond to sketch a colorful and loquacious fisherman ("the oracle of the tap-room") wandering the English countryside in what amounts to a tribute to the great Izaak Walton himself. Irving instills in his narrator, like Walton's protagonist/narrator Piscator, an appreciation for the "brotherhood of the angle."

The unnamed Catskill stream in "The Angler" sounds very similar to the stream near which Rip Van Winkle slept for twenty years. My guess is that both were inspired by the Kaaterskill, or a stream much like it. The lower, flatter portion of the Kaaterskill flows through the town of Catskill and is stocked with brown trout, while the upstream portion at Palenville and in the steep gorge above holds wild rainbows and brook trout, according to Tom Gilmore in *Flyfisher's Guide to the Big Apple*.

No longer the quiet country lane of yesteryear, Route 23A, known as the Rip Van Winkle Trail, is a well-traveled state highway that climbs steeply from the Hudson Valley following the Katterskill. As I motored along, I wished I had time to explore the stream with a fly rod in hand, like the characters in "The Angler." Two miles above Palenville there is a parking area and trail to Kaaterskill Falls. This part of the stream seemed too steep to hold fish, but I just had to take a few minutes to see the falls. At 231 feet in two drops, this is the tallest waterfall in New York, even taller than Niagara Falls (which is a mere 167 feet).

Kaaterskill Falls was one of the biggest tourist destinations in the United States during the height of the Hudson River school of painting in the mid-nineteenth century. Thomas Cole (1801–1848) painted the falls in 1826 as one of the earlier examples of this style. Cole and his fellow artists were Thoreau's and Charles Orvis's contemporaries, and thus had as much impact on America's relationship with nature as Thoreau and his fellow philosophers. All this nature-loving allowed Orvis to take advantage of the romanticism of the wild American landscape and the burgeoning interest in fly fishing.

I parked my car, dug out my camera, and hiked the half mile up to the base of the falls. The azure sky was dotted with white puffy clouds, and the falls thundered down from above, high enough to be neck straining. It wasn't hard to imagine thousands of tourists and artists coming here almost 200 years ago, and, before that, the Native Americans who lived in these mountains for thousands of years. There are times when one can truly feel the history of a place. This was just such a time. The scene hasn't changed much since Cole's time, thank goodness.

After basking in the rainbow-shrouded mist for twenty minutes, I strolled back to the car, intent on getting to the West Branch Angler cabins in Hancock before dark. I was jonesing to cast a fly before joining Craig Sutton for a late dinner. The winding road continued for another two hours through the Catskill highlands, past Hunter Mountain ski area, through picturesque Phoenicia, and along the very fishable-looking Esopus Creek.

About halfway to Hancock, Route 30 hugs the shore of the Pepacton Reservoir for twenty miles to the Downsville Dam, where the East Branch of the Delaware emerges wild and free-flowing all the way to its confluence with the West Branch in Hancock. Craig and I would be floating this section the next afternoon with our guide. My maiden journey up and over the Catskill Mountains was almost complete.

- 6 -

Bug Soup on the East Branch of the Delaware

Monday evening, May 15

Like backgammon and cribbage, fishing is a pleasing combination of strategy, skill, and chance. Fortune can fall either way, so it's best to keep your hopes high but your expectations in check. As I had joked with Norm at Walden Pond, it would be just my luck, everyone telling me day after day, "You should have been here last week!" Now, several days into my trip, I was feeling like it was time for some serious serendipity.

I pulled into the West Branch Angler on Monday evening just before my soon-to-be fishing partner Craig Sutton came back from an afternoon fishing on the Beaverkill. The West Branch Angler is a comfortable, Orvis-endorsed fishing resort on the banks of the West Branch of the Delaware River in Hancock, New York, about an hour east of Binghamton. After checking in and unloading my gear onto the cabin porch perched atop the river bank, I pulled on my waders and walked down to the river to make a few casts. The sun was barely peeking through the treetops. Craig drove in moments later and came down to join me.

Drift boats floated gracefully by in the twilight, oars a-clunking and anglers casting toward shore, their voices carrying across the water. One fellow, who was wading upstream from me and smoking a cigar, landed a fish but I couldn't see what kind or how big. The much-anticipated Hendrickson mayflies were hatching on schedule, so the fish were active. Craig and I moved downstream a bit to get away from the cigar.

A few well-meaning trout were rising to emerging mayflies near shore as the sky faded to dark. We each made a few casts, but very soon it was impossible to see our flies drifting on the surface. Our stomachs began rumbling in unison for dinner, and we longed for a cold brew, so we stashed our rods on the cabin porch and walked over to the pub, chatting rapid-fire about what was in store for tomorrow: a float trip down the East Branch with Rich Hudgens, the head guide at the Beaverkill Angler shop in nearby Roscoe.

Craig caught the fly-fishing bug from me about twenty years ago. Our families vacation the same week in August at Silver Bay YMCA Conference Center on Lake George in the Adirondacks, along with several other families who have become dear friends. Craig and I often bring our bicycles and ride through the hills around the lake. He and his wife Susan are also avid tennis players. Their three children overlap in age with our two.

One evening after dinner, Craig was watching me fly cast for bass on the lake and peppered me with questions about fly fishing. I showed him how to cast, which was enough to spark his addiction to this crazy sport. He has since fished all over Pennsylvania and, now and then, with his brother in Colorado and Montana. Craig and I had been talking about fishing together for years, and this was our first opportunity. He had stayed at the West Branch Angler and floated the West and East Branches of the Delaware several times with Rich as his guide. Craig was nice enough to arrange everything for this stop on my tour. I hadn't planned to hire any guides on my trip but was happy to split the cost with Craig, given his experience and enthusiasm.

Tuesday morning, May 16

Before meeting Rich at noon the next day, Craig suggested we make a few casts into the Beaverkill just above its confluence with the East Branch. We finished up breakfast quickly, picked up a few flies at the resort's well-stocked shop, and headed down the highway a few miles before turning onto a shady side road that Craig had scouted the afternoon before.

We caught up on family news while we sat on my tailgate pulling on our waders. The river glistened and gurgled to our left. After climbing down the bank, we crossed a wide gravel bar and, with a ceremonial high five from Craig, I waded into the world famous Beaverkill—considered holy water by many—for the first time.

Craig waded downstream, searching for an eddy or seam in the current where fast water meets slow water behind a rock or near shore. The river was knee- to thigh-deep and about twenty yards across. Using my wading staff to steady me in the quick current, I set my sights on a smooth glide over a deeper slot between submerged rocks in the middle of the river. We both chose to start with dry flies on floating line. After a few minutes of seeing no signs of hatching bugs or rising fish, I switched to my sinking line with a streamer which I danced in the current, hoping to attract an interested trout hiding among the rocks. We fished in the bright sunlight for about forty-five minutes, each trying a handful of different flies and retrieves, but still with no success. Doubtful refrains of "last week . . . last week" began to echo in my head. I also heard myself muttering the well-worn cliché, "That's why they call it fishin' and not catchin'!"

Craig waded back upstream, shrugged with his ubiquitous smile, and said, "Well, I think it's supposed to cloud over a bit this afternoon. Let's hope!" Craig is one of the most persistently optimistic and good-natured people I've ever met. Yes, I've heard him grumble a few times or talk seriously about weighty topics, but he can somehow make even a sober statement or a sarcastic aside sound positive.

We climbed back into the car and motored up the East Branch to rendezvous with our guide, trusting that Rich might have a few tricks up his sleeve for the afternoon.

Tuesday afternoon, May 16

Craig had worked with many fishing guides here and out west, and he told me that Rich was by far the best he'd seen. Rich's knowledge and excitement were clearly evident as we loaded our gear into his truck with his boat on the trailer behind. As we drove upstream toward Shinhopple with the river on our right, I noticed a dozen flies stuck into the ceiling fabric above his rearview mirror—a sure sign of a busy guide who doesn't mind coaching less-experienced clients who don't know enough to stow their flies properly before putting their rod into the vehicle. A touch of gray in Rich's beard told me he'd probably had his share of difficult clients on challenging days. Guides earn their gray hairs the hard way. Yet his smile lines indicated that Rich keeps a proper attitude and a sense of humor in a profession many people think of as their dream job.

"We've had great luck the past couple of weeks," Rich told us. This somehow sounded much more hopeful than "You shoulda been here last week."

"This stretch of the East Branch is my favorite when there's this much water. The conditions have been excellent all year; the water has stayed high and cold. The river is 51 degrees and running at 850 cfs [cubic feet per second]. This time of year, it's usually 250. We should have a great day!" I liked that assessment. He, too, had Craig's knack for optimism.

We crossed the historic Corbett suspension bridge just after noon. Rich backed the trailer down the gravel ramp underneath the bridge. While he slid the boat off the trailer, he explained that the Hendrickson mayflies had been emerging all week, but wind and rain over the past few days had kept the duns (submature winged stage) from molting into spinners (mature adults) and mating.

"The duns and spinners have been hanging in the trees, waiting for the right conditions to do their sky dance and mate," Rich explained. "With clouds and a light breeze, we should see a good spinner fall this afternoon." When the spinners fall to the water to deposit their eggs, they die and become delectable trout food. "And we may still see more duns emerging if we're lucky. If so, the fish will be taking both dries on top and nymphs underneath the surface."

When someone mentions "the Delaware," it's easy to picture George Washington standing in a boat crossing the river in winter. But we were far upstream from that event, which was down close to Trenton, New Jersey. The Upper Delaware far above the Delaware Water Gap forms the border between New York and Pennsylvania. It splits into the East Branch and the West Branch at Hancock, New York.

The Upper Delaware region had its chronicler in John Burroughs (1837–1921), one of the most influential naturalists and essayists of the nineteenth century. In his writings, he sang the praises of the Delaware, Neversink, Beaverkill, and other trout streams in the area. In his story "A Summer Voyage" (1881) in his book *Pepacton*, he told of a solo trip he took down the East Branch. It began:

When one summer day I bethought me of a voyage down the east or Pepacton branch of the Delaware, I seemed to want some excuse for the start, some send-off, some preparation, to give the enterprise genesis and head. This I found in building my own boat. It was a happy thought. How else should I have got under way, how else should I have raised the breeze? The boat-building warmed the blood; it made the germ take; it whetted my appetite for the voyage. There is nothing like serving an apprenticeship to fortune, like earning the right to your tools. In most enterprises the temptation is always to begin too far along; we want to start where somebody else leaves off. Go back to the stump, and see what an impetus you get. Those fishermen who wind their own flies before they go a-fishing,—how they bring in the trout;

Our guide, Rich Hudgens, launches his drift boat on the East Branch of the Delaware River with a hand from my friend Craig Sutton.

and those hunters who run their own bullets or make their own cartridges,— the game is already mortgaged to them.

When my boat was finished—and it was a very simple affair—I was as eager as a boy to be off; I feared the river would all run by before I could wet her bottom in it. This enthusiasm begat great expectations of the trip. I should surely surprise Nature and win some new secrets from her. I should glide down noiselessly upon her and see what all those willow screens and baffling curves concealed. As a fisherman and pedestrian I had been able to come at the stream only at certain points: now the most private and secluded retreats of the nymph would be opened to me; every bend and

eddy, every cove hedged in by swamps or passage walled in by high alders, would be at the beck of my paddle.

Today the upper reaches of the Delaware are not the same wild rivers that Burroughs celebrated. Several have been dammed to provide water to New York City, including the inundation of the Neversink with a dam and reservoir in 1952, the Pepacton Reservoir on the East Branch at Downsville in 1955, and the Cannonsville Reservoir on the West Branch built in 1964. The Pepacton Reservoir displaced over 900 residents and flooded four East Branch towns: Pepacton, Union Grove, Shavertown, and Arena. Many stories, both told and untold, including the carefree

From afternoon into evening, we enjoyed "bug soup" on the East Branch of the Delaware.

days of John Burroughs's boyhood, were lost beneath 200 feet of water.

In his essay "Speckled Trout" in *In the Catskills* (1910), Burroughs glorifies the brook trout that he loved to chase on these rivers before they were dammed:

I have been a seeker of trout from my boyhood, and on all the expeditions in which this fish has been the ostensible purpose I have brought home more game than my creel showed. . . . But I early learned that from almost any stream in a trout country the true angler could take trout, and that the great secret was this, that, whatever bait you used, worm, grasshopper, grub, or fly, there was one thing you must always put upon your hook, namely, your heart: when

rainbow trout. "The Pepacton Reservoir is the most pristine water of all the reservoirs that supply New York City," Rich explained. "Because of the cold bottom-water releases, the East Branch is full of wild brown trout feasting on tons of bugs under ideal conditions."

We didn't build our own boat, as Burroughs did, but we were on our own enterprising voyage in Rich's drift boat, giving us full access to the "private and secluded retreats of the nymph." And we hoped that would make the trout "jump clear from the water" after our flies. As the bridge disappeared behind us, we spotted a mink scooting along the shoreline among the rocks and logs, hunting for frogs, minnows, crawfish, or anything else to make a good lunch. In a blur, it vanished into the vegetation.

We started off under a milky blue sky as the afternoon warmed. The air was muggier than in the morning. Perfect for hatching bugs. The river in the first part of the trip was four or five feet deep, so Rich had set up our fly rods with three nymphs each to start out. We lobbed the weighted rigs out a few yards to drift with floating lines alongside the moving boat as we watched our strike indicators for any kind of herky-jerky motion. Within the first ten minutes, I scored the first fish of the day, a porky 14-inch brown trout that took the second nymph on my line: a bead-head pheasant tail. Next, I caught an 18-inch brown on the lowest nymph, a regular pheasant tail. Hey, wasn't I loving this guided drift-boat thing!

Soon we started seeing rises everywhere. Rich told us to switch to the dry flies he had tied onto our own rods. He gave me some welcome pointers on how to improve my long casting with a "reach cast," which arcs the fly line upstream of the fly for a better drift to the wary brown trout holding in place, often near a submerged rock that breaks the

you bait your hook with your heart the fish always bite; they will jump clear from the water after it; they will dispute with each other over it; it is a morsel they love above everything else.

Thankfully, the East Branch below Downsville dam is still wild and free, with thirty miles of world-class fishing for wild brook trout, wild and stocked browns, and the occasional

Where & How—
Upper Delaware River

Under the right conditions, a float trip down the East Branch or the West Branch of the Delaware is an unforgettable experience well worth some travel and a chunk of cash. Book well in advance, as prime time fills up quickly, especially during May and June when the hatches are hot. Beaverkill Angler trips (full day or half day) are catch-and-release fly fishing only. The guides working out of the West Branch Angler resort are Orvis-trained instructors. There are many more qualified guides in the area.

What Works: The most important thing to prepare for a float trip like this is to practice casting beforehand. Practice a lot; be the best you can be. Rich said it is painfully obvious when someone hasn't cast a fly rod since their last fishing trip a year ago. A good guide will offer helpful tips and instruction, as Rich did for me. But the guide shouldn't be teaching the basics while you are paying for the guide, the boat, and the fishing.

Rich provided us with rods set up with triple nymphing rigs to dead-drift in some deeper runs at the beginning of our trip on the East Branch. The top nymph was a tungsten Prince Nymph, the second was a Bead-Head Pheasant Tail, and the bottom was a regular Pheasant Tail Nymph.

Our guide was really good at spotting fish, and he explained what he was looking for. After a few hours, Craig and I were getting the hang of it, but Rich could see many more rising fish than we could. He could also judge the size by the rise form and behavior. Then, he'd anchor the boat so we could make long casts at the proper angle to get a good drift down to the fish.

When we were fishing dry flies, fly choice was less important than a proper drift. We had to switch flies a few times if we had a refusal, but when bugs are hatching, it is all about controlling your casting loop, hitting upstream of the target, mending line to prevent drag, and having good timing on the take.

Rich reminded us that the rise ring moves along with the current, but the fish stays in one place. If I aimed for the rise ring that a fish just created, I was usually downstream of the actual fish. This was important to remember so we could cast far enough upstream to drift the fly down to the fish.

In short, an experienced guide is well worth the money on a river like this. ■

current. The wild brook trout I was used to catching are not quite as predictable in their rising patterns, nor as finicky about the fly's drift as were these East Branch browns. These fish were experienced and spooky. They required a perfect dead drift right onto their nose or they would ignore the fly.

Craig promptly caught three in the 12- to 14-inch range from a pool with over a dozen rising fish. This was getting fun! We were fishing with heart, as Burroughs might say.

By 3:00 p.m., there were massive clouds of spinners swarming overhead, both male and female mayflies undulating up and down to an ancient rhythm. At first, they weren't falling onto the water, but by 4:00 we saw trout feeding on spent spinners. Incredibly, recently emerged duns were also floating by on the glassy water among the spinners.

"This is epic!" Rich exclaimed, looking all around, beaming. "It's like bug soup out there! Mayfly duns and spinners, caddis, midges, even a stonefly or two!"

The spinner fall continued until dark. Rich couldn't get over it. "Wow, I don't think I've seen so many spinners so consistently for so long. Ever!"

With so many fish active, Rich had us hunting for the biggest fish. He knew where and how to look, and soon we were learning the subtle skill of scanning the water. We found a few big trout rising right up against the left bank. Rich pointed out a cavernous mouth slurping flies, with a big tail and dorsal fin breaking the surface now and then. He anchored the boat in about three feet of water, giving Craig the best angle to cast to one big fish. Craig's casts were excellent, but he missed the fish on the strike. Remarkably, the big brown came back to the fly twice more. After the third miss, Rich scolded Craig with a laugh, "Stop flossing the fish and bring one in!"

On the next cast, Craig reeled a chunky brown trout to the boat. Then it was my turn. I took an 18-incher on a small dry fly: a size 14 Red Quill, tied Catskill-style. And so it went, with Craig and me taking turns casting to rising fish, until dark. We dodged a few sprinkles at some point, but nobody cared, as the fishing couldn't have been better. The cloudy, humid conditions with temperatures in the low 60s were perfect. The challenge wasn't finding fish that were actively feeding. The problem was putting your fly in front of the correct (i.e., the biggest) fish. If Craig or I missed by a foot or two, a smaller fish would

take the fly, resulting in a friendly reprimand from Rich. "No! Not that one!" It was a kick-ass challenge to have.

We weren't the only ones on the river that evening. We had to pull in our lines as we drifted past a pod of eight fly fishers and two other drift boats at a place called Long Flats. Despite Rich's skilled efforts to courteously hug the far bank, we earned a few scowls from our wading brethren.

Beneath the flats, towering swarms of spinners persisted. Rich looked up and declared morbidly, "Every one of these bugs will be dead in an hour."

Well, that's a nice thought, I said to myself, realizing that it was indeed true. Mayflies live most of their lives underwater in the larval and nymph stage. Their time as adults is very brief. They "hatch" from nymphs into adults, they fly off the water, they mate, and they die in a day or two. Brief, but blissful, we might imagine.

We landed our last two fish of the day just as it was getting too dark to see our flies on the surface. Craig hooked a 19-inch brown and landed it after a tense ten-minute battle. Rich dropped anchor and jumped out of the boat to get it in the net. On the next rising fish, I wrestled with an 18-inch brown that had confidently slurped my size 14 Hackle Wing Rusty Spinner. Rich seemed as excited as I was when he netted my final fish of the day. It was satisfying to see a man enjoy his job.

"You know, I'm glad this incredible day wasn't wasted on two newbies who didn't know how to fish," Rich admitted with a wry smile. We took that as a sincere compliment and also a frank confession from a seasoned guide who has probably seen many fine opportunities "wasted" when the clients weren't quite up to the task. Probably like Pete Kutzer must have felt when I lost that big brown on the Battenkill two days before.

The author glows from the thrill of catching a brown trout "of voting age," as Robert Traver would say, on the East Branch of the Delaware.

What a loser! Literally. But thanks to Pete's and Rich's coaching, my skills were improving by the hour, especially with respect to these wily brown trout, which I don't encounter very often in Maine. I was proud that Craig and I could rise to the occasion.

We got off the river at 9:00 p.m. straight up. That's when we discovered the only real downer of the day: The designated shuttle guy had failed to move Rich's truck and trailer back down to the take-out point. Luckily, Craig and I had dropped our car there, so we drove Rich back up to the bridge to get his truck before dashing back to camp hoping to get there before they stopped serving food at 10:00.

High fives and handshakes seemed grossly inadequate to celebrate what Rich said was about the best day of fishing he could imagine on this river. Despite the truck mishap, he was still totally pumped about the great day.

We made it to the pub in time. As we ordered our burgers and Southern Tier IPAs, I commented to Craig that, sometime next week, maybe Rich would be telling the sports in his boat, "Boy, you should have been here last week!"

- 7 -

Beaverkill Blues

Wednesday morning, May 17

Craig had to go home on Wednesday, so I was on my own to explore the Beaverkill. We checked out of the West Branch Angler mid-morning and said our good-byes, and I drove toward Roscoe, where the Beaverkill and Willowemoc meet at the famous Junction Pool.

The Beaverkill earned its well-deserved fame starting in the 1870s, when the Ontario & Western (O&W) Railway began its run from New York City through Roscoe. Easy passenger rail access to this (then) remote and wild river drew pioneers like Theodore Gordon (1854–1915), who introduced the dry fly to American fishing in the 1890s. Gordon's articles in both *Fishing Gazette* and *Forest and Stream* popularized the area, creating a generation of disciples who revered the Beaverkill, the Willowemoc, and the Neversink rivers. He also tinkered with English dry-fly patterns to better imitate the local bugs and thus established the tradition of Catskill-style fly tying.

Corey Ford (born James Hitchcock Ford Jr., 1902–1969), one of my favorite outdoor writers, loved the Beaverkill. Ford lived in New York City and wrote for the *New Yorker* in the 1930s, bestowing on that fine publication his snarky wit and the top-hatted mascot Eustace Tilley. He also wrote for *Vanity Fair*, *Collier's*, *Life*, and many other magazines that were a main form of visual entertainment before television. A noted humorist and satirist, he also wrote Hollywood screenplays and some thirty books.

Ford escaped the city often enough to become a serious fly fisherman. The O&W brought him and his fishing friends to Roscoe, where they waded in the famous pools of the Beaverkill and swapped stories in smoke-filled rooms at Ferndon's boardinghouse. In his essay "Profile of a Trout Stream," written in the 1950s and reproduced in *Trout Tales & Other Angling Stories* (1995), Ford recounts the history of the Beaverkill, as well as his own history of falling in love with the river.

I suppose it's the historic American trout stream. Generations of anglers have floundered through its rapids, and stepped over their waders in its cold deep holes, and hung up their backcasts in the balsams along its banks. Leading sportsmen from all over the world have come to whip its legendary pools. . . .

I was born on the Beaverkill myself, in a manner of speaking. I learned to cast a dry fly over Barnhart's Pool under the choleric instruction of Ted Townsend, the old master. . . .

The stream has changed since the good old days, of course. The fishing isn't what it used to be, they tell you today. . . . I suppose that when Hendrick Hudson sailed up to the Catskills the Indians told him: "You should have discovered this place a hundred years ago. That's when the fishing was really good." It doesn't matter: A trout stream is more than the fish in it.

As a renowned writer, Ford moved to Hanover, New Hampshire, in 1952. There he began writing a regular feature in *Field & Stream* magazine that delighted readers with

Corey Ford. INK WASH AND CHARCOAL DRAWING BY *JILL OSGOOD*

tall tales about the antics and misadventures of the colorful characters of the Lower Forty Shooting, Angling and Inside Straight Club, which was based on his group of friends in the Hanover area. The Lower Forty stories have been collected into various anthologies, including *You Can Always Tell a Fisherman (But You Can't Tell Him Much)* (1958), *Minutes of the Lower Forty* (1962), *Uncle Perk's Jug* (1964), and more recently in *The Corey Ford Sporting Treasury* (1987). The opening from his story "Uncle Perk's Splitting Wedge" provides the feel for his characters and style:

Gloom hung in a pall over the Lower Forty Shooting, Angling and Inside Straight Club. Normally June would have been a month of carefree angling, with mayflies hatching and trout rising eagerly to the lure; but now a mood of black despair gripped the membership, as the date of the Widow Libbey's nuptial ceremonies drew nearer. As soon as she and Deacon Godfrey sealed the matrimonial bonds, they knew, there'd be no more hunting or fishing on the Libbey farm. "The moment that old skinflint gets his hands on her property legally," Judge Parker said grimly, "he'll put up signs over every last inch of it, just for spite."

"Including our favorite woodcock cover down in the Libbey lower forty," Doc Hall mourned. "He'll probably cut out all the alders and drain the swamp for pasture."

"He couldn't do that!" Cousin Sid gasped. "Why, that's where the Club first got its name."

"I wouldn't put anything past Ira Godfrey," Colonel Cobb frowned. "I heard the other day that he's planning to subdivide the land and sell it off for building lots."

"Maybe we could talk to the Widow Libbey," Dexter Smeed urged, "and explain that the Deacon's only marrying her for her money."

Judge Parker glared at his wife's nephew. "She'd suspect we were trying to break up the marriage so the Club could keep on using her land."

"Now, what would ever make her think a thing like that?" Doc Hall protested in a hurt tone.

I first heard of Corey Ford when I played rugby at Dartmouth College in the late 1970s. Ford had developed a passion for Dartmouth rugby after watching the team practice across the street from his house in Hanover. Even though he had never played, he considered himself the informal "coach" of the team and was instrumental in organizing the club's first tour to England in 1958, the first ever for a US side. Thanks to his connections, Dartmouth's tour was written up in *Sports Illustrated*, and the team appeared on the *Ed Sullivan Show* upon their return. When he died in 1969, Ford left his estate to Dartmouth with instructions to use the funds from the sale of his house to build a rugby clubhouse.

When I played, a clubhouse was a far-off dream. The team used part of the interest earned from the Corey Ford Fund to go on tour during spring break, and I was fortunate to tour to England my sophomore year, just as the club did in 1958, thanks to Ford's beneficence. It took a while, but in 2005, Ford's vision became a reality when the men's and women's rugby clubs and generations of generous alumni dedicated the magnificent Corey Ford Rugby Clubhouse on a sunny September Saturday. Ford would have been thrilled.

While I'd known since my college days that Corey Ford was a famous writer, it was not until just a few years ago that I learned he wrote about fly fishing. *Hel-LO! How did I miss*

that? When I finally read his stories, it was a thrill to discover I had much more in common with Ford than I'd ever imagined. And now, here I was following in his footsteps in the Beaverkill.

As I drove into Roscoe, I passed the historic rail station downtown where Ford and other anglers would disembark. The "Old & Wobbly" operated until 1957, when the railroad was liquidated. The former station now houses the O&W Museum. A few railcars are on display just off the main drag, including the old trout car that hauled fish from various hatcheries to stock rivers along the route.

After getting my bearings in Roscoe, aptly nicknamed Trout Town, I decided to start my explorations by visiting the Catskill Fly Fishing Center & Museum (CFFCM), home of the Fly Fishing Hall of Fame, on the banks of the Willowemoc, just four miles to the east in Livingston Manor. Museum director Glenn Pontier had heard about my Storied Waters journey from an American Museum of Fly Fishing post on social media and invited me to the museum in the Catskills with the promise of a personal tour of the exhibits. I had arranged to meet him there at 11:00 a.m.

The Catskill museum was the brainchild of Elsie Darbee. Elsie and her husband Harry began a fly-tying business in 1935, and their flies were coveted by anglers around the world. When the museum was founded in 1979, Elsie was elected the first president. Elsie and Harry were enshrined in the Hall of Fame in 1999, and Elsie's fly-tying desk is a centerpiece in the main museum building. A similar desk on display is from Winnie and Walt Dette's Fly Shop in Roscoe, the oldest family-run fly shop in the world.

Walt Dette was good friends with Corey Ford and developed a fly in the 1930s he named the Corey Ford Fly, which Ford described in several articles about the

The Theodore Gordon exhibit at the Catskill Fly Fishing Center & Museum includes a mystery photo of an unknown woman fishing with Gordon, apparently in the Neversink River.

Beaverkill, including (according to Mike Valla in his book *The Founding Flies*) a 1931 article in *Vanity Fair* and a 1952 article in *True* magazine called "The Best Loved Trout Stream of Them All." Ford wrote, "Mr. Dette, it appears, has succeeded in manufacturing a Corey Ford Fly. Now if he would only manage somehow to manufacture a Corey Ford trout, which can be guaranteed always to take this lure, my satisfaction will be complete."

Glenn walked me down the porch where seventy brass plaques memorialize the names of other members of the Hall of Fame, including Theodore Gordon, Art Flick (conservationist, fly tier, and author of *Streamside Guide to Naturals and Their Imitations*), Sparse Grey Hackle (journalist and writer), Carrie G. Stevens (professional fly tier and angler from Maine), and many more. I was hoping to see

one for Corey Ford and was disappointed to learn that the museum had no artifacts or exhibits on display about my hero. Perhaps I should start a petition to nominate him for the Fly Fishing Hall of Fame. But at least he has a rugby clubhouse named after him. And as I learned later, he was inducted in 2006 into the Fresh Water Fishing Hall of Fame in Hayward, Wisconsin.

Also front and center in the main museum are flies tied by Theodore Gordon himself, along with some of his letters and other personal papers. The late Alfred W. Miller, known to most as Sparse Grey Hackle, wrote a reverent treatise in 1954 called "The Quest for Theodore Gordon," which recounts Gordon's life and importance to the sport.

Despite all we know about Gordon, I learned during my tour that there is, in fact, one notable mystery at the Catskill museum. A much-published photo of Gordon fishing with a woman in the Neversink River, standing in mid-stream dressed to the nines, has baffled experts for years. Nobody has been able to identify the woman in the photo from around 1895. It serves as a reminder that there are countless untold stories from these waters, far more numerous than the stories that have been written and published over the decades.

A second newer museum building houses the Wulff Gallery with exhibits on Lee Wulff (1905–1991) and Joan Wulff (b. 1928). The Wulffs brought fly fishing into American living rooms through magazines and television. Lee, the author and film producer, flew his own float plane to destinations across North America to make films about fly fishing that were featured on *The American Sportsman* TV show. An innovator all his life, Lee Wulff created several new types of flies, including the popular Royal Wulff, and is even credited with inventing the ubiquitous and always fashionable multipocketed fishing vest. Sadly, Lee crashed his plane near Hancock, New York, in 1991, and whether he died before or after the plane crashed remains a mystery.

Joan, known as the First Lady of Fly Fishing, won the national casting championship seventeen times, including a record cast of 131 feet against an all-male field, and later an unfathomable 161 feet. For decades, she toured the world giving casting demonstrations and has written books and produced videos about fly-casting techniques. In 1979, she and Lee founded the Wulff School of Fly Fishing in Lew Beach on the upper Beaverkill. I had tried to arrange a time to drop in to meet her while I was in the area, but unfortunately her busy speaking and travel schedule—even at age ninety—didn't align with mine.

Downstairs in the same museum building is a workshop where students learn to make bamboo rods on vintage equipment previously owned by the great rod maker Everett Garrison (1893–1975). My stop happened to be on a day when the CFFCM was hosting a group from Back in the Maine Stream, a program that encourages disabled veterans to get involved in fly fishing. When I met the trip leader, Marc Bilodeau, we quickly realized that we lived only ten miles apart in Maine. The world of fly fishing can be small indeed.

With my tour complete, I thanked Glenn for his hospitality and picked up a map and a few souvenirs in the gift shop before moving on to explore the Beaverkill's famous pools.

Wednesday afternoon, May 17

The temperature was approaching 90 degrees as I climbed into my car. I thought I would beat the heat by wading in the cool river, despite the bright afternoon sunshine. Junction Pool seemed like the proper place to start. As I pulled into the parking area, a gentleman, maybe in his seventies, sat on a rock, fly rod in hand, looking discouraged and disappointed.

I walked over and introduced myself. Ed Andrejko was from Burnt Hills, New York. He sighed and expressed his frustration with both the heat and the tree catkins covering the water. "I can't drift a dry fly or nymph without fouling the hook," he grumbled. Looking over his shoulder, I saw several people fanned out across Junction Pool; I was in no rush to join them only to share Ed's frustration.

Ed cheered up as I told him about my grand Storied Waters excursion and asked him about his favorite fishing stories and writers. He was a John Gierach fan. "I love reading his stories during the winter.

A cadre of optimistic anglers await an evening hatch in Barnhardt's Pool, where Corey Ford first learned to fly-fish, just upstream from Hendrickson's Pool.

Gierach is surely one of today's most popular fly-fishing writers who I assumed would find his way into my trip, but I hadn't found any stories of his that intersected with my itinerary. Most of his story settings are out in the Rockies, on the West Coast, or in Canada—fodder for another trip someday west of the Mississippi. Plenty of Gierach fans out there.

But," Ed confessed, "my favorite stories are my own." He said he sometimes publishes short pieces in his local *Trout Unlimited* (TU) chapter newsletter. "Will you tell me a couple?" I asked. His first story he called "A

a sandwich and having a drink, I heard a noise and saw a horse coming toward me. The horse must have smelled my food. He stuck out his tongue and was begging to be fed, but I had no food left. The persistent horse started pushing me backward toward the river with his nose. When I got to the edge, I turned and he pushed me into the bushes and started nipping me. I called my friend to come help me. As soon as he got there, the horse turned and trotted off.

A second story he called "Fishing to Music," which went something like this:

I was fishing the Big Hole River, also in Montana, where I came upon a wedding party in a big field under a tent. As I fished about a hundred yards away, the band struck up a tune and the bride and groom danced while I stood in the river casting my line to the music. The band played on until dark and I remember that beautiful river and the musical evening like it was yesterday.

After the impromptu streamside yarn-fest, Ed's friend Kevin Baughman came up from the stream, equally frustrated. They posed for a photo before they headed off to look for some shade and quiet water. Junction Pool was still too crowded for my taste, and I was further disappointed to see that Route 17, a four-lane divided highway, crossed above the pool. The roar of eighteen-wheelers detracted mightily from the historic ambience of the setting. I climbed back into my air-conditioned car and pulled out my map.

Horse's Tale," about a fishing trip on the Big Horn River in Montana.

A friend and I had walked up the trail from the river access and we started fishing. We were waiting for the Trico hatch to start. A little later, I took a break, left the river, and climbed up the bank. I sat on the trunk of a fallen cottonwood tree. After eating

It looked like a short drive to the upper Beaverkill and the Covered Bridge Pool that was Theodore Gordon's favorite. The road along the river wound through a much quieter, scenic countryside, but for several miles the river was posted by private trout clubs.

Where & How—
Beaverkill and Willowemoc

Admittedly, I didn't have stellar results on the Beaverkill. But timing can be everything, so avoiding the middle of the day when it is really hot and sunny is one lesson learned. Had I been able to fish from 6:00 a.m. to 8:00 a.m., or 6:00 p.m. to 8:00 p.m., perhaps I wouldn't be "Goin' Down the Road Feeling Bad" with the Grateful Dead jamming on my car stereo.

It is always wise to carry a stream thermometer to check the water temperature. Trout and bugs are both very active when the water is 50 to 60 degrees. When the water is above 60 degrees, the trout are more likely to stay deeper or in cooler, more oxygenated water; bigger fish are less willing to move very far to get a bug. If the river water gets much above 65 degrees, think about going bass fishing or playing golf.

What Works: The hot fly of the week or month is usually just what someone says is the hot fly. Flies, of course, come in and out of fashion. Sparse Grey Hackle argued that what works depends on what is used. Here's what he had to say about which trout flies work best in the Catskills (from his chapter "Minor Mysteries" in *Fishless Days, Angling Nights*):

Trout fishermen with long memories can recall the rise and fall in popularity of quite a few flies. The Quill Gordon, the fan-wing Royal Coachman, the long-hackled variant, and longer-hackled spider, the Ratface Macdougal, with a unique body composed of the bristling ends of deer hair, the parachute fly with its hackle horizontal on it back instead of vertical around its neck, the Bivisible hackled from end to end with a white "indicator" for the front face, even George LaBranche's once-famous Pink Lady, each had its turn at being the irresistible, surefire, creel-filling wonder. And after this success had set every angler on the stream to using it, each in its turn became just another fly, good on its day but no better than any other over an extended period.

I wish I had picked local guide Rich Hudgens's brain a bit before my outing on the Beaverkill to get his recommendation for the hot fly on a hot May day. When I spoke with him after my trip, he said that the Beaverkill, a freestone stream, gets a good March Brown hatch, especially in areas with fast flow and large, uneven cobbles. The Hendrickson hatch often ends earlier on the Beaverkill than on the dam-controlled rivers nearby, but then March Browns start coming off sporadically during the day, not in consistent clusters like Hendricksons. Rich recommends nymphing in faster water with a double-rig of size 12 March Brown nymphs or small brown stoneflies that look similar. A large Pheasant Tail Nymph can also imitate a March Brown. And, yes, he agreed, it would have been best if I'd fished in the evening when the sun was lower. ■

A truck roars over the fabled Junction Pool where the Beaverkill and the Willowemoc rivers join forces.

I'm sure the clubs do the river and the trout therein a great service by keeping fishing pressure down. By preserving the undeveloped shoreline, they protect the overall water quality and wild fish population. But the signs, mile after mile, seemed a little menacing and reminded me of the signs at the entrance to the haunted forest in *The Wizard of Oz*. I kept thinking I'd see one that said "I'D TURN BACK IF I WERE YOU."

I drove past the bucolic Beaverkill Community Church where, I suppose, everyone prays to the fishing gods. Then I came upon the famous covered bridge, or rather the recently reconstructed version of the bridge where Gordon liked to fish. It was so new that it was not yet open to traffic. It's no longer possible for pilgrims like me to walk the same worn planks as generations of fly-fishing royalty, but I'm guessing the bridge was in really bad shape, so the reproduction covered bridge will have to serve for the next one hundred years.

I parked in the shade and tied a Quill Gordon onto my floating line. I wasn't sure if that was the proper fly for the conditions, but it seemed like the right thing to do at that time and place. There was no one else foolish enough to be casting into the slow, clear water in the blazing sunshine, but, hey, here I was in Gordon's pool. I had no luck with the Quill Gordon (nothing appeared to be hatching in the heat), so I tried a Royal Wulff, since I was already name-dropping my fly selections. When that didn't work, I switched to a couple classic wet flies like the old-timer Thaddeus Norris might have suggested to use in Catskill streams in *The American Angler's Book*, published in 1864.

I was not at all surprised that there were no signs of fish where I was casting, but a guy fishing with a worm and bobber above the bridge pulled in a sizeable trout as I was walking back to my car. It was good to know there were fish in there, I suppose, but my fly-fishing fantasy world was momentarily shaken. I stashed my rods and waders in my car and meandered back down river.

Finally, as the sun slanted low in the sky throwing sharp shadows across the Battenkill, I pulled up to Hendrickson's Pool, which was the favorite pool of Alfred Hendrickson, for whom the famous Hendrickson dry fly pattern is named. He didn't create the fly nor did he tie it himself; it was originally tied streamside below Junction Pool in 1916 by Roy Steenrod, a protégé of Theodore Gordon, who later named it after his friend Hendrickson. So, Steenrod invented the famed pattern, and Hendrickson got the glory.

Fortunately for me, the pool was far enough from Route 17 that the traffic noise was well muted by the riffle at the head of the pool. Another fisherman arrived as I was getting settled and kindly gave me some pointers on where the fish tend to lie. I looked upstream at Barnhart's Pool, which was growing crowded with a half-dozen anglers who I guessed were casting to rising fish. Or waiting for them to start rising in the twilight. Did I start with a Hendrickson, you might be wondering? No, actually, I started by swinging a couple streamers with sinking line before tying a Hendrickson dry fly onto my floating line rod when the light got lower.

Sadly, I failed to raise a fish in the legendary pool, and I had to leave before the prime hatch time at dusk. With the heat, however, there was no guarantee of a hatch anyway. I'll never know. I drove off into the sunset without having seen a rise or felt a strike in the few hours I fished the Beaverkill. But I'm sure the fish are in there. The water was clean, clear, and gorgeous. The people flocking to the pools were a clear indication that it's still a mecca for the fly-casting faithful.

Chalk my misfortune up to a scorching sunny day or insufficient guile in my approach or both. Timing, as we know, can be everything. And skill is everything else. The harder we work, the luckier we get. Or some cliché like that.

The railroad helped to create the Beaverkill as an iconic destination. The periodic rumble of the trains was eventually replaced by the steady whine of the four-lane highway that crisscrosses the Willowemoc and Beaverkill for miles in the narrow valley. Why is it that a train whistle in the distance has a romantic edge, while the roar of an eighteen-wheeler dulls the charm of a place? Perhaps the people driving over from Long Island or New Jersey don't heed the road noise, or they tune it out as they focus on the fishing, the hills, and the other scenery, but I found that the highway robbed the river of some of its mystique.

Maybe if I had caught a couple big browns, I wouldn't be singing the Beaverkill Blues. Regardless, the Beaverkill is a remarkable river with a singular place in fly-fishing lore. It was an honor to wade in her waters and soak in her history.

I'll go with what Corey Ford said: "The fishing isn't what it used to be."

- 8 -

Mud Run in the Poconos: A Touch of Graystones

Wednesday evening, May 17

After the Catskills, my next stop was the Poconos in eastern Pennsylvania, where my friend Ed Baldrige belongs to Graystones Preserve, a fishing club nestled next to the 16,000-acre Hickory Run State Park, on a small stream called Mud Run. I was planning to meet Ed and several other friends from college there, a fly-fishing reunion of sorts.

But first the drive from Roscoe to Graystones was about two hours. I followed my GPS faithfully through the Pennsylvania countryside and was flabbergasted when suddenly I was driving through Carbondale, where my mother grew up, a coal-miner's daughter during the Depression. I'd never been there, but I had vivid images of her childhood town etched into my mind. The dozens of stories Mom had told us tumbled through my mind as I rubbernecked through downtown, searching for landmarks—the five-and-dime, the viaduct, her old high school—that I might recognize. It was an eerie, emotional experience seeing her hometown with nobody there to guide me. Sometimes you just have a few minutes to absorb the spirit of a place and move along. And so I did, on through the rolling hills.

Pennsylvania is often called the bedrock of American fly fishing. If so, that bedrock is as folded and wrinkled as the fishing clothes stuffed in my duffle. Sandstone, shale, and limestone create the landforms, shaping the watersheds and streambeds of the creeks (pronounced "cricks" around here) and runs (local vernacular for a faster stream) that hold brook trout, rainbows, and some notoriously big brown trout.

Hickory Run State Park and the neighboring Graystones Preserve were once land owned by Ed's great-grandfather's brother, industrialist Henry Clay Trexler. Trexler was a founder of Pennsylvania Power & Light and Lehigh Portland Cement, at one time the world's largest cement producer, among other successful enterprises, including the consolidation of Bell Telephone. Trexler was a noted philanthropist, supporting many organizations, including the Boy Scouts, hospitals, and universities. He was also an outdoorsman.

According to the Lehigh County Historical Society and the Pennsylvania Department of

Conservation and Natural Resources, Trexler purchased the land around Hickory Run starting in 1918 specifically to provide recreation opportunities for nearby communities. In his words,

> We are only a short distance from the anthracite coal region where there is scarcely a blade of grass growing. In the not too distant future, the men will be working shorter hours and they will have more leisure time. Rather than have them loafing in pool rooms and saloons fomenting anarchism, I would like to see Hickory Run developed into a state park where families can come and enjoy wholesome recreation.

So Trexler purchased the land and opened it to the public for hunting and fishing, an unusually selfless thing to do. Well, okay, he was trying to prevent idleness and anarchy, but it still seems pretty generous to me.

After Trexler's death in 1933, the Hickory Run parcel was acquired by the National Park Service. In 1945, after the Second World War, Hickory Run was turned over to the state to become a state park. An adjacent tract, including the lower portion of a stream called Mud Run, was sold to the Bronstein family, who in 1934 founded Graystones as a private fishing preserve. When I visited, Graystones Preserve still leased the club's land from the Bronsteins. The upper portion of Mud Run is in the state park and open to the public (delayed harvest, artificial lures only) and nearby Black Creek and Hickory Run, also in the state park, provide fine fishing for stocked and wild browns. In his *Flyfisher's Guide to Pennsylvania*, Tom Gilmore calls these "three of my favorite wild trout streams."

Mud Run is so-called because in the 1800s the steep sides of the valley were heavily logged. As a result, the stream would run brown with mud before joining the equally murky Lehigh River. Today, the name is a misnomer. Mature forests have regrown, protecting the watershed from erosion and shading the stream to keep it cool. Mud Run is now superbly clear, holding both wild brook trout and stocked rainbows and brown trout. The nearby Lehigh River and several tributaries, including Mud Run, are now designated by the state as a scenic river corridor.

Private fishing clubs are common throughout the Poconos and much of Pennsylvania and the Catskills. As development spread west in the 1800s, land was being heavily harvested for timber, converted to farms, and mined for coal. In response, wealthy businessmen and entrepreneurs began buying up large tracts along the rivers during the late nineteenth and early twentieth centuries to offer rustic fishing getaways—camps, clubs, and lodges—to people looking for an outdoor adventure. Thaddeus Norris and Theodore Gordon fished Brodhead Creek in the late 1800s, which was celebrated as the cradle of American fly fishing in Ernie Schwiebert's encyclopedic work, *Trout* (1978). As trout fishing grew in popularity in the late nineteenth century, streams were heavily stocked with brown trout and rainbow trout to keep the clientele happy. Browns and rainbows tolerate warmer temperatures better than native brook trout and so have done particularly well across Pennsylvania.

The first time I ever fished in Pennsylvania was in the 1990s on Tobyhanna Creek with Sim Savage, a friend from Maine who worked at L.L. Bean at the time. His family belonged to a private club, so we had the opportunity to fish their club's section of the river. That historic fishing preserve seemed like a Disneyland for anglers. The streams were engineered by carefully placing rocks

Norm and Ed casting for browns or rainbows in the stretch below the dam on Mud Run at Graystones Preserve in the Poconos.

to form perfect pools and cascades. I noticed that I didn't have to worry about my backcast because the vegetation had been manicured to remove all obstacles behind the favored casting spots. We all caught fish and had great fun that trip, but I prefer things a little wilder and woolier.

Like the streams at other fishing clubs, Mud Run at Graystones has been "improved" over the years, but in ways more subtle than Sim's club on the Tobyhanna, with the notable exception of a stone dam built in Mud Run to create a deep pool to hold larger trout. There happen to be convenient openings in the underbrush in prime locations, but still plenty of overhanging branches to steal your fly. A few of the bigger pools have some very large feed-fattened fish. In most places, though, the fish have grown accustomed to

foraging for natural food sources. They can be quite picky and well-educated about which flies are real and which were made by the hand of man.

And there was still plenty of unimproved pocketwater up and down the three miles of stream where wild and wary fish hide under vegetated cutbanks and in deep plunge pools. It's also important to note that these private clubs protect and improve the water quality and the spawning and rearing habitat, benefiting the entire watershed for miles upstream and downstream.

I pulled into the access road to Graystones about 9:00 on Wednesday night and rumbled down the two miles of twisty, narrow dirt road to the cottage that Ed had rented for a couple nights. I thought for a minute that I was at the wrong place, because through the screen door I saw a bunch of gray-haired guys sitting around the dinner table. But then I realized that these were, no surprise, my college classmates who had come down to join me for this stop on my Storied Waters journey.

My own reflection in the window reminded me that I'm no longer the strapping young dark-haired dude I continue to picture in my mind's eye. I recall something I heard Andy Rooney say years ago: "I'm every age I've ever been." My friends and I are still young at heart, even if our cranky joints complain from time to time.

After a round of handshakes and proper man-hugs, I popped a cold beer and pulled up a chair to scarf down a plate of the lasagna someone had brought, now just above room temperature. There was a big bowl of salad and enough Italian bread to make a hearty meal. I was hungry.

Ed had been fishing that evening with Norm Richter, Dave Klinges (whom we call Klingon), and my longtime fishing buddy from Maine, Lou Zambello. Norm, you may recall, had fished with me at Walden Pond and had stopped in to fish with us on the way to visit his father near Philadelphia. Klingon lives nearby in New Jersey, so it was an easy hop over to join us. Lou had come down to make a full swing across Pennsylvania and would be tagging along with me for the next few days.

Ed, Norm, and Klingon are all coauthors of *The Confluence*, so we had managed to assemble four of the seven "Boys of the Grant" for this particular outing. Lou, a Maine guide, fly-fishing author, and fishing celebrity in his own right, had written the foreword to our book, so we consider him an adjunct member of our gang.

As Klingon poured himself more cabernet and refilled several glasses, it was heartening to hear that the trout were rising and the

Boys had each caught a few that evening. Given the heat wave we were experiencing, Ed suggested we get up and out early the next morning before the sun hit the water. Everyone agreed, and we all soon hit the hay, saving the hard, late-night drinking for another time.

Thursday morning, May 18

At 5:00 a.m., some durn bird was chirping incessantly outside my open window. Now I love birds, don't get me wrong, but I didn't immediately recognize this one's call or I might have cut it some slack. Maybe it annoyed me precisely because I couldn't identify it. Anyway, five comes too early, even for a fly fisher and bird lover, so anyone has a right be a little grumpy at that hour.

Everyone was up and we had coffee brewing by six. Lou was already on the stream, as he doesn't drink coffee like the other Boys and can't wait to get going. After enjoying a steaming mug on the front porch, the rest of us headed out into the morning mist, hoping for some early action. Lou was somewhere upriver, and the rest of us spread out within shouting distance along the bank below the cottage.

Ed had the first fish of the morning, a 14-inch rainbow trout. Tally one in the coffee-drinker column. Next up, Norm whooped joyfully when he got his first strike, but he didn't manage to set the hook quickly enough. It was a clear case of premature e-whoop-ulation.

Soon we noticed fish rising in the long glide below the dam. Several of us moved down and started to toss dry flies out just upstream of the rise rings. We couldn't see what was hatching, but Ed guessed perhaps a Blue-Winged Olive or March Brown hatch might be starting. We had little response from the rising fish before human stomachs started to rumble. Just as the others started to head back for breakfast, I hooked a peppy 17-inch brown trout on a Parachute Quill Gordon mayfly pattern. I quickly landed it with my net and snapped a picture of the golden, glistening trout so the others would believe me. Otherwise, a resounding round of "Sure, Dave, sure!" would be in the offing upon my announcement.

After breakfast, we all spread out, some upstream and some down, looking for shady water. Apparently Lou had trekked a long way up to the wilder pocketwater and had not returned, which could have been either a sign of success or sheer stubbornness, but certainly stamina. Klingon and I together worked a couple deep shady pools, where I hooked a big rainbow that threw my hook on the fourth jump. I still call that a success: an LDR (long distance release) counts in my book, especially after four jumps. And Klingon was a witness.

After lunch, the day grew very warm. Klingon decided to pass on fishing in the heat and head back to New Jersey for a business meeting. My business for the day was on the water. Ed, Norm, and I went bouncing down the road in Ed's Suburban to explore where Mud Run enters the Lehigh River under an old limestone arch bridge.

The Lehigh River's recent recovery is a success story for the Clean Water Act, as it was once highly polluted from municipal sewage, industry, and coal mine waste. Today, thanks to strict discharge limits for industry and treatment plants constructed since the law's passage in 1972, the river is now clean enough to get heavy use from rafting, canoes, and kayaks. According to Tom Gilmore, author of the recently updated *Flyfisher's*

A willing brown trout brought to net just before breakfast at Graystones.

Where & How—
The Poconos: Mud Run

It's tempting to think that fishing on private, stocked water is too easy, like shooting fish in a barrel as the cliché goes. There is a distinct advantage, no doubt, when you know the fish are there, that they are bigger than most wild fish, and there is less fishing pressure from the general public. But that doesn't guarantee success on any given day or in any given pool. As our group demonstrated, it is possible to fish diligently for hours and only catch one or two trout. The fish, it seems, learn to key on real food rather than artificial flies. They cue in on movement or color or drift or action in the water.

What Works: Ed Baldrige has been fishing in the Poconos his entire life. When nothing else works, he says, the best technique in a smaller stream like Mud Run is nymphing. With a 10-foot rod, an angler can easily get the fly almost anywhere on either side of the stream without a long cast. The trick is to get the fly down near the trout's nose, so it makes the trout's decision to take a bite that much easier while expending little energy.

According to Ed and some well-known guides he has worked with, like George Daniel, the emphasis should be on the presentation, depth, and size of the fly and less on the particular pattern. That said, Black Stonefly Nymphs (sizes 12-16), Zebra Midges (18-22) and Pheasant Tails (12-18) are staples for Pennsylvania fly fishing. In heavily pressured water, Ed says, avoid brightly colored bead heads, which seem to alert the trout; instead use black bead heads or split shot to get the flies down to where the fish are eating.

Ed often fishes with Tenkara gear, which is a good fit for a stream like Mud Run, although it can be a challenge to land a bigger fish without a reel. Tenkara is a traditional style of fishing used on small mountain streams in Japan with a long (11 to 13 feet) telescoping rod that is a very flexible rod and collapses down to about 20 inches. The light line is about the length of the rod, and there is no reel or spool of line. The casting stroke is similar to a Western rod, but the fly can be dapped on the surface, twitched, or pulsed while it drifts.

Traditional Tenkara flies, called *sakasa kebari*, look like soft-hackle spider flies, which originated 200 years ago in England, but with the hackle reversed on the hook. They can be drifted like a nymph, skittered, or retrieved in the current in a very lifelike pattern. Hopefully, that will fool some fish. ■

Ed leads the way to the confluence of Mud Run and the Lehigh River under a stone railroad bridge.

Guide to Pennsylvania, the Lehigh has some excellent trout fishing, although we didn't have a chance to explore it on this outing. Maybe next time I visit Ed, we'll give the Lehigh a try.

The early evening hatch on Mud Run gave us all a few more gray hairs. The fish were rising steadily to what we ultimately determined to be tiny, nearly invisible midges, but none of us could get them to take a fly, no matter how small. I had only one or two short hits in ninety minutes. Later, during dinner, Lou said he had finally figured out that the trout were keying on motion, so a tiny twitch of his fly would sometimes result in a strike. He managed to hook a few but wasn't able to land more than a couple before it got dark. He also reported that he had caught several fish upstream earlier in the day, which accounted for his prolonged absence.

By the time we cleaned up the dishes, we were all exhausted. We celebrated the day with a round of Bell's Two Hearted Ales—with the awesome fish logo—that Norm had picked up in anticipation of my journey to Hemingway country on the Upper Peninsula of Michigan. Lou and I had to be up and out early to get to State College for our next stop, so after a final toast to a great day, we hit the hay.

As we loaded our cars the next morning and said goodbye to Ed, Lou and I agreed that it was a pleasure and privilege fishing at Mud Run, a gem of a stream.

- 9 -

Spring Creek & Spruce Creek: Fine Fishing in State College, Pennsylvania

Friday morning, May 19

"I'll meet you at Fisherman's Paradise," Phil said.

At first, I thought it was some kind of inside joke or a nickname for his favorite fishing spot. I assumed he would give me specific directions later. But then he explained that Fisherman's Paradise is actually a well-known public fishing park near State College, home of Penn State University.

Lou Zambello and I left Graystones mid-morning, and after several hours of driving west across Pennsylvania, we saw a directional sign on the highway that said "Fisherman's Paradise 1." That, of course, is where we exited.

Fisherman's Paradise is on a highly productive limestone stream with classic milky water called Spring Creek that runs north from State College through neighboring Bellefonte. Its nearby cousin, Spruce Creek, flows south on the other side of the Penn State campus. Phil's plan was to show us around Fisherman's Paradise, take us to Spruce Creek in the afternoon, then return in time to catch the Sulfur hatch on Spring Creek that evening.

Charles Philip Boinske—Chas to some, Phil to most—was introduced to me by Ed Baldrige. Both are Pennsylvania natives, both work as investment advisors, and the two friends share a passion for fly fishing. Phil, a friendly, outgoing man in his fifties, had enthusiastically agreed to show Lou and me around his local stomping grounds. When we pulled into the parking lot at Fisherman's Paradise, he was waiting for us by his olive-drab Toyota Sequoia. He greeted us with a warm cherubic smile and a strong handshake.

Phil told us that George Harvey used to sit right there by the stream in Fisherman's Paradise and sell flies while giving out advice. Known as the Dean of American Fly Fishing, Professor Harvey taught what is believed to be the first college-level course in fly fishing at Penn State. Many of his students went on to become notable instructors and authors.

Harvey also fished with Presidents Eisenhower and Carter on the various limestone creeks in the area. In the spirit of Professor Harvey, Phil handed Lou some flies he had tied himself: a selection of small bead-head nymphs, Sulfur emerger patterns, and a couple soft-hackle Sulfur flies.

Sulfurs are a species of yellow mayfly about the size of a dime. They emerge from the stream predictably at dusk in mid-May in this part of Pennsylvania, causing a feeding frenzy among the trout. The Sulfur hatch is much anticipated by fly fishers, who flock to the stream for the chance to catch multiple fish and possibly bigger fish that move in to feed on these sizeable bugs. With a hatch expected that evening, the nymphs would be active beneath the surface during the day, and the trout would be looking for them.

As he handed Lou the flies, Phil explained that Fisherman's Paradise was set aside by the Pennsylvania Fish Commission (PFC) many years ago as a special regulations area near its Bellefonte fish hatchery, right across the stream from where we were chatting. Ironically, the PFC stopped stocking fish here at one point because of pollution from commercial and suburban development in the watershed around the university. Despite occasional insults from upstream, the water quality is now good enough to support a naturally reproducing population of brown trout, with rainbows swimming in their midst. "Wear waders," Phil advised, "especially in the warm weather" because of possible bacteria in the water from storm sewers. Good advice.

"Even with the occasional water-quality issues, Spring Creek has the highest density of trout per mile in the commonwealth," Phil continued. Once he heard that last tidbit of information, Lou decided to stay at Fisherman's Paradise and hike upstream to a section that gets less pressure. With Phil's flies in hand, Lou was ready to roll.

Phil hands Lou some hand-tied flies for the upcoming Sulfur hatch at Fisherman's Paradise on Spring Creek in Bellefonte, Pennsylvania.

Phil and I climbed into his vehicle to go to Spruce Creek for the afternoon. But first he wanted me to meet Steve Sywensky, another former Penn State fly-fishing instructor and proprietor of a nearby fly shop, Flyfisher's Paradise, that was on our way across town. When we walked into the shop, Steve was tying flies at a table up front while listening to tall tales from two local guys seated on each side. Phil introduced me around and gestured for me to sit down with the group. He mentioned that I was on an epic fishing adventure and wanted to meet some of the local experts. But Phil could barely get a word in, and my unfolding Storied Waters odyssey was summarily ignored. Instead, I was impressed with how the two guys watching Steve tie flies simply couldn't wait for the other to stop talking so he could jump in with a whopper of his own to try to top the previous story.

As the tall tales continued nonstop, I got up and strolled to the counter to buy a few flies before Phil quietly ushered me back out into the bright sunlight. As far as I know, those guys are still in there talking. We got back into Phil's truck to go meet a couple more friends at the Spruce Creek Tavern for lunch a few miles south of town.

We drove past old farmhouses built from cut limestone blocks and an enormous dairy farm that Phil said was owned by Wayne Harpster. According to Phil, the Harpster family takes great pride in protecting Spruce Creek, which meanders along the edge of their 1,600-cow farm, with state-of-the-art conservation practices to shade the stream and reduce soil erosion. This stretch of mostly private water is another mecca for fly-fishing fanatics and can be accessed through Harpster's Evergreen Farms either with a day fishing permit or by staying in one of their rental units. Phil turned down a side road to

"The Cottage," with its broad porch that over-looks the scenic creek and a covered bridge.

The most notable visitor to Spruce Creek and the Harpster's Evergreen Farms cottage was President Jimmy Carter, who began fishing in this area when he was our thirty-ninth president. President Carter became close friends with Wayne Harpster and George Harvey while fishing the clear, cold water for wild trout over many years. Phil pointed to the field behind the cottage where the presidential helicopter would land and showed me the plaque that explained how Jimmy and Rosalynn Carter had helped Wayne build the covered bridge across the creek.

Jimmy Carter recounted his fishing success here in his memoir *An Outdoor Journal*, in a chapter called "Trout Fishing and a Birthday: Spruce Creek." One year, the Carters timed their visit in late May to celebrate Wayne's birthday while fishing the Green Drake mayfly hatch. In reading his account, I was impressed with President Carter's detailed descriptions of hatches, fly selections, tackle, and tactics, including fishing into the evening darkness. I was also pleased to learn that the First Lady was a first-rate fly fisher as well, often outfishing her husband. Carter's three sons and their families also joined in the action on Spruce Creek. Young Amy never took much to fly fishing, according to her dad.

President Carter recalled how he learned nymph fishing from another Pennsylvania icon, Joe Humphreys, author of *Trout Tactics* (1981) and also a professor at Penn State. As related in the president's book, before going out one day, Joe asked Jimmy,

"What's your favorite kind of fishing?"

When I [Carter] told him, "Dry fly, rising trout, long leaders, fine tippet, deep water," he said, "Then let's try nymphs

Phil gently handles a wild brown trout landed and released on Spruce Creek near State College, Pennsylvania.

on the bottom in the riffles in shallow pocket water!"

It was the first time I had fished this way. In a few minutes, I was using Joe's tuck cast . . . trying to remember to keep my rod tip high as the nymph floated toward me. . . . The fish seemed to be waiting for us and took the nymphs regularly. The trout we caught were larger, on the average, than our usual daytime catch on dry flies.

The president also told of hooking his first really big trout in Spruce Creek but losing him in a tangle of brush. "I had more than met my match," he admitted. "For a few moments I forgot the church sermon and my Baptist training and said some choice words that disturbed the former quiet of the murmuring stream."

Amen.

At Spruce Creek tavern, Phil and I met Skip Galbraith, a local guide and commercial fly tier who has been fishing this stream for thirty years. Also joining us for lunch was Kevin Compton, who owns another fly shop next to the tavern. When I described my combined fishing and literary quest, Kevin eagerly told me that he had met author Jim Harrison years ago and had given Jim some flies. We chatted about Harrison's books—*True North* and *Legends of the Fall*—during lunch; I told him I planned to fish the Yellow Dog River, which appears in *True North*, when I visited the Upper Peninsula.

Skip was a very soft-spoken guy who looked strikingly like my brother: white beard and white hair in a ponytail with a rocky, bow-legged gait. While quiet, Skip seemed well-equipped to give me some good pointers for fishing Spruce Creek. After lunch, Phil and Skip took me to a place simply called Jack's, behind a house owned by a friend of theirs (yes, Jack) on the bank of the slightly milky creek. Skip directed me to a beautiful little pool about as wide as my driveway and ten yards long. I approached it cautiously, flipped my fly across the pool, and promptly missed a splashy strike by a good-size trout. These wild fish didn't mess around. With less fishing pressure in this private stretch, they seemed very enthusiastic.

We plied several more pools in the narrow stream with Phil landing four to my none. I missed another quick strike, then hooked a feisty fish for a moment but lost it when it threw the fly on its third jump. There seems to be a pattern here for me with the jumping fish and the hook-throwing thing.

Before I knew it, we had to say our good-byes to Skip in order to meet Lou at Fisherman's Paradise as arranged. In spite of all the expert advice, I hadn't caught a Spruce Creek brownie, but the wild trout certainly were willing participants, if perhaps a bit too quick for me that day. With a little patience and better timing, I would have had more chances and eventual success. But so it goes when you're on a schedule.

When we got back to Spring Creek, Phil pointed out some private water below the public park where Lou and I could fish the evening hatch with less competition from the crowd. Phil said he knew the landowner and had gotten the okay for us to fish there. At precisely 5:00, we rolled into the Paradise parking lot, where Lou was waiting. The place was swarming with fly fishers gearing up to stake out a spot in the creek for the famous evening Sulfur hatch.

Lou was a little down after a challenging afternoon with the bright sunshine and competition for pools and runs, even in the upper sections, but as always, he was anxious

to fish through to the evening hatch without a break. That man can go days on just snacks and Diet Coke. Phil had to head home to an evening event with his wife, so we thanked him for all his help and advice (and his flies) before heading downstream to the run that Phil had pointed out earlier.

Friday evening, May 18
Lou and I were standing in Spring Creek still waiting for the Sulfur hatch to start. It

Two anglers chat amiably while awaiting the Sulfur hatch on Spring Creek below Fisherman's Paradise.

was now almost 8:00 p.m., so we were wondering if the hatch would happen at all. The day had been very warm and I wondered aloud if perhaps the mid-May heat had thrown the bugs off, but Lou reminded me that in a spring creek the water temperature tends to stay cool. A few fish were rising sporadically. We each landed a small brown trout in short order, but so far things were pretty quiet.

Two men were sitting on rocks in the middle of the creek a hundred yards downstream from us, waiting for the hatch to start while chatting away like they were in a hotel lobby. We could faintly hear their voices above the burbling water. Another man and woman cast languorously in the run below them.

Lou decided to go back downstream to Christian's Pool, so named by Phil after his son's success there, where we had started

Where & How—Spruce Creek & Spring Creek

Spruce Creek is thirteen miles of Class A wild brown trout water, but unfortunately nearly all of the land on either side of the stream is privately owned and posted against trespassing. Some private landowners, including the Harpsters, charge a fee for access to the creek

There is a half-mile public stretch that is owned by Penn State University, named in honor of George Harvey, which gets heavy use at certain times. Still, the best way to access the river is to book some time with a local landowner and/or guide. Most of the spring creeks in Pennsylvania are fishable year-round.

What Works: Spruce Creek has reliable hatches of the same species found in other local streams: Blue-Winged Olives, Sulfurs, Green Drakes, March Browns and Light Cahills. Of course, hiring a guide will increase the chance of success at any time of the year.

Public access is less of a problem on *Spring Creek*, but expect to have plenty of company on the stream. Fortunately, despite the pressure, the fishing is still excellent.

What Works: When I was in Steve Sywensky's fly shop, I picked up a book called *Fly Fishing Pennsylvania's Spring Creek* by Daniel L. Shields (2003), a true local expert. Lou and I were lucky to be there during a hatch, but Shields offers this advice for fishing when hatches aren't happening:

Hatches are fun, but what really grows Spring Creek trout is its supply of freshwater crustaceans and aquatic worms. These critters fill voids between hatches, and only the strongest emergences override trouts' predisposition to them. . . . Sowbugs are the staff of life for Spring Creek trout. . . . Its numbers peak in late summer and early fall, when other food forms are less available. . . . Muskrat nymphs imitate sowbugs very well. . . .

Freshwater shrimp, or scuds . . . .are more numerous than sowbugs in many parts of the stream. . . .

The most important [baitfish] is the sculpin, which exists throughout the watershed. Shenk's Sculpin is my favorite imitation. ■

---

earlier around 6:00 p.m. I stayed put and continued casting rhythmically to a pair of rises in the faster water on the far bank, when suddenly—*yikes!* I was startled from my trance by my cell phone ringing in the breast pocket of my waders. I sometimes carry my phone along in its waterproof case to take pictures or a video, but this was the first time it ever rang while I was fishing.

I thought it was Lou calling to give me an update on conditions in his pool below. Reluctantly, I answered, "Hello?"

I really hate that cell service commercial that brags about putting cell towers everywhere; they show a fisherman talking on the phone, sending texts and pictures from the middle of a stream. I would never be that guy. But now I *was* that guy.

This part of Spring Creek runs through a suburban neighborhood where the smell of burgers on a grill wafts downstream from nearby yards, so talking on the phone didn't seem quite so out of place. But still.

The call wasn't from Lou, it was Bill Skilton, director of the Pennsylvania Fly Fishing Museum in Carlisle calling to confirm our meeting time the next day. As I talked to Bill, holding the phone in my left hand, I was casually flipping my fly into the current with the rod in my right hand. I noticed a couple Sulfurs fluttering in the air while I finalized arrangements with Bill.

Just then a brown trout took my fly. And he hooked himself solidly.

There I was, standing in the river talking on the phone with one hand, trying to keep the line tight on the fish with the other. I blurted to Bill that I needed to call him back, just as the phone beep-beeped again; the screen showed that this time it was Lou. Two calls at once while playing a fish. A busy day at the office. Maybe I should hire an assistant to screen my calls:

"Mr. Van Wie, there's a Mr. Brown holding on line two! I'll tell Mr. Zambello you'll call him back shortly."

I stuffed the phone into my waders, ignoring Lou, and managed to land the fish, ten inches of pure exuberance. Now the Sulfur hatch was finally starting. Time to get dialed into the fishing. I released the fish and called Bill back to say a proper goodbye. He laughed when I told him a brown trout had connected on my other line.

I called Lou back to tell him, "Get your ass up here! The hatch is starting!" He had just landed a 12-inch brownie in the lower pool but was coming back up anyway. In the next forty-five minutes, until dark, Lou and I each landed a half-dozen fish, including one final 12-inch brown that hammered my fly even though it was so dark I couldn't see the fly on the water. The fish splashed and hooked himself so well that I had little trouble landing him, but I could barely see the fly in the fish's mouth to remove the hook. I flipped on my headlamp, unhooked the fly, and released my last fish into the dark water of Fisherman's Paradise.

Now it was 9:00 and time for dinner. We grabbed a table at Otto's Pub and Brewery for—what else?—fish tacos and a Spruce Creek Lager. Lou and I had quite a pleasant meal catching up on the adventures of the day. Phil was a fabulous guide, far more help than we had ever hoped. And the fishing more than lived up to the reputation that the Pennsylvania limestone creeks so much deserve. And there was more to come.

- 10 -

Yellow Breeches & the Letort Spring Run

Yellow Breeches,
Full of stitches,
Mammy sewed the buttons on.
Daddy kicked me out of bed
For sleeping with my breeches on.
(Traditional song)

Saturday morning, May 19

The origin of the creek's name is uncertain, but it is unquestionably colorful. According to the Yellow Breeches Watershed Association, the name Yellow Breeches dates back to the 1700s, when it appeared on various deeds and maps. The origin of the silly song is unknown. No matter where the name came from, the Yellow Breeches is a fine fishing creek.

After an educational day and evening fishing in the State College area, Lou and I drove south two hours on Saturday morning over the accordion hills of central Pennsylvania toward Boiling Springs and Carlisle. Saturday was overcast and a tad muggy. Perfect for fishing. The Allman Brothers Band serenaded me with "Seven Turns" as the road twisted through a maze of steep valleys with at least "seven rivers to cross."

Neither of us knew where we were going exactly, but we both wanted to try the Yellow

Breeches before my scheduled meeting at the Pennsylvania Fly Fishing Museum, which had recently relocated from the banks of the Yellow Breeches in Boiling Springs to a new home on the banks of the Letort Spring Run in Carlisle. Thanks to *Flyfisher's Guide to Pennsylvania*, Lou and I were able to navigate quickly to a parking lot at "the Run" below the small lake, called Children's Lake, which is fed by several artesian springs in the center of scenic Boiling Springs (pop. 3,225). A historic gristmill graces one end of the lake, and a number of buildings around it are built from limestone blocks. I was surprised to learn that the Appalachian Trail passes through town (as did the Underground Railroad) following the edge of the lake right past the TCO Fly Shop (formerly Yellow Breeches Outfitters) and the Boiling Springs Tavern.

The Run is a short section of stream—just a few hundred yards—that flows from the dam at Children's Lake down to the main stem of

Yellow Breeches Creek, a classic slightly milky limestone creek, one of only thirteen rivers designated as a scenic river under the Pennsylvania Scenic Rivers Act. The cool, clear spring water from the Run enhances the trout habitat downstream in the main stem of "the Breeches," as it is called. The Run and a one-mile section of the Breeches downstream are catch-and-release fishing only.

When Lou and I pulled into the parking lot near the dam, we admired the old stone ironworks furnace that towers over the Run. Nearby, two fishermen were chatting at a picnic table at the edge of the parking area. Lou strolled right up to "to the fishiest-looking guy" (as he explained to me later, he's done this many times) to ask for help orienting ourselves and to maybe get a tip on fly choices to get us started. It doesn't always work, but this time he struck pay dirt.

Jim Marafka, a loquacious fellow in his sixties with a trimmed gray goatee, was wearing a camo cap and shirt sporting the logo of the Yellow Breeches Anglers and Conservation Association, which, he proudly said, had just stocked thousands of trout in several sections of the river, including the Run. He pulled binders of info about fishing in the area from his car and spread across the picnic table his impressive collection of books by Pennsylvania authors—George Harvey, Jim Leisenring, Vernon "Pete" Hidy, Vince Marinaro—who had written about the Breeches and the Letort. Jim's vehicle was literally a library and fly shop. Who carries a library in his car when he goes fishing? Well, other than me?

Jim showed us his collection of flies, mostly traditional wet flies, flymphs, and streamers. Flymphs are sort of a cross between a wet fly and a nymph, meant to imitate insects that

Jim's fly box is bursting with flymphs he tied for fishing on Yellow Breeches Creek.

"The Run" feeds into Yellow Breeches Creek from Children's Lake in the center of Boiling Springs, Pennsylvania. The Carlisle Iron Works Furnace is in the background.

are metamorphosing from swimming stage to flying stage. Jim gave Lou a couple flies, including a big ugly streamer Jim called "The Spook," which had a 2-inch-long yellow foam body and long gray mallard-down wings, similar to a large pale version of a Wood Special. Lord knows what it imitates, but Jim assured us that The Spook would prove effective on the Breeches.

When we asked why there were so few anglers at the Run on such a perfect Saturday morning, Jim explained that "everyone is up in the general regulation area where we just stocked. Most of them are chasing the trucks

Lou stayed behind a few more minutes chatting with Jim. I found where the Run enters the Breeches and waded across the knee-deep creek under a full canopy of streamside trees to cast, as instructed, toward the bank where cool water entering from the Run lowers the temperature of the water in the main stem flow.

I had one strike almost immediately on a March Brown wet fly swung in the current but failed to hook up. Rats! Soon Lou came by to check in, then wandered farther downstream from me as I kept working my way toward him. As so often happens, just five minutes after I had moved thirty yards down to the next run, a young man waded into the same spot where I had that first strike and caught a plump trout on a spinning lure. Probably the same fish I had missed, a brown trout I think. Grrrr!

When I reached Lou, it was time for me to go. He stayed to explore more water and try some different flies, while I departed for the museum to meet Bill Skilton.

Saturday afternoon, May 20

The newly relocated PAFFM is a beauty of a place with glass-encased exhibits that look like shrines to the greats of Pennsylvania fly fishing: George Harvey, Joe Humphreys, Vince Marinaro, Charlie Fox, Jim Leisenring, Ed Shenk, Ross Trimmer (Bill Skilton's great-uncle), Lefty Kreh, and even Bill Skilton himself.

Tall, with a trimmed beard and a rumpled fly-fishing shirt, Bill is himself an important piece of fly-fishing history in the commonwealth and knew most of the museum's honorees personally. He grew up working in the fly shop in Boiling Springs, learning from many of the greats who stopped there regularly. In addition to his duties as museum director, Bill now sells flies and fly-tying

so they can catch fish to keep." We were glad we timed our visit so perfectly, as we had the catch-and-release section almost to ourselves.

There was only an hour to fish before I was to meet Bill Skilton at the Pennsylvania Fly Fishing Museum (PAFFM) in Carlisle, about fifteen minutes away. I extracted myself politely from Jim's clutches so I could get started down the path where he pointed.

materials online and trades in fly-fishing memorabilia.

While showing me around the museum, Bill provided some insightful lessons in the history of bamboo and graphite rod construction, and thus solved the mystery from the American Museum of Fly Fishing in Vermont about why the male and female ferrules on bamboo rods were switched on modern rods. Bill said it has to do with how the metal would wear with use. Metal-on-metal wears out over time and can be replaced on bamboo rods. A male end on the bottom/reel section was easiest to work with and more convenient to replace when it would wear down. "For a few years, there were hybrid setups—some manufacturers experimented, especially with fiberglass rods—until graphite took over, eliminating the metal altogether, and the current system of female on the bottom section became the standard."

There you have it. One mystery at the museum solved. Bill couldn't help me with the mystery woman in the photo with Theodore Gordon. But I was pleased that my quest had been fruitful. I couldn't wait to tell my wife about my successful sleuthing!

With that one solved, I couldn't help but notice another mystery at the Pennsylvania museum: Why were no women included in the exhibits? I noticed just one photo of Chauncy Lively's wife, Marion. There have always been women who love fly fishing and certainly some famous, skilled women have cast a rod in the Keystone State; Rosalynn Carter comes immediately to mind. A growing number of women are out on the water today, but it was clear from my brief visit to the PAFFM that our sport needs to work much harder, as Orvis and Trout Unlimited are trying to do, to reach out beyond the current core demographic of middle-aged white guys to include more women, young people, and people of color. It would be very good for the sport.

After the tour, Bill and I walked down to the lawn behind the building to where the Letort Spring Run flows past the museum. Bill indulged me by taking a few photos of me casting and drifting some flies in the famous stream. I lamented having no time to actually fish the river. But everything I'd read indicated that the Letort is one of the trickiest streams to master. For many it is a long-term, if not lifelong, project. Here is Vince Marinaro's assessment of the Letort in his seminal 1950 book, *A Modern Dry-Fly Code*:

What can I say of the Letort? Certainly it is beautiful, not with the wild beauty of our mountain freestone streams, decked out in their garish display of laurel and rhododendron, but rather with the calm and serene beauty of pastoral scenery. Nestled in a little valley, with gently rolling hills on both sides, it meanders slowly and evenly, its placid surface hardly ever ruffled even by the westerly winds. . . .

The reader must not suppose, however, that these features indicate a lack of character in the Letort. It could not be so, in consideration of its great depth and vast weed beds and channels exerting their subtle influence underneath the calm exterior, creating currents and crosscurrents, intermingling them in a sinuous manner which, barely noticeable to the casual visitor, causes no end of astonishment and despair in his efforts to overcome drag. The Letort is a hard taskmaster and does not treat lightly any violation of dry-fly technique. Any suggestion of drag, heaviness in the cast, or thick gut [leader] is magnified many times on such a calm surface, and the penalty is absolute and total failure.

The author makes some ceremonial casts on Letort Spring Run behind the Pennsylvania Fly Fishing Museum in Carlisle.

Marinaro and his close friend Charlie Fox spent many hours studying the Letort and its fickle fish, testing various techniques including tiny flies (Fox called it "the Art of Diminution") or grasshopper patterns on thin leaders. I love Fox's story of an enormous trout, estimated at 8 to 10 pounds, that he called Vesuvius. After watching it feed on real hoppers, then refuse several imitations, Marinaro eventually hooked it on an artificial hopper on a superthin 5X tippet, only to have the fish break the line. They never saw the fish again.

In passing up on my chance to fish the Letort Spring Run, I chose to forego the frustration of this "hard taskmaster." I calculated that "absolute and total failure" would likely have been the outcome of my efforts to try to solve the Letort in just one afternoon.

After my ceremonial photo op, I returned to the Yellow Breeches to catch up with Lou before he drifted back to Maine. As I climbed into my car, Lou texted me that he was catching fish, and they were rising to dry flies. Now I was pumped to hook one or two trout under the favorable conditions in the Breeches before moving along to my next stop: Wisconsin.

I parked again at the Run and worked my way back downriver, looking for Lou. As I waded quietly, trout were rising along the far bank. I noticed a few mayflies in the air, so I switched to a light green mayfly pattern. I was rewarded for all my effort with a solid strike by a 9-inch wild brown trout with bright red spots and a golden belly. What a striking beauty! It was even more fun to watch it dart back across the river when I released it.

Where & How—Yellow Breeches

Jake Villwock, a young guide working at the TCO Fly Shop in Boiling Springs, told me that the catch-and-release, artificial lures only section near the Run in Boiling Springs is consistently productive, and is a mix of stocked and wild fish. But Jake also likes to fish in the Upper Breeches, about ten river miles upstream from Boiling Springs beyond Mount Holly. "While there is more private water in that area, the ecosystem is healthier and there are lots of wild fish ten inches and under," he says.

What Works: Jake has found that nymphing is the most consistently productive method in the Yellow Breeches, especially when the water is a little high, "unless there is a crazy, crazy hatch," he said.

"We've got lots of bug life on the Breeches: Sulfurs, Grannom caddis, golden stoneflies, Hendricksons. And when the caddis and mayflies start coming off, the wild trout respond first to dry flies and are the most playful. The wild fish also tend to be tight to the bank when stocked fish push them out of the more obvious holes." Jake said he prefers cul de canard (CDC) patterns for dry flies; CDC Sulfurs and Grannom caddis work well.

The Breeches is a fine example of how Pennsylvania spring creeks can bring year-round fishing pleasure—in spring and fall, midsummer, and even midwinter, a good trip to make when the northern rivers are locked under several feet of snow and ice. Or . . . maybe when spring starts a month or two earlier down there than is does in New England, I'll find my way back to Boiling Springs. ∎

Lou made his way upstream to me, and soon said his goodbyes after telling me about all the fish he'd caught, of course. After he left, I stayed to cast for another thirty minutes and had a few more chances at rising fish, but wasn't able to get another hookup. But, hey, at least I didn't experience absolute and total failure! I was satisfied with my hectic day.

When I arrived at my car, buzzing from nine days (so far) of intense fishing and driving, the parking lot was filling up with anglers getting ready for another Sulfur hatch. I was tempted to stay, but wanted to get some rest before the long drive to Wisconsin, so I sat down on my bumper to shed my waders and pack up my gear.

As I slipped into my shoes, a car backed into the spot next to me. I did a quick double take, as the gentleman at the wheel looked remarkably like my late father-in-law, Wilbur Bascomb, even down to the cigarette between his fingers. This was doubly odd because not only was the fellow Wilbur's doppelganger, but it is rare for me to see an African-American man geared up for fly fishing, at least in New England, where I do most of my fishing. I could hear him talking on his cell phone and he gave me a little wave when he caught my eye. I felt a bit awkward, as if I were gawking at him as I had seen many times in Maine, when people would cast sidelong looks at my wife because, for many years, there were so few black people in Maine that she was literally the first dark-skinned person that some native Mainers, especially children, had ever seen in person. For this reason, I was self-conscious about being rude, especially sitting so close that I could hear him telling his wife he would wait a half hour to see if the Sulfur hatch started on schedule. I was still packing up my stuff and just wanted to be neighborly.

When he ended the call, I introduced myself and conveyed that I'd seen a few random Sulfurs fluttering about as I left the stream. I chuckled and said, "Ya know, you look like you could be my father-in-law's younger brother." He smiled and shook my hand; "I'm Rowland Harrison."

Rowland said he lived nearby and once owned the Yellow Breeches Outfitters fly shop in Boiling Springs just a few blocks away. He often came down to the Run to see if anything interesting was happening, especially when a hatch was expected.

When I told him where I was from, Rowland was excited to tell me he'd been to Maine and had eaten so much lobster he thought he would burst. I explained my Storied Waters journey and the invitation from Grace Voelker Wood to visit Frenchman's Pond on the U.P. in Michigan, which elicited another big grin: "My favorite writer is Robert Traver! Well . . . John Voelker. I have his 'Testament of a Fisherman' on my wall at home," he said proudly. "I told my wife, 'You better read that at my funeral!'" he laughed again with a big smoky rumble.

I wish we could have kept chatting, but Rowland had to go chase some fish, and I was ready to ride west in to the setting sun. I waved goodbye to a kindred soul as I wheeled out onto the road, leaving the Yellow Breeches behind.

- 11 -

The Limestone Creeks of Southern Wisconsin

Saturday evening, May 20

After getting off the Yellow Breeches at about 6:30 p.m., I drove only a few hours before I was ready for dinner and a good night's rest. Using an app on my phone, I booked a discounted hotel room that turned out to be on a noisy and dingy truck-stop strip just off the Pennsylvania Turnpike. Maybe I was already spoiled by "the environs where trout are found, which are invariably beautiful," as John Voelker observes in "Testament of a Fisherman," but this place seemed particularly ugly. So, idiot that I am, I decided to stay there for an extra day to catch up on my writing about the trip.

Sunday morning, May 21

The next morning I drove around town looking for someplace quaint to sit and drink coffee while writing (think Hemingway sipping espresso at a café in Paris . . . while writing on his laptop), but couldn't find anything remotely suitable. Even the Starbucks was sketchy. I went back to my room with a take-out coffee and a scone and made the best of it.

My laptop had been giving me fits the entire trip. My hard drive was nearly full and, as I was uploading photos daily, I had to continually offload files onto my external drive. With only 100 gigabytes (GB) of storage on my secondhand laptop and with programs expanding like the universe at the speed of light, I was down to just 1 GB available. Uploading photos to my website was a dubious proposition, and editing videos was out of the question. My computer tech had warned me to upgrade both my RAM and disk storage before I left, but that didn't happen in the hectic run-up to departure. Oops. Now my laptop took forever to boot up or would choose inconvenient times to do system upgrades over a slow WiFi network. Not good. I was worried that the whole thing would crash and I would lose pictures and notes and more from my trip.

I found myself limping along, cursing and muttering, barely able to post periodic updates, all the while assuming I'd never be able to upgrade on the fly while driving from town to town and state to state every day.

Sunday evening, May 21

After a frustrating day of writing and wrestling with my computer, I went looking for someplace to have a decent dinner. Given that my hotel was in McPlace, as I call these generic commercial districts, I had few choices nearby besides havin' it my way at the Golden Arches, eatin' good in the neighborhood at Applebee's (er, what neighborhood?), or a gambling on the "local landmark restaurant" that probably hadn't changed its decor or its menu since the 1950s.

Always in search of local flavor, I took my chances at the landmark eatery with its musty wood paneling and limited choice of beers. While waiting for my totally forgettable meal, I overheard a couple guys at the bar talk about their work "fracking" for oil and gas. Southern Pennsylvania was abuzz with this latest energy boom. These two worked for a company that was drilling horizontally through the Marcellus and Utica shale deposits, injecting a slurry of water, chemicals, and sand under high pressure to hydraulically fracture the bedrock and then pump out natural gas and sometimes oil that is released through the fractures. I'd spent several years studying the regulations to reduce the risks of this controversial technology, which, when everything goes right, can be done safely. But, if anything goes wrong, and it sometimes does, fracking can have devastating effects on water resources, groundwater quality, and wildlife. These two fellows didn't sound like they cared much about the environment. They were in it for the other kind of green. Why would I be surprised?

I went back to my hotel room with indigestion, for a variety of reasons.

Monday morning, May 22

I was up early the next morning, raring to push through to Wisconsin. After wrestling with my computer again for another hour, I filled up my travel mug at the sketchy Starbucks and hit the highway. I rocked out to my Storied Waters music playlist as I crossed into West Virginia, where I stopped at a huge Cabela's store in Wheeling to pick up a few flies (which turned out to be very handy soon enough). I played John Hiatt's *Crossing Muddy Waters* as the Fort Henry Bridge carried me into Ohio, then on to Bloomington, Indiana, and north on I-39 through Illinois. It was a verrrrrry long day on the road, from 10:00 a.m. to 11:00 p.m., with a few breaks to stretch and admire the endless cornfields.

Monday afternoon, May 22

As I drove through Rockford, Illinois, I remembered that Thoreau had passed through this town on his way to Minnesota while on his last major excursion. In fact, he came through here on May 23, 1861: 156 years ago, almost to the day. When he was here, the Civil War was but a month old. Thoreau's companion for his westernmost trip was young Horace Mann Jr., a budding young botanist. They traveled by train from Massachusetts and Albany, New York, all the way to the Mississippi River, then up to St. Paul and Minneapolis by riverboat. The two naturalists returned by steaming across the Great Lakes through the Straits of Mackinac to Toronto, then by train to Ogdensburg, New York, and Lake Champlain, and finally south through White River Junction, Vermont, to Boston. Their route was roughly the same big loop I was following, except I would be returning to New England through the Adirondacks to White River Junction before exploring the Northeast Kingdom of Vermont, across New Hampshire to Maine.

Thoreau never had a chance to write a book about that excursion before he died of tuberculosis in 1863. Only the more serious

Thoreau scholars have followed Henry's and Horace's accounts of that last trip in their journals. Fortunately, Corinne Hosfeld Smith decided to retrace his route, which she described in her 2012 book *Westward I Go Free: Tracing Thoreau's Last Journey*, highlighting his journal entries and what has changed in the towns along the way since the mid-1800s.

When his train left Chicago heading west, Thoreau noted the topography of northern Illinois in his journal: "Very level 1st 20 miles—then considerably more undulating. Greatest rolling prairie without trees just beyond Winnebago. Last 20 miles in NW of Ill. quite hilly."

That hilly area Henry described is now called the Driftless Area, which is where I would be fishing for the next few days. For those not familiar with it, the Driftless Area comprises portions of southwest Wisconsin, southeast Minnesota, northwest Illinois, and northeast Iowa. This region was sort of an island in the middle of the last ice age; the continental glacier did not cover this area and thus neither scoured the landscape nor left behind deposits of sand and gravel, called glacial drift by geologists, hence the name "Driftless Area."

The landscape was indeed undulated, as Thoreau described, and scenic with low hills, steep bluffs of sandstone and limestone, and deep valleys dotted with farms, although it was still mostly native prairie when Thoreau and Mann passed through. The Driftless Area is noted for its numerous spring-fed creeks emanating from the limestone bedrock, making for ideal trout habitat.

As I got off the highway, I was pretty psyched that I had crossed paths with Thoreau once again in the space-time continuum, almost to the day of his trip in May 1861. We would cross paths several more times before my Storied Waters odyssey concluded.

At almost midnight, I rolled into another cheap chain hotel in South Beloit, Illinois, just a mile short of the Wisconsin border. I was exhausted and slept like a rock, with dreams of Driftless Area trout in my head. This hotel also had a fitness room, so I was happy to get in some much-needed cardio the next morning after the long drive. A free breakfast, hot shower, decent bed, and a workout. Not bad for $60 a night.

The wary wild trout in Mount Vernon Creek, portions of which are classified Outstanding Resource Waters, sometimes required a long drift with a dry fly.

Tuesday morning, May 23

After a solid day of driving, I really wanted to get out fishing on Tuesday. I homed in on Mount Vernon Creek, just twenty miles southwest of Madison on the eastern edge of the Driftless Area. I had learned from the good folks at the Aldo Leopold Foundation that Dr. Leopold (1887–1948) had been a driving force in restoring Mount Vernon Creek during the 1940s, which was chronicled by Harry Peterson in the fall 2003 issue of *The American Fly Fisher*. The Wisconsin Department of Natural Resources website had a good map of this Class 1 and 2 stream that showed several places for public access and sections designated as Outstanding

Resource Waters, affording it higher levels of protection. I found it with little trouble.

Pulling into the empty parking area, I tried to picture what this place looked like during the Dust Bowl of the 1930s, before Dr. Leopold and his colleagues began their restoration efforts. Billions of tons (several feet) of topsoil had eroded from both wind and rain because of poor tilling practices, overgrazing, and overharvesting of timber. Leopold worked here while he was formulating his notion of a "land ethic," which gained renown as an essay in *A Sand County Almanac*, considered by many as the Old Testament of the modern environmental movement. Leopold and his colleagues successfully convinced farmers to try new methods to protect the soil and restore water quality in the streams. His theories laid the groundwork for our modern notions of environmental stewardship and sustainability.

Leopold also was a fly fisherman. In *Sand County*, he wrote about a memorable fishing trip to a favorite stream in a passage called "The Alder Fork—A Fishing Idyl." There is some debate among scholars about the setting for that story, whether it was an actual place called Alder Fork or Alder Creek, or if it was the pseudonym for a favorite spot that Leopold wished not to divulge. In the story, after catching nothing but a chub on his previous outing on a warm afternoon, Leopold found a rising trout the next day in the cooler waters upstream:

In the fresh of the morning, when a hundred whitethroats had forgotten it would ever again be anything but sweet and cool, I climbed down the dewy bank and stepped into the Alder Fork. A trout was rising upstream. I paid out some line—wishing it would always stay thus soft and dry—and, measuring the distance with a false cast or

two, laid down a spent gnat exactly a foot above his last swirl. Forgotten now were the hot miles, the mosquitoes, the ignominious chub. He took it with one great gulp.

As I hiked across a marshy meadow to the creek, I noticed that Mount Vernon Creek could well be the stream described in Leopold's Alder Fork story, as could hundreds of other creeks in this part of Wisconsin. I decided it didn't matter where his story was set; as he said, his tale was more "a happy meditation . . . upon the ways of trout and men. How like fish we are: ready, nay eager, to seize upon whatever new thing some wind of circumstance shakes down upon the river of time! And how we rue our haste, finding the gilded morsel to contain a hook."

With Dr. Leopold's spirit guiding me, I had a refreshing and gratifying afternoon on Mount Vernon Creek with perfect conditions: overcast, a bit muggy and threatening

Aldo Leopold. INK WASH AND CHARCOAL DRAWING BY *JILL OSGOOD*

I landed my first Wisconsin brown trout on a flying ant pattern.

rain, with naturally milky water and a good current in the spring creek. Trout were rising all afternoon, up and down the stream in all the classic spots: undercut banks, near submerged logs (some obviously placed there to improve habitat), and under overhanging trees. It was challenging to get the fly where it needed to go; I kept snagging in the tall grass and branches overhead, but I appreciated the warblers flitting and chipping in the bushes and red-winged blackbirds scolding me at every turn.

I caught the first rising fish I saw: a sprightly, glistening wild brown trout of about seven inches. A second one rising a few feet away took the same fly, a small size 18 Foam Flying Ant that I had purchased the previous day at Cabela's, and promptly went under some alders. Leopold had found himself in a similar situation and declared, "No prudent man would risk a dollar's worth of fly and leader pulling a trout upstream through the giant toothbrush of alder stems comprising the bend of that creek. But, as I said, no prudent man is a fisherman."

I was lucky that the fish unhooked himself; I wasn't going to get him out of there—at least I got my fly back. And, for the record, the flies I bought at Cabela's were $12.99 a dozen, so it was indeed "a dollar's worth of fly."

I caught another half-dozen red-speckled wild browns, missed three more, and was unable to fool another dozen fish rising energetically to the plentiful bugs on the water. Quite an afternoon! I was loving Wisconsin already. It was a pleasure to experience firsthand how Dr. Leopold's hard work restoring this stream was still paying forward.

Tuesday afternoon, May 23

My next destination was Baraboo, where I planned to spend the night near the Leopold Center because I had an appointment to meet some Leopold scholars on Wednesday. I had considered camping at Devil's Lake State Park, but the forecast called for thunderstorms and heavy downpours, which sounded ominous and rather soggy. I passed up the opportunity to get drenched in my tent and booked another discounted two-star hotel while I ate my lunch.

I was happy to stay on the back roads toward Baraboo, which are more scenic and more fun. My cross-country route took me through Mount Horeb, a suburb west of Madison, at about 5:30. Rush hour, if you could call it that. I slowed in traffic as I approached a roundabout, when, to my left, I noticed a friendly looking computer shop called Troll-Bytes. (Mount Horeb is the self-proclaimed Troll Capital of the World). Through the open front door, under a sign that said Sales & Service, I saw a guy standing at the counter looking bored. *What the heck!* I thought. *Let's give it a try.* I circled a full loop around the roundabout and pulled in to the shop.

"I'm on a fishing trip and I need more bytes," I told the sales and service guy, "Can you help?"

The kind young man, hardly a troll, looked at me quizzically, pondering my pun, and said, drolly, "Let me chew on it a while." He inspected my laptop while pretending to listen while I recited my punch list of problems. Mostly, he was ignoring me while checking specs and running diagnostics.

"Yes," he said kindly, "we can upgrade you to 500 GB disk storage and 8 MB of RAM. Come back at 10 a.m. tomorrow, and we can have it done in a couple hours."

"What? Really!?! Wow. You must have magic trolls working in the back. It'll require a tad more driving than I'd planned, but I can make it work. I'll be back in the morning."

In Baraboo, there was a decent-looking pub across the street from my hotel. The skies opened up in a ferocious downpour while I was enjoying a burger and a couple tall Spotted Cows (New Glarus Brewing) for dinner. Good thing I didn't camp out in the park. I had to dodge some serious raindrops to get back to the hotel, where I thoroughly enjoyed my comfortable bed and hot shower in the morning.

Wednesday morning, May 24

It was a short drive back to Mount Horeb after breakfast. I dropped off the laptop and, with time to kill, ventured to the Vermont Creek Fishing Area that I'd passed coming into town. It was a very small spring creek, running clear despite the heavy rain showers overnight. Spring creeks are often slightly milky but unaffected by rainfall and runoff because of the porous limestone bedrock. This stream was no more than ten feet wide with tall grass and sedges overhanging steep banks. The pools and runs were about the size of my kitchen table, so it was tough to get a fly on the water without hitting the overhanging vegetation. In the light drizzle, my morning was all about sneaking up on very spooky fish and precision casting. Several times I blundered near the bank only to see small shadows scatter like tiny, dark bolts of lightning.

I did manage to get five or six trout to splash at my fly, but every one was a short hit with no firm bites. I'm guessing they were wild brook trout, maybe brown trout, but I'll never know; they were too quick and too wary. I tried the foam ant and a small caddis pattern that had worked on Mount Vernon Creek. No luck. It was, nevertheless, great fun stalking these trout and doing my best to hit the small targets hoping to fool them. But so far on this trip, I had scored a goose egg for Vermont; strikes, yes, but no fish caught, on either the Battenkill in the state of Vermont or on Vermont Creek in the state of Wisconsin.

As I walked back to my vehicle, I recalled another Leopold quote from his essay "The Alder Fork": "What was big was not the trout,

Where & How—
Wisconsin Spring Creeks

According to the Wisconsin Department of Natural Resources, there are over 13,000 miles of trout streams in the state that are classified as Class 1—High Quality, No Stocking (5,365 miles); Class 2—Stocked, with Some Natural Reproduction (6,120 miles); and Class 3—Stocked, No Natural Reproduction (1,786 miles). Public access to trout waters is generally well marked, with excellent detailed county-by-county maps available in PDF online, showing state lands, access easements on private lands, and parking areas. It doesn't get any simpler than that to find fishing anywhere in the state.

Mount Vernon Creek and Vermont Creek were easy to find and had ample parking. Yes, it was midweek, but I crossed paths with only one other angler on Mount Vernon Creek during prime time. I had plenty of open water to choose from on both creeks.

What Works: Both spring creeks had rising fish midday. They were very wary, so approaching from a distance required accurate casting. Choosing the right approach can be the key to success in these tight quarters.

Casting from downstream, it was a real challenge to get a long enough drift without spooking the fish with my line. I had some success casting from upstream and feeding the fly line out to drift the fly down to the rising fish with just enough slack to let the fly and line follow the foam line. On some longer runs, I played out ten to twenty yards of floating line to get a long drift to a rising fish at the tail of a run.

In "Alder Fork," Aldo Leopold described the same challenges of upstream and downstream casting. To catch one fish upstream of him, he waited for a puff of breeze to riffle the water "for an instant," so his line and fly wouldn't spook the fish. He had to time the cast perfectly: "The last three yards shoot out, the fly falls gracefully at the feet of the laughing alder—he has it!"

Leopold spotted another rising fish but had no approach from below. He noticed an opening twenty yards upstream where he might approach the fish from above: "Fish a dry fly downstream? It cannot, but it must, be done."

He moved cautiously upstream through the thicket: "With cat-like care not to roil his majesty's bath, I step in, and stand stock still for five minutes to let things calm down. . . . I blow on my fly to give it one last fluff, lay it on the stream at my feet, and quickly pay out coil after coil." The fly carried downstream into a dark tunnel of brush: "It rounds the bend [and] . . . reaches the black pool. I hear, rather than see, the rush of a great fish; I set hard, and the battle is on." ■

but the chance. What was full was not my creel, but my memory; full of the stuff that fishermen's dreams are made of."

Before picking up my computer, there was one more public access spot on Black Earth Creek I wanted to try, about five miles away. Heading north again, I crossed the very railroad tracks that Thoreau and Mann had traveled when returning from Minnesota later in June of 1861. Their train followed the Wisconsin River and came through Black Earth on its way to Madison. Henry had noted in his journal a "great abundance of tall spiderwort—also red lily—rudbeckia" as he and Horace botanized through the train window as it rolled along. I'll admit, I didn't specifically notice any of these particular plants, but they very well could have been what I had snagged my fly on at Vermont Creek.

Vermont Creek feeds into Black Earth Creek, which is much larger. While the smaller spring creek was slightly milky, Black Earth lived up to its name. It was running up to the top of its banks, the color of Hershey's Syrup. I guess soil erosion is still an issue in parts of the valley that are more heavily cultivated. I parked at a fishing access area and walked across a bridge with the forbidding water swirling underneath.

I found a safe place on the bank, plunked a green-and-black Woolly Bugger into the fast-moving current, and promptly snagged a sizeable stick, breaking off my fly. The second Woolly Bugger lived through a few more casts, but the fishing seemed futile.

I shambled back to the car, wondering if I smelled bad from the sorrowful skunking I had just experienced. But heck, at least my computer would be ready soon. Off came my musty waders, in went the rods (they had remained fully rigged since Walden Pond), and back to TrollBytes I went, listening to Johnny Copeland and Stevie Ray Vaughan sing "Don't Stop by the Creek, Son."

Wednesday afternoon, May 24

Success! Incredible. After just three hours, my laptop now sported a beefy new hard drive and a RAM boost. I was back in business. What are the chances? If I had tried to find someone to do this at home in Maine, I might still be waiting. Many thanks to the talented technical trolls from Mount Horeb.

Glancing at my watch, I saw that I had just enough time to make to the Leopold Center for my appointment. I punched the address into my GPS and headed back north. The route took me past the Sauk Prairie State Recreation Area, where the Sauk Prairie Conservation Alliance is working to restore the native prairie ecosystem that Thoreau and Mann had witnessed and that Leopold worked to preserve, and Devil's Lake, the only non-man-made lake in the Driftless Area. Soon I was in the heart of Leopold country. This was another major landmark in my literary and piscatorial pilgrimage, a chance to visit the Leopold Center and see the "Shack" where Dr. Leopold actually wrote *A Sand County Almanac*.

- 12 -

Leopold's Driftless Area Legacy

Wednesday afternoon, May 24
Everyone has a hero, or so we say. My heroes are not your typical sports or military heroes, nor people who performed superhuman or ultra-courageous feats. They are people who change the way we think about the world, thereby making our world a better place. Sometimes changing the way people think takes great courage. My heroes are people who give society hope for a brighter future.

It should come as no surprise that many of my heroes have made great contributions to how we think about nature and the environment. My list includes Henry David Thoreau (obviously), John Muir (who will become pertinent in a moment), Teddy Roosevelt (a courageous leader for conservation who gets extra credit for traditional hero status), Rachel Carson (of *Silent Spring* fame), and many others who have been voices for the Earth.

One of my greatest heroes is Aldo Leopold. His masterpiece, *A Sand County Almanac*, published in 1949, is considered a bedrock of the conservation movement and a stepping-stone toward the environmental movement of the 1960s and '70s.

Leopold was a lifelong hunter and fly fisherman, a forester and wildlife ecologist who was appointed the nation's first professor of wildlife management at the University of Wisconsin at Madison. He pioneered new forms of forestry, ranching, and agriculture that featured a holistic watershed approach to protect soils, vegetation, habitat, and water quality. A founder of the Wilderness Society, Leopold was a big fan of John Muir's groundbreaking mission to protect wilderness areas in the latter years of the nineteenth century.

Coincidentally, Muir grew up fifty miles from Madison (note: he was born in Dunbar, Scotland, and spent his boyhood there up to the age of eleven). In a second coincidence, he had just finished his first year at U of W in 1861, the same year Thoreau came through Madison on his way back from Minnesota. It's interesting that all three men had a connection to modest Madison, Wisconsin. Muir and Thoreau never met, but Muir later visited Walden Pond after Thoreau's death. Leopold built on the foundations laid by both of these two philosopher-conservationists in his own work. In his famous essay, "Thinking Like a

The Shack where Aldo Leopold wrote A Sand County Almanac *is a big draw for Leopold aficionados who visit the Leopold Foundation near Baraboo, Wisconsin.*

Mountain," Leopold slightly misquotes Thoreau's dictum, "In wildness is the preservation of the world." (Leopold used "salvation" rather than "preservation.")

Many have compared the three men in their writing, their careers, and their philosophies. They had much in common, but there remain important differences in style and focus. Leopold relied on his observations, lyrical descriptions, and ecological parables to make his key points, while Thoreau and Muir were more evangelical in their particular doctrines. All three men were important advocates for understanding and respecting nature. Leopold also put his theories into action on the ground.

In 1935, Professor Leopold bought a desolate, worn-out "sand farm" near the Wisconsin River so he could practice his land management principles on his own property. His family planted trees and worked to restore native prairie vegetation. They turned an old chicken coop into a cabin, called the Shack, where Leopold eventually wrote his master work. Part memoir and part manifesto, *Sand County Almanac* recalls Leopold's long career, including his early years with the US Forest Service, working to restore lands damaged by destructive management practices. In his most important essay, "The Land Ethic," Leopold expressed what many of us feel: that humans must consider themselves to be a part of the natural community around us, not separate from it.

He argued that the well-being of human society depends on the well-being of the physical and ecological systems that support us. He recognized the value of keystone species and apex predators. He appreciated the essential roles that tiny unnoticed plants and creatures played in the complex web of life. In a beautiful, lyrical style, Leopold conveyed his love for the natural world and his wonder at the mysteries of ecological systems. He translated his love and wonder into an ethical framework of respect for animals, plants, soil, and waters, which he called the "land ethic."

The land ethic is a moral code of conduct—a way to distinguish right and wrong actions—that grows out of our interconnectedness with the land and the recognition that humans and the land are part of a singular community: "A thing is right when it tends to preserve the integrity, stability and beauty of the biotic community. It is wrong when it tends otherwise."

With example after example, Leopold illustrated the disastrous consequences that occur when we fall short in this ethical code and instead exploit the land and our natural resources solely for their economic value. Or when we fail to consider the sometimes predictable, but often unforeseen, impacts of our actions, like polluting the waters and the air, or draining wetlands that support a diversity of flora and fauna. Soil erosion, invasive species, and plant and animal extinction are but a few of the resulting consequences.

Sadly, almost seventy years later, Leopold's land ethic remains an elusive ideal. Today, we find our progress in environmental protection and land conservation compromised by those who are motivated more by self-interest and economic gain than by an appreciation of what is right and wrong for the natural systems critical to our very existence.

The Aldo Leopold Foundation is an educational center near Baraboo, north of Madison. The Shack where Leopold wrote the book is a prime attraction, a short stroll from the Wisconsin River. The similarity of the Shack to Thoreau's cabin on Walden Pond is striking, although I doubt it was on purpose. Dr. Leopold and Thoreau were, at least in this regard, two birds of a feather seeking solitude in nature to think and write.

I had read *A Sand County Almanac* in college. Leopold's argument for a land ethic certainly had a major impact on my life and career in environmental sciences and policy. While teaching *Sand County* in my Introduction to Environmental Issues course at the University of New England, I found his work every bit as inspiring today as when I first read it.

Curt Meine, Senior Fellow at the Leopold Foundation, greeted me at the center and shared some insights about Leopold's contributions to land conservation. While we walked among the native prairie wildflowers that surround the Shack, Curt noted that Leopold's land ethic included soil and water and native plants, birds and wildlife and fish.

According to Curt, rivers and fishing were "in Leopold's DNA," as he had grown up in Iowa near the Mississippi River. His writings include essays on numerous rivers: the Rio Grande, the Gila River, the Flambeau River, the Wisconsin River, and his brilliant parable of the Round River, which flows in a circle into itself, much like the circle of life. Curt told me about a vintage film clip available on YouTube showing Dr. Leopold on a 1927 family fly-fishing trip to the Lily River in northeast Wisconsin. The opening sequence in the clip looks much like how I had imagined Alder Fork would look.

Early in his career Leopold started thinking about how changes in the landscape and vegetation within a watershed affect water quality and aquatic habitat, particularly trout habitat. He had advocated for protecting native trout populations—long before Trout Unlimited was founded—with a paper called "Mixing Trout in Western Waters," published

Timber Coulee is a blue-ribbon spring creek in Coon Valley, Wisconsin, where Aldo Leopold and colleagues completed the first watershed restoration project during the Dust Bowl in the 1930s.

in 1918. Later, in 1944, he wrote a short paper called "Sick Trout Streams" that included a strategy for restoring headwaters, streambanks, and buffer strips around streams.

I mentioned to Curt that my next stop after touring the Leopold Center was the Flambeau River, which Leopold describes in his essay of the same name in *Sand County*. But Curt was adamant in steering me first toward the Coon Valley, deep in the Driftless Area, northwest of Viroqua. "Coon Valley didn't make it into *Sand County*," Curt noted,

project. Leopold and his colleagues at U of W sought to engage farmers in better agricultural practices to allow rainwater to seep in, cool off, and run out into the spring creeks that flow through the deeply incised valleys among the hills of this beautiful landscape.

The result of their efforts was a model for soil conservation that became the standard for improved agriculture and better wildlife and fish habitat management across the nation. The streams in Coon Valley are now blue-ribbon trout streams teeming with wild, naturally-reproducing brown trout and even some persistent native brook trout.

Coincidently, I had been listening to a recent Orvis podcast with Tom Rosenbauer during my drive across Ohio. In that episode, Tom interviewed Mat Wagner, proprietor of the Driftless Angler fly shop in Viroqua, Wisconsin, about fly fishing in the area's spring creeks. This fortuitous convergence of advice by Curt and Mat pointed me to Viroqua and Coon Valley to stalk some of those wild trout.

After thanking Curt for his time and enlightenment about Leopold, I spent Wednesday night at the 1950s throwback Hickory Hill Motel in Viroqua. I'll give Hickory Hill three stars with one of those stars strictly for the nostalgia.

Thursday morning, May 25

The next morning, I stopped in to see Mat at the Driftless Angler, one of the best fly shops I have ever seen, on the quaint Main Street of this picture-postcard Midwestern town. Mat gave me some detailed and enthusiastic advice about where to fish and which flies to use, including a crane fly imitation I had never used before. I also bought a couple cool Driftless Angler T-shirts; their best-selling shirt says, "Your Skills Suck and Your Fly Is Ugly. Fish Off!" Mat circled some prime locations on a map of the area and, after a

"but it was a huge part of Dr. Leopold's legacy to fly fishing and the environment."

The Coon Creek valley was the location of the nation's first soil-conservation project during the height of the Dust Bowl in 1933, a cooperative effort of the federal Soil Erosion Service and the University of Wisconsin–Madison, where Leopold was advisor for the

Where & How—
Coon Valley, Wisconsin

In the heart of the Driftless Area, the tiny hamlet of Coon Valley is eight blocks long, with a handful of markets, banks, and churches; two pubs; a feedstore; and a scattering of auto repair shops and gas stations. But what is most unusual is the Coon Valley Veterans Memorial Park behind the American Legion hall. The ten-acre park includes a mile-long paved path with two bridges across Coon Creek and a dozen handicapped-access fishing pads and ramps down to the water. The park draws physically challenged anglers from a wide radius who can't otherwise access the many spring creeks in the valley.

Northeast of town, County Road P first crosses Spring Coulee, then Coon Creek, Poplar Coulee, and Timber Coulee. Other county roads branch off to access numerous other creeks and coulees that flow out of the hills and limestone bluffs that characterize the Driftless Area. The Wisconsin Department of Natural Resources maps for Vernon County show many public access lands and easements in this area.

What Works: Mat Wagner, owner of the Driftless Angler, introduced me to his Coulee Cranefly pattern. I took three with me and later wished I had bought a dozen. Here's what Mat says about crane flies:

Crane flies are one of the most unrecognized, underutilized species. If the trout are making random splashy and sporadic rises, chances are they're eating crane flies, which don't come off in big numbers that block out the sun like some of the other big hatches. They tend to pop randomly through the entire day. It's more of an all-day, all-season type thing. Skitter them, swing them downstream, cast upstream, and dead drift with a twitch now and then. Movement is important!

When I was there in May, the mayfly hatches were later in the day. Mat insisted I take some caddisfly patterns, as the caddis were hatching pretty much any time. Elk Hair Caddis are a go-to fly here, as they are in Maine and New Hampshire. I had plenty of those. But Mat recommended his gray CDC (cul de canard) caddis emerger pattern, which proved *very* effective on the remainder of my trip. I only had one left by the end and did everything I could not to lose it. This is a first-rate fly. Once you catch a fish on it, however, you need to switch to a dry one, as the fly won't stay in the surface film when it is saturated, so it's always good to have a few on hand. ■

bite of lunch in Viroqua, I cruised on down the road to the Coon Valley.

Thursday afternoon, May 25

My afternoon was a mix of warm sun, swarming gnats, and rising fish—nothing short of spectacular. I caught several vigorous 10-inch brown trout in Spring Coulee, a one-lane spring creek that flows through a tallgrass meadow. Moving to Timber Coulee, a slightly bigger stream, I was entertained for hours by some lightning-fast browns who seemed

The spring creeks in the Driftless Area near Coon Valley are filled with beautiful brown trout.

to enjoy slamming my flies without actually eating them. Ultimately, I landed a dozen fish on the day, mostly on caddis patterns, and missed many more. I was thrilled when I caught my first trout ever on the crane fly pattern that Mat had recommended. I'll have to get more of those.

One memorable piscine foe short-hit at least a dozen different flies before I finally hooked him on a caddis pattern that I had also purchased from Mat. That fat 12-inch fish was one of the most satisfying on my entire Storied Waters trip. My persistence and its patience (the trout was clearly waiting for me to figure out which was the correct fly) made for quite the chess match.

A steady hatch of March Brown mayflies, a few Sulfurs, and caddis was still going strong when I heard a deep growling. A few casts later I heard it again. What was it? Yes, it was . . . my stomach announcing that it was time

to get some dinner and a local brew. I know I should have fished through the evening until dark, but I needed to make some headway toward the northwest Wisconsin woods to meet my next host, Ron Weber, and visit the Flambeau River.

On the way to the car, a steadily rising fish made garish rings in a pool near the road. I couldn't resist one more jousting match before leaving the beautiful Coon Valley. I watched the fish make two or three sonorous slurps before putting a long cast up and over the rising trout.

Ba-BING! An exciting way to end the day. Who doesn't love shaking hands with a muscular 12-inch brown trout? The stout fellow bid me goodbye before swimming off. I returned to my car and wheeled into Coon Valley for dinner before pointing my car north to explore the Flambeau and Namekagon Rivers.

- 13 -

Exploring the Flambeau & Namekagon Rivers

Friday, May 25

In *A Sand County Almanac*, Aldo Leopold explained how his father "used to describe all choice camps, fishing water, and woods as 'nearly as good as the Flambeau.'" The father's reverence was reflected in the son's description from his own canoe trip on the wild river years later:

Paul Bunyan was too busy a man to think about posterity, but if he had asked to reserve a spot for posterity to see what the old north woods looked like, he likely would have chosen the Flambeau, for here the cream of the white pine grew on the same acres with the cream of the sugar maple, yellow birch, and hemlock. This rich intermixture of pine and hardwoods was and is uncommon.

I wanted to visit the Flambeau to experience the river Leopold and his father described and see what had happened in the seventy years since he published his essay "Flambeau" in *Sand County*. Leopold was worried about the future of the Flambeau River and lamented the encroaching development and loss of wilderness values. He wrestled with the uncertainty about the river's future as a political battle raged over preserving the free-flowing Flambeau River versus developing it for hydropower.

The good news is that the impoundment of the Flambeau did not unfold as Leopold feared. Today, the lower Flambeau is mostly "flowage" (an impoundment) behind two dams near Ladysmith, but the North and South Forks of the Flambeau above the fork remain wild and wildly popular for canoeing and fishing. Leopold's work as a member of the Wisconsin Conservation Commission and his published concerns played an important role in saving the river. Fifteen miles of the South Fork and over seventy-five miles of the North Fork are now protected within the Flambeau River State Forest.

In March, when I was planning my trip, I called the Flambeau River State Forest headquarters to get advice about where to stay and how to get on the river. Two staffers, Curtiss and Judy, made a few suggestions for where to stay and which section might be best to paddle by myself. A few days later, Curtiss called back and said I needed to talk to Ron Weber, a state forester at the Department of Natural Resources in Ladysmith; Curtiss said Ron was an enthusiastic Aldo Leopold fan like me. I gave Ron a call.

Ron had taught high school science for twenty years and included *A Sand County Almanac* in his classes about ecology. It was clear from the get-go that he was very excited about my Storied Waters tour. We spoke for almost an hour about my destinations and writers on my itinerary. To my surprise and pleasure, Ron offered to personally show me the Flambeau and paddle a section with me if the weather and water cooperated. He ended the call by asking if I had ever read any stories by one of his favorite authors: Gordon Mac-Quarrie. I had not.

"Well," he said in his ambling Wisconsin drawl, "you need to get ahold of MacQuarrie's *Sporting Treasury* book and read 'Now, in June.' It's about trout fishing on the Namekagon River, not far from the Flambeau. My family has a camp near there. You can come stay with me, an' I'll take you to the spot where the story takes place." I said I would and got ahold of a copy that week.

I loved MacQuarrie's story and knew I had found a kindred spirit in Ron. I was honored to take him up on his generous offer and even more excited to see the Namekagon, which I had never heard of before.

Sometimes you have to celebrate the little things, like doing laundry after two weeks on the road. After staying at the Holiday Inn Express in Eau Claire, Wisconsin, on Thursday night, I was feeling smart enough to wash and dry a couple loads at the hotel on Friday morning. Cheryl was happy to hear that I was starting afresh and wasn't stinking up the entire Midwest with bug dope and fish smell on my clothes. I, on the other hand, consider that fishy fragrance to be a sign of my great skill and success. Bug dope is my signature scent. But it was nice to have clean clothes.

On Friday afternoon, I motored north to Ladysmith and turned left into the Wisconsin Department of Natural Resources (DNR) driveway. I wandered around the lobby, looking at stuffed critters, posters, and publications about Wisconsin wildlife and fishing opportunities and regulations while waiting for Ron, who soon came out to greet me with a big smile. He's a tall, lanky man, about my age, with a long, easy stride. He'd told me earlier in the week that the Flambeau was running very high after several inches of rain, so canoeing and fishing it would not be advisable. Instead, he said, he'd show me the Flambeau State Forest and take me up to his camp to fish for trout on the Namekagon River, which was running at a wadable flow.

I followed Ron in his truck as he took me first to Little Falls and Slough Gundy on the South Fork of the Flambeau. Ron was interested to learn that there's also a Slewgundy on the Dead Diamond River in New Hampshire. *Slewgundy* was a word used by river drivers across the Northeast to describe any narrow, winding place where logs would bottleneck to create dangerous logjams. Apparently, they spell it differently in Wisconsin.

Little Falls was roaring with tea-colored water, the natural result of tannins from the cool northern Wisconsin forest. I could see and feel the wild river that Leopold admired. Ron and I pulled out our fishing rods to make some hopeful casts for smallmouth bass in the strong eddy above the falls near Slough Gundy. I cast a Woolly Bugger on sinking line, while Ron threw a Rapala lure with his spinning rod. Neither of us had any luck in the swirling current, but it was worth a shot.

The author casts a streamer into the high waters of the Flambeau River near Little Falls.

Next stop was the Flambeau River State Forest Headquarters on the North Fork of the Flambeau in Winter, Wisconsin, where Ron introduced me to his colleague, Dianne Stowell. Dianne confirmed that Aldo Leopold was instrumental in protecting the river from damming and the forest from development. She noted that there are now fourteen beautiful, free canoe campsites along the Flambeau River in the state forest. She also mentioned that her husband is the elk biologist on the forest.

"Elk biologist?" I asked. I knew that there are wolves in northern Wisconsin, but had not heard that elk were again wandering the woods in this part of the state. In his essay

state exports some of the animals to replenish herds in other states. Elk from the Michigan herd were reintroduced in Chequamegon-Nicolet National Forest near Clam Lake, Wisconsin in 1995, with additional elk added more recently in the Flambeau River State Forest. A second herd was imported from Kentucky and released in the Black River State Forest. In 2018, the Clam Lake herd was estimated at 185 animals and the Black River herd at 55 individuals. I'm sure that Leopold would be thrilled to know that such a prominent species is again part of this impressive wild ecosystem.

Oddly, moose are very rare in Wisconsin, even though they are plentiful in neighboring Minnesota and Michigan. Minnesota also has a wild herd of elk, which were reintroduced there in 1935.

Ron and I soon left the Flambeau behind to get to the Namekagon River to fish before dusk. I followed Ron's truck through the national forest down forty-some miles of remote roadway, watching all the while for elk, deer, bears, and wolves along the roadsides and in the clearings. I saw two deer, a Coopers hawk, and few crows pecking at a dead porcupine, but no elk. We stopped briefly at Ron's family camp on Namekagon Lake to unload some gear and park my car. I then climbed into his vehicle for the ride to the Namekagon River.

The narrator in Gordon MacQuarrie's "Now, in June" was driving to the same place Ron and I were headed while he pontificated to his companion about the fine art of the fly angler:

"Good Oak," Leopold mentioned that the last native Wisconsin elk was killed in 1866. Like a proud mother, Dianne showed me and Ron recent photos of several elk, one of the largest members of the deer family in the world, that now live in the Flambeau valley.

Elk were reintroduced near Wolverine, Michigan, on the Lower Peninsula in 1918. The Michigan herd has thrived, and that

"Trout fishing is not like drinking beer," he lectured as the car sped south and east. "It's more like sipping champagne. A good beer drinker just sits him down and lays into it. You hear the first one splash. But you just sip champagne. You take a tiny leetle bit and smack your lips.

"So with trout. You don't want too many. . . . I'm for filling frying-pans, you understand. But only now and then. More often I'm for picking out a trout so smart he thinks of running for the legislature."

Ron told me that Gordon MacQuarrie (1900–1956) was the outdoor editor of the *Milwaukee Journal* and a friend of Leopold and supporter of his land ethic. Although he is not as well-known east of the Great Lakes, MacQuarrie's best-loved stories feature the semi-fictional and humorous Old Duck Hunters Association, which is similar in spirit and wit to Corey Ford's Lower Forty Shooting, Angling and Inside Straight Club. MacQuarrie, a 1998 inductee in the Fresh Water Fishing Hall of Fame in Hayward, Wisconsin, also dazzles with first-rate fishing tales chock-full of his personal philosophy and musings:

Trout waters can be very personal places. The best trout streams are the ones you grow up with and then grow old with. . . . You develop a profound affection for them, and you think maybe before you die you will even understand a little about them.

MacQuarrie's "Now, in June" is set near a place called Squaw Bend, just below the tiny town of Cable. The two fishermen in the story waited for the bright day to turn to dusk on "a night for blankets" so the bigger fish would come prowling. Night fishing for big brown trout is quite popular in Wisconsin and Michigan. I learned later that another Hall of Famer, Ernie Schwiebert, also wrote a fine story in 1972 about fly fishing for big brown trout on the Namekagon River in the dark. In "Night Comes to the Namekagon," Schwiebert tells how he and his guide/

companion, Art Besse, landed several browns between three and six pounds each after sunset near the railroad trestle above Hayward, about twenty miles south of where Ron and I would be fishing.

Ron and I weren't patient enough to wait until dark for the biggest fish, and neither of us was prepared for the night-fishing strategy. Plus, it looked like a storm was coming, so we wasted no time getting on the water. Ron parked near the bridge, which we crossed on foot.

As we scanned the water from the bridge, trout were rising steadily upstream in the foam line to a steady hatch of mayflies and the occasional caddis. The sky was darkening more from the approaching thunderstorm than from the setting sun. We scrambled down the bank, sloshed through the weeds along shore, and waded quietly to the head of the pool above the bridge. I picked a spot, thigh deep, near the base of two small islands, which created triple channels that merged together with multiple seams in the current. Trout were feeding steadily in every seam.

I worked the water "methodically, persistently," to borrow MacQuarrie's words, letting my fly drift down to the rising fish. Occasionally I gave the fly a twitch with a short flick of the rod tip. It didn't take long before I had my first Namekagon brown. Not big, but brightly spotted, and "bucking like a mule," as MacQuarrie wrote. And soon enough, I had four more, all about 10 to 14 inches and "built like tugboats" but perhaps a bit smaller than the fish in the story. I caught them all on a single size 12 Adams dry fly. As dusk settled into dark, thunder rolled ominously enough that we decided we should avoid mid-river electrocution and get ourselves some dinner.

At the Pla-Mor Bar and Restaurant near Ron's camp on Namekagon Lake, the

Friday fish fry of local walleye was the obvious choice, washed down with a Wisconsin Brewing Company pale ale. While we were waiting for our meals, Ron's nephew Gary came in with two friends—Dan and Chris—who were all up for the weekend to fish for muskies and northern pike on the lake and also to replace the ancient, well-worn carpeting in the family camp with new flooring. This wasn't part of Ron's plan during my stay, but he couldn't discourage free labor. Regardless, the five of us had a cozy time squeezed into the camp, while the three guys worked almost to midnight tearing up the carpeting. My hosts graciously gave me my own bedroom, where I slept soundly. No complaints here.

Saturday morning, May 26

After coffee and scrambled eggs, Ron took me out on the lake in his open motorboat on a bluebird morning to try tempting any one of a half-dozen game fish to our flies: muskies up to 50 inches are in the lake, northern

pike over 30 inches, smallmouth up to 4 or 5 pounds, crappies, walleyes, and battle-ready bluegills. With all that competing fish flesh, we had to get something, right?

Wrong. No luck for us, but it was fun trying. The lake water was still cold, so the fish were less active and uninterested in flies. Later in the day and that evening, Gary and the boys hooked a few pike using baited lures. C'est la vie.

After a quick lunch, Ron took me out to pursue some native brook trout in tiny 18 Mile Creek in the Porcupine Lake Wilderness Area of the Chequamegon-Nicolet National Forest. That stream is not far from Washburn, Wisconsin, where O. W. Smith, former angling editor of *Outdoor America* wrote his 1917 book *Trout Lore*, which conveys the author's particular admiration for stalking "speckled trout" in small streams with dry flies. And here we were, exactly one hundred years later, doing the same thing. On the short drive there, we crossed the

Raindrops landing just a few feet apart along the Great Divide will travel on remarkably different journeys to either the Gulf of Mexico or the North Atlantic.

Ron wades along the Namekagon River at dusk looking for a promising lie for brown trout.

Great Divide (yup, there's a big sign), which separates water that flows to the Mississippi River and the Gulf of Mexico from land that drains to the Great Lakes, the St. Lawrence River, and the North Atlantic. I always find that kind of geographic landmark interesting when you think of the very different journeys in store for two raindrops falling a few feet apart.

A tannin-stained stream, 18 Mile Creek is only five to ten feet wide in some places, that runs through a tangle of mature conifer forest. Casting was impossible, so we just flicked our flies out into the current and let our lines run downstream toward cutbanks, downed trees, and submerged logs.

No more than fifty yards from the road, I caught a young beauty of a brook trout, just 5 inches long, on an Elk Hair Caddis, which I had dead-drifted dry and retrieved wet. This was a fun change of pace that yielded

another half-dozen brookies (and one chub) for the two of us, taken on either the float or the retrieve, depending on the mood of the fish. After two weeks of catching brown trout, it was a joy to see some wild, speckled brook trout again, my usual quarry at home.

Bratwurst is king in Wisconsin, so it was no surprise to find it on our dinner menu that evening, cooked on the grill. We cleaned up quickly and then motored hastily back to the Namekagon River for the evening hatch. Mr. MacQuarrie's spirit again kept us company as we geared up by the bridge. This time we started higher upstream, where Ron caught a couple modest-size browns before I moved back to the same pool I had fished the night before.

The fish were pickier tonight, scorning my fly most of the time until a fat 13-inch brown took me for a fun run around the pool. "He's

Where & How—
Namekagon River, Wisconsin

First of all, don't fret about the spelling. It's either Namekagon or Namakagon (pronounced "NAM-uh-KAH-gun"), depending on where you look. I could find no official distinction one way or another, but the plurality seems to lean toward Namekagon. This is the Anglo spelling of an Ojibwe word meaning "place of the sturgeon," so the spelling is only an approximation anyway. I was pleased to learn that there is an ongoing program to restore a self-sustaining population of sturgeon in the lower Namekagon River below Hayward. And enormous 50-pound sturgeon can be caught (and must be released) in the St. Croix River, into which the Namekagon flows.

Ron and I were fishing in the upper Namekagon in a cold-water section (with no sturgeon) below Namekagon Lake. The entire river is part of the St. Croix National Scenic Riverway, and the cold-water reach is carefully managed by the National Park Service and Wisconsin DNR. The river here holds some native brook trout, wild brown trout, and rainbow trout.

What Works: Timing is (almost) everything. And location is everything else.

Ron and I hit two evenings with perfect late May/early June conditions, just as the anglers did in MacQuarrie's story "Now, in June." Both mayflies and caddisflies were on the water, so we really couldn't miss with fly choice. An Adams and a Hornberg both worked well—nothing fancy there. We applied exactly zero entomological expertise to fool fish with these tried-and-true patterns. And we both caught plenty of trout.

Wading wasn't a problem, as we had a very favorable flow. The US Geological Service (USGS) river flow gage on the Namekagon makes it easy to check both the flow and the water temperature, two keys to a successful outing. We could wade almost anywhere we wanted to go, yet the current was strong and the water released from Namekagon Lake was cold. That allowed us to move into position to reach fish that were rising. We caught some on 10-foot casts and some on 20-yard casts, with most of my fly line played out into the current. As long as we could drift a fly into the trout's window, we had a chance.

When fishing unfamiliar water, I've learned that the key is to find a seam and work both sides of the foam line, and right in the foam line itself. Usually fish prefer to slurp the fly on the slack side of the seam, but sometimes they'll take it in the faster water.

We also explored around underwater structure, including rocks and deeper slots in the bottom. Sometimes the fly had to be just inches from a submerged log to bring the fish to the fly and to the net. In short, location of the cast was every bit as important as the fly used. ■

fast and he's heavy and he's going places," to borrow another quote from MacQuarrie. As dusk grew thicker, I waded to shore, reflecting on another line from "Now, in June":

> I have caught more fish than I deserve to catch. And always and forever, the good ones like this fellow put me on edge, send me hippity-hopping to a boulder or the bank to sit down and gather my wits.

Ron and I pulled off our dripping waders just after 9:00 p.m. He was closing the tailgate when a young man in full fly-fishing regalia came up the trail from downstream. It's always encouraging to see a younger person who has taken seriously to fly fishing. We said hello and introduced ourselves. Rob Novak, we learned, was born and raised in nearby Hayward, where he was now working as an insurance agent. He happily shared that his hot fly for the night was "the smallest Blue-Winged Olive that I had." Who knows if our paths will cross again, but it is always fun to meet another "Brother of the Angle," to quote Izaak Walton.

Back at camp, Ron and I sat and chatted a while before bed. Ron's excitement about my adventure was heartening, and his generosity in showing me his piece of Leopold and Mac-Quarrie country was truly a gift. He was an engaging and thoughtful host. While we sat there sipping our cans of Two Hearted Ale at almost 11:00 p.m., his nephew's friend Chris came out of the bathroom with the toilet in his hands! He announced that he was changing out the old one for a newer model. Ron and I exchanged glances as we both realized that the only crapper in the camp had just waltzed out the front door. "Sure hope the new one goes in without a hitch," I said, "or we could all be in for an interesting morning."

Chris soon walked back into the camp with a brand-new Glacier Bay throne. Thankfully, the installation went smoothly and, just fifteen minutes later, I was privileged to test-drive the sparkling new loo before retiring for the night. With that potential nightmare averted, we were all soon sound asleep, dreaming of big fish and happy days.

Ron cooked another hearty breakfast on Sunday, and at 9:00 a.m. sharp, I shook hands with Ron, waved goodbye to the boys, and pointed my nose east toward the Michigan UP to meet Gracie Voelker Wood and her husband Woody for my long-awaited visit to Robert Traver's legendary Frenchman's Pond. Even with a four-hour drive ahead of me, my mood was as bright as the morning sun, thanks to Ron's exuberant generosity and such a memorable time in the Wisconsin woods.

- 14 -

Onward & UP-ward: Amazing Grace

Sunday afternoon, May 28

This whole Storied Waters trip was Gracie's doing.

After Grace Voelker Wood gave us permission to reprint "Testament of a Fisherman" in *The Confluence*, I sent her a copy of our book when it was released. In a lovely handwritten thank-you note, she suggested I come visit her in Ishpeming. She promised her husband, Woody, would take me out to Uncles, that famously secret fishing spot her father, John Voelker, called "Frenchman's Pond" in many of his stories that were written under the pen name Robert Traver.

I don't think Gracie expected I would take her up on her offer. But I couldn't resist, and the entire Storied Waters adventure started with her generous, friendly proposition.

The other five weeks of the trip were essentially the means to an end: to get myself to the U.P. and Uncles (no apostrophe, no "pond," according to Woody). At some point in my planning, Gracie invited me to stay a few nights at their home in Ishpeming. That, too, was a kind offer, and I really couldn't say

no. Still, I left my plans a little vague in case I felt I was imposing on them, or things got awkward and I needed to find an excuse to move on. We all had fly fishing and a love for writing and her dad's stories in common, but we were otherwise complete strangers, although Gracie and Woody knew more about me from reading *The Confluence* than I realized. Conceivably, we could have been like oil and water on other dimensions: politics (especially in this polarized era), religion, pets, you name it.

When I got on the road after leaving Ron's camp on Sunday morning, I texted Woody to tell him my approximate arrival time. Woody replied, "David can u plz be here no later than 3? Let me know. We are all going to dinner at friends. Thanks Woody."

Oh dear. Now I was imposing on their friends, too. But, heck, I was game and willing to meet more interesting people. Things had been working out well so far, so why not? I replied to Woody in the affirmative.

Woody, Gracie, and I hit it off right from the start. When I pulled into their driveway, I was greeted with a big hug from Gracie. Both are seventy-something, and after so many years together, they orbit each other like twin stars, beaming out goodwill and big smiles. Within minutes, I felt very comfortable in their home. They were informal and relaxed, and their two dogs, Inky and Jenny, were friendly and polite. Soon, Woody was giving me grief like the older brother I never had. I felt perfectly at ease as Gracie showed me to my room.

Sunday evening, May 28

Around 5:00 p.m., Woody drove us to nearby Marquette for dinner at Rich and Susan Vander Veen's beautiful home in town. Susan and Rich were gracious hosts and anxious to hear all about my adventure. Susan is a talented professional chef, so the food was phenomenal. Rich is an attorney who now develops wind-power projects in upper Michigan, so he and I shared an interest in both fishing and renewable energy. He chairs the John D. Voelker Foundation, which sponsors the Robert Traver Award for Fly Fishing Writing and provides scholarships to Native Americans who are attending law school. Rich is a regular at the Opening Day gatherings hosted by Woody at Uncles, a continuation of the tradition that Voelker began many years ago to celebrate the new fishing season with his fly-casting friends.

Two other guests, Bob and Peggy Jensen, had recently moved to Marquette from North Dakota. Both were fly-fishing fanatics and had traveled all over the world for business, so they had interesting stories to tell. The wine flowed. The conversation was effervescent. We all enjoyed the evening immensely.

Later during my stay Woody admitted, over a post-fishing breakfast at the local diner, that he had the same muted worry about my visit being awkward. He was kind of nervous about what Gracie had signed him up for. But, as Woody correctly observed, "Gracie is a pretty good judge of people." As we talked

Gracie and Woody carry on the legacy of warmth, caring, and good humor that Gracie's father, John Voelker, crafted into his writing.

more about our families and other things new friends explore, he chuckled and commented, "It appears you and I both married over our heads." I couldn't disagree.

Gracie took me under her wing and treated me like family. She even insisted on doing my laundry. Her offer reminded me of some sage advice I once saw on a roadside sign: Never refuse a breath mint. I think she was just being nice, but for the rest of the trip, I was constantly sniffing myself and doubling up on deodorant, wondering if I might have a problem. When I got back from fishing on Monday, my clean clothes were all folded neatly on my bed.

In their living room a carved name board that says "Amazing Grace" hangs over the sofa. Woody told me that when he bought a thirty-six-foot Cape Dory sailboat many years ago, he knew that Grace might not be too enthusiastic about the idea, so he named the boat *Amazing Grace*. This shrewd move went a long way toward earning her reluctant acceptance of his big toy. Clever fellow, that Woody. He no longer owns the boat, but the nameplate from his boat says it all.

Woody is a diehard devotee of John Voelker's life work and legacy. Woody always refers to his late father-in-law as "John," so it wasn't long before I started to do the same, which sounded odd, as if I had known him myself. Even so, I still think of him mostly by his pen name, Robert Traver, because that is how I came to know him first, by reading his stories.

I asked Woody if he had fly-fished before he met Gracie. He had not. He got the bug from John, whom he admired deeply. Woody loves Uncles as much as John did. Well, I can't say that for sure, but I can't imagine anyone loving Uncles more than Woody. He and Gracie are ardent advocates and defenders of John's place in fly-fishing history, especially his special sanctuary at the pond.

Reading a favorite author, especially one who writes very personally, as much memoir as entertainment, we sometimes come to feel we know them. That's certainly how I felt about John Voelker, whom Charles Kuralt called "the greatest man [I've] ever met" after filming a segment about John in his TV show *On The Road*." After meeting Gracie and Woody and hearing their stories and insights about John, my impression of the man was on the mark. He opened his soul to the world through his writing, which I think is a large part of his lasting appeal. Here are a few words from the preface to *Trout Madness*:

To this fisherman, the fish in fishing happens to be what the onion is to onion soup: one of the main ingredients, yes, but far from everything. I fish mainly because I love the environs where fish are found. . . .

Successful fly fishing for trout is an act of high deceit; not only must the angler lure one of nature's subtlest and wariest creatures, he must do so with something that is false and no good—an artificial fly. Thus fake and sham lie at the heart of the enterprise. . . .

In this book, I will lie a little, but not much, and I would prefer to hide my lapses under the euphemism "literary license," my excuse being that I find it difficult to inject drama into a series of fishing stories unless somebody occasionally gets on to a good fish. Quite frequently, you know, we fishermen don't.

Monday morning, May 29

Come Monday morning, we loaded up Woody's fish-mobile and set out to Uncles. We made a quick stop at the Huron Mountain Bakery for coffee and a muffin; the sign read "Muffins so good the Muffin Man is jealous." As I sipped my coffee, Woody gave

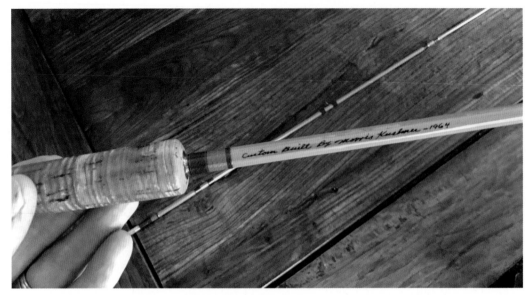

Woody proudly showed me John Voelker's custom bamboo rod handmade by Morris Kushner, subject of the story "Morris the Rodmaker" in Trout Magic. *Yes, that's my hand touching it.*

me a quick driving tour of Ishpeming before heading to the pond.

Woody pointed out the local landmarks from John's fishing and writing career, including the clapboard house where Gracie first lived as a young girl, the post office where John collected rejection notices and an occasional royalty check, and the Rainbow Bar (named after the trout) where John would meet up with fishing buddies. The house appeared in the 1959 film *Anatomy of a Murder*, shot on location in Ishpeming and Marquette and based on Voelker's bestselling book of the same name. The success of the book and the Academy Award–nominated film allowed Voelker to retire from his job as Michigan Supreme Court justice and turn full-time to writing and fishing.

The evening prior, on our way to dinner, Woody had showed me the courthouse in Marquette where they filmed Jimmy Stewart as defense attorney Paul Biegler squaring off against high-powered prosecutor Claude Dancer (played by George C. Scott) in the murder trial of Lieutenant Frederick

John Voelker, pen name Robert Traver. INK WASH AND CHARCOAL DRAWING BY JILL OSGOOD

Manion (Ben Gazarra), whose wife, Laura Manion (Lee Remick) was allegedly raped by the murder victim. If you haven't read the book or seen the movie, it is a classic of the black-and-white era, directed by Otto Preminger with music by Duke Ellington (who appears in a cameo). *Anatomy of a Murder* is still considered one of the best court trial movies ever.

The story is based on a real case that Voelker tried and won in 1952. Voelker, of course, made his protagonist, Paul Biegler, a fly fisherman. In the opening scene of the movie, Biegler (Jimmy Stewart) returns from a fishing trip, cleans a trout that looks to be about 16 inches, wraps it, and puts it into the fridge. In the book, there is a passage where Paul, who was still considering whether he would take the murder case, called his assistant, Maida (played in the movie by Eve Arden) on the phone from the jail. She asked him, "Will you be back this afternoon?"

"No, I'll work here and then I'm going fishing tonight."

"Fishing, fishing, fishing," Maida said. "You just had a long weekend of it. Look, Boss, are you mad at the trout?"

"I'm afraid it's a blood feud, Maida. For years I caught them and now they've caught me. I'm getting to hate 'em worse than women. And there'll be damn little time for fishing once I dive into this case—if I take it."

During breakfast, before we went out to Uncles, Woody and Grace lovingly showed me some of John's prized possessions, including his custom bamboo fly rod made by "Morris the Rodmaker," signed copies of his books, and a special commemorative print of "Testament of a Fisherman." After letting me fondle the hallowed fly rod, Woody pulled up on YouTube a short film called *Trout Madness* (after the book of the same name) from the 1960s, narrated by John Voelker himself. The color clip is quite a throwback, showing John leaving the same house where I was sitting to drive out to Uncles in his Jeep. After watching the film, Woody and I got up and made that very same drive. I was bristling with anticipation.

Fantasy Fulfilled at Frenchman's Pond

Monday, May 29

I felt like I had walked onto the pages of *Trout Magic.*

There I was: casting into the fabled French-man's Pond, aka Uncles, at last. The pond is a long, narrow beaver flowage that is shallow but spring-fed, where John Voelker discovered trout that benefit from the cold water refuge and stay active all summer. The location of Uncles is still a closely guarded secret. Woody blindfolded me and locked me in the trunk on the way there. Figuratively, of course. He told me I could say that the pond is roughly an hour's drive due north of Marquette. (Hint: That would put it somewhere in the middle of Lake Superior.)

As we were driving, I was enjoying our chat, looking out the window but not paying much attention to the many twists and turns along the way, so I wouldn't be able to find Uncles now if I tried. We bounced along a two-track woods road through scrub pines and down a hill to a small clearing where Voelker's cabin stood, adorned with a handmade sign that announced "Royal Coachman Inn." Several ramshackle sheds and an outhouse stood nearby. A pleasant-looking screened gazebo and an outdoor bar with wooden stools were more recent additions built by Woody to make it more comfortable for entertaining guests.

Following the financial success of *Anatomy of a Murder,* Voelker was able to acquire the land around his favorite beaver pond that was tucked far into the backcountry. He soon built a camp there. He also constructed a footbridge across the pond, and several small casting platforms along the marshy edges among the alders.

John's camp itself hadn't changed much in the twenty-six years since he died at age eighty-seven. Jim Enger described it perfectly in "The Master of Frenchman's Pond," a touching tribute to his good friend John in his own collection of fine stories, *The Incompleat Angler* (1996). The single room is chock-full of his memorabilia: books, photos, statues of mermaids (per a reference in "Testament"), his old saloon table, cribbage boards, a couch, and a woodstove. The cramped cabin is filled with John's spirit and boasts a decent stock of bourbon left behind

John Voelker's eclectic cabin sits near the shore of Uncles, aka Frenchman's Pond, a remote beaver pond on the Upper Peninsula of Michigan.

by visitors who came here to raise a glass in his honor with his spirit of choice.

I found it impossible not to make a connection between Voelker's small cabin by his pond, Thoreau's small house next to Walden Pond, and Leopold's Shack on the Wisconsin River. All three men were very different in personality, but each had a special relationship with his own remote surroundings, closely observing the landscape, studying the fish and wildlife, contemplating his own connection to nature, and reveling in the "haunting quiet water" (Voelker), the "tonic of wildness" (Thoreau), and "the orchestra of evolution" (Leopold).

Woody was casting about ten yards to my left. A trout had just short-hit his fly—a Betty McNault, or simply a Betty: a down-wing, caddis version of a Royal Wulff similar to a Royal Trude that was one of John's favorites, tied by his friend from Ishpeming, Bill

Woody and I both caught fish near the old beaver dam at Frenchman's Pond, where John Voelker had fished with Art Flick.

Nault. After his miss, Woody urged me to try my fly—the gray CDC Caddis Emerger that I bought at the Driftless Angler—where the fish had just risen.

Two casts later, a stout 11-inch brook trout was in my net. This was a special moment, almost surreal. I was laughing and grinning like a madman as I played that magical trout across the glistening surface of Frenchman's Pond! To double the pleasure, a few minutes later I caught a 6-inch native brookie close to the same spot. I really couldn't believe that, after all those months of planning and dreaming, I was actually in the shadow of John Voelker catching fish.

Woody and I moved down to the old beaver dam as a brief rain shower gave way to patches of sun. In his story "A Flick of a

hottest spot in the very hottest fishing place that I knew."

Because I had caught two fish from under Woody's nose, he had the honors of the first try here.

His casts were slow and graceful with his 8-foot Orvis bamboo rod and vintage reel, as he aimed to put the fly near a downed tree under some overhanging dead branches. I couldn't resist shouting, "Watch your back-cast!" just *after* he caught his fly in the alders behind us. I extracted his fly for him, and two casts later he hooked up with a hefty brook trout, right where Art Flick had missed the big one on his Grey Fox Variant in the *Trout Magic* story.

Landing Woody's trout was a bit compli-cated, because Jenny, his gentle aging hound and regular fishing companion, decided she wanted to sniff the fish. We finally convinced Jenny to move out of the way so I could net the brook trout, a twin of the one I had caught earlier.

It was proper that Woody and I both had success on this special outing. Even though I had traveled far, the fishing was far from lousy.

The rain started again, so Woody and I retreated to the cabin. John came here when the fish weren't "in the mood" and drank his bourbon straight up or mixed in his sig-nature old-fashioneds—the official camp cocktail—while playing cribbage with com-panions. Woody poured me some bourbon in a tin cup, well aware that I knew the line from "Testament": "Bourbon out of an old tin cup always tastes better out there." I was in heaven.

As I looked around the single room, Woody pointed out pictures of characters that appear in John's stories, including Danny Spencer from John's first novel *Danny and the Boys*. A carved mermaid sat on a shelf next to several of John's books. Woody pulled out

Favorite Fly," John had fished this exact spot with Art Flick, author of *Streamside Guide to Naturals and Their Imitations*. In anticipating Art Flick's arrival, John remarked that, when visitors come from far away, the fishing often turns lousy—"the farther, the lousier." And so it had on that fabled outing. The old beaver dam was John's last and best shot at getting Art Flick a fish. Woody and I were standing in that exact place: the "bottom is a vast tangle of crossed logs," the "very a copy of one of John's journals, and I flipped to an entry from the same date on which I was visiting, May 29. I don't remember the year, but on that day, John and his pal Vic Snyder drove in his Model A "fish car" to the Big Escanaba River near Gwinn. Here's part of John's entry:

Went up to the car to get a beer. Looked down the river & saw a rising fish. Forsook the beer. Went down and cast over the rise. Nothing. The fish rose again. Cast again. Nothing. A fish rose above me. Nothing. Put on a #16 dry fly (I do not know the name of it, which was part of its charm) and on the 3rd try over the bottom fish got a pass. Missed. Three more casts. Nothing. One more. Clap. Three minutes of doggy underwater fighting: one 12 inch brook.

I'm not much of a cribbage player, so I passed on taking an inevitable whupping from Woody. But I was more than happy to sit at John's saloon table, sip some bourbon, and make a toast to all the fishing madness and magic that he shared with generations of readers, recognizing as he did that "fishing is at once an endless source of delight and an act of small rebellion."

Before I left, I signed the log book of visitors, one among many, including bamboo rod maker and Michigan/Maine resident Kathy Scott, who shares a deep appreciation for this storied place. I left behind a signed copy of *The Confluence* for the bookshelf.

Above all, it was a privilege to be there with Woody, an irrepressible man who keeps John's spirit alive with the same passion that his father-in-law passed on to him. I'll never forget my special day at Uncles with Woody and Jenny. And I thank Gracie for her kind invitation.

Tuesday morning, May 30

The next day Woody and I trekked to the Yellow Dog River, west of Marquette. This river appears in Jim Harrison's 2004 novel, *True North*, which coincidentally my friend Paul

Woody's faithful dog, Jenny, has accompanied him on many successful outings.

Woody ties on a Betty on the bank of the Yellow Dog River.

Cain had just finished reading the night before I was telling him about my plans to visit the UP. He loaned me the book to read before my trip. David Burkett, the antihero of this captivating but contemptuous story set in and around Marquette, loves fly fishing (as did Harrison, who died in 2016), thus *True North* serves as kind of a trout fishing guide to the UP.

When I mentioned that I wanted to fish the Yellow Dog, Woody reminded me that the Yellow Dog was the setting for Voelker's story called "The Old Fox" in *Trout Madness*, in which John's companion introduces him to the virtues of the Betty McNault, the same fly Woody had been using (size 16) the day before. Voelker had called it a "fabulous little rocking-chair stream . . . the kind of seductive trout stream that keeps fishermen misty-eyed and mumbling to themselves trying to fathom its tempestuous mood and to realize its promise."

On our way down the 510, a wide dirt road suitable for big trucks, Woody stopped to show me Little Pup Falls, a tumbling cascade dropping thirty or forty feet in one hundred yards through the beautiful Michigan forest. The new leaves were still a few weeks behind the trees in Pennsylvania, glowing with a dozen shades of pale green.

At the Yellow Dog bridge, we geared up and clambered down the bank on the downstream side. We waded across the shallow stream and walked quietly up under the bridge to toss our flies to the pool above it, which Woody said was a reliable spot for stocked rainbows. Casting under the bridge was a little tricky, but sure enough, a rising rainbow took that same CDC Caddis Emerger I was using the day before. Woody scoffed that the 8-inch hatchery fish was "factory fresh," but I was thrilled to catch a trout out of the Yellow Dog, a doubly storied water, even if it wasn't a wild trout on a Betty.

Where & How—
Uncles & Yellow Dog

Woody swore me to secrecy. I can't even find the place on a map, so he doesn't have to worry about my spilling the beans about where to find Uncles/Frenchman's Pond. There are hundreds of similar beaver ponds and flowages dotting the landscape in that part of the UP, so it hardly stands out, except in literary history.

Many remote ponds and streams in Michigan require the landowner's permission, so getting into backcountry bogs is not always an easy proposition. Michigan's laws around access versus trespass are complicated, so it's best to get some local advice about how to access waters that are not specifically marked as public land or public access. The Michigan Fishing Information System (MiFISH) has additional information on stream-specific regulations.

The Yellow Dog River, however, is accessible by several public roads, including the 510. The upper portions of the river fall within the Ottawa National Forest, but the river there is extremely rugged and remote. Four miles of the Yellow Dog are designated as part of the National Wild & Scenic River system.

What Works: John Voelker swore by a local fly tier named Bill Nault, who tied for John many of the patterns he found in Art Flick's *Streamside Guide*.

Bill Nault also tied a fly that Woody calls the Betty McNault, or simply a Betty, one of Voelker's favorites and the subject of his story "The Old Fox." Voelker tells how his friend Carroll Rushton introduced him to the fly after catching numerous trout on the Yellow Dog, while John had been skunked. Carroll gave John a few Betties to try. John "took the flies humbly and followed instructions" and promptly caught a half-dozen trout in thirty minutes.

Here is what Voelker has to say about the Betty in "The Old Fox":

It is a dainty little hackled hair fly, tied and appearing much like a minor variant of that old reliable, the Royal Coachman. It is a tremendously versatile fly, one that can be fished either wet or dry. Oddly enough, like so many effective flies it looks like no natural fly I've ever seen floating on a stream. Carroll always carries oodles of them, in all smaller sizes, but the number 16 is far and away his favorite.

The Betty McNault (I've also found it called a Betty McNall or a Betty Nault) is similar to a Royal Trude, but with a red tail instead of a golden pheasant tail. It's seems to imitate many things: a stonefly, a big caddisfly, or a grasshopper. Woody has a friend who ties a version of a Betty with weighted wire so it sinks quicker, and he retrieves it like a Muddler Minnow, a Hornberg fished wet, or a small streamer. Best of all, it is visible even to aging anglers in low-light conditions.

Don't fish the UP without a fistful of Betties. Fish 'em dry, fish 'em wet. John and Carroll Rushton, the Old Fox, would be proud. ∎

Woody and I waded upstream, flipping various dries and nymphs into the small runs and deep holes under downed trees. Just as Voelker described in "The Old Fox," our casts had to be short—less than 15 feet of line at any time, letting the current take the fly, with a quick retrieve so we wouldn't get hung up in the branches or roots.

The naturally stained water gave the sandy bottom of the river a striking yellow-orange hue, which may have something to do with the name. The water was cold (50 degrees), and there were few bugs in the air. We saw no rising fish, nor did we have any real action on the way upstream or back down, except near the bridge where Woody and I each caught another small rainbow before heading back into town for a late breakfast and a restful afternoon.

That evening, we had a home-cooked dinner, with Woody manning the grill and making the old-fashioneds, while Gracie and her sister Julie shared stories about growing up in the house where I had been staying. Julie told me of hours spent outdoors and a world opened to the Voelker children by two interesting and enlightened parents.

The next morning, I was up early, ready to head east for the next leg of the journey. It was difficult to say goodbye to Gracie and Woody, my new, dear friends. After my visit to Uncles, I resolved to find my own tin cup for future bourbon sipping. And now and then, I call or text Woody to remind him to watch his backcast.

- 16 -

On Hemingway's Fox River

Wednesday morning, May 31

It had been a cool, wet spring in northern Michigan. The rivers were running high, and the bug hatches were off by about a week. Even the black flies and mosquitoes had been tempered in their typical early June attack.

After fishing the Yellow Dog River the previous morning, Woody and I had stopped in at Down Wind Sports in Marquette (a historic port town on Lake Superior with a hip vibe, much like Portland, Maine, or Portsmouth, New Hampshire) to check out their fly-fishing section. There we chatted with the shop owner, Bill Thompson, who casually mentioned that steelhead were still running in local rivers because of the late spring. My ears perked up. Bill reported that he'd just seen a photo of an impressive steelhead someone had recently caught in the Carp River, right near the edge of town.

I'd never fished for steelhead, and catching a steelhead in the Carp River had a nice ring to it. "Hmm," I said to Woody as we climbed back into his truck, "I wouldn't mind hooking into a steelhead before getting back on the road." Woody gave me directions where

to go on my way out of town on Wednesday morning. "Park across from the ski hill," Woody instructed.

The water was fast and broken into rapids and plunge pools not much bigger than the rug in my living room. I tried to imagine a 10-pound steelhead sitting in one of those holes waiting to slam my fly.

Following Bill's advice, I swung a few streamers and high-sticked some nymphs in the faster current, and floated a big fluffy Royal Wulff with a nymph dropper in the deeper pools, anticipating a wild ride at any minute. I am sad to report that I didn't hook a supersize steelhead, but I did catch a 7-inch rainbow on a red nymph dropper similar to a Candy Striper that John Voelker favored. I guess I was a little relieved that I caught the Mini-Me version rather than a 2-foot trout-osaurus ready to run me into my backing under downed trees and sunken logs. Simply put, I was satisfied that I had caught something, anything to start my day.

My next stop was Seney, Michigan, where Nick Adams, Ernest Hemingway's semiautobiographical character, embarked on his cathartic fishing trip after returning home from World War I in the incomparable short story "Big Two-Hearted River." There happens to be a Two-Hearted River in upper Michigan, but scholars agree that the actual river in Hemingway's story is the Fox River that runs through Seney. According to Carlos Baker's biography of Hemingway (*Ernest Hemingway: A Life Story*), after being wounded in Italy in World War I, Ernest made a trip to the U.P. in 1919 with companions Al Walker and Jack Pentecost. During a week spent on the Fox River, young Hemingway and his friends together caught nearly 200 trout. Or so they claimed. In the story, Nick did pretty well, too.

On my way to Seney, ninety miles east of Ishpeming, I passed through the Ottawa and the Hiawatha National Forests, the third and fourth national forests, respectively, that I'd driven through so far on this trip. The land on that part of the UP is flat as flat can be,

and the "Seney stretch" of Highway 28 is straight as an arrow, crossing multiple alder-choked rivers and streams, which were running high. I stopped to make a few casts in one promising looking river, and later spotted a sandhill crane on the side of the road as I was driving. It flew off gracefully when I stopped to get a photo.

Wednesday afternoon, May 31

Nick Adams stepped off the train in Seney where the train depot is now a museum. In the story, the town where Nick disembarked was recently burned from a forest fire:

> Nick looked at the burned-over stretch of hillside, where he had expected to find the scattered houses of the town and then walked down the railroad track to the bridge over the river. The river was there. It swirled against the log spiles of the bridge. Nick looked down into the clear, brown

The train station museum in Seney is where Hemingway and Nick Adams disembarked to fish on the "Big Two-Hearted River."

water, colored from the pebbly bottom, and watched the trout keeping themselves steady in the current with wavering fins. As he watched them they changed their positions by quick angles, only to hold steady in the fast water again. Nick watched them a long time.

Nick walked north out of town and into the woods to fish for trout and recover from his wounds and the war. The war is never directly mentioned in the story, but is clearly an undercurrent. For example, Nick noticed as he walked through the charred countryside that "the grasshoppers were all black now. He wondered how long they would stay that way."

Once he was beyond the burned land, Nick walked all day through a pine plain, then made camp by the river before fishing the next day. Although Nick was clearly a fly fisherman, he used live grasshoppers instead of flies. He released some of the fish he caught, but kept a few of the bigger ones for dinner.

On my way out of town, I stopped at the highway bridge over the river and looked for trout. I saw no trout under the bridge, as the water was high and cloudy. I followed the Fox River from the bridge along a dirt road and pulled into a parking area where a sign indicated that, in 2005, the Nature Conservancy consummated a public-private partnership to protect over 270,000 acres in the Fox River watershed, surrounded by both state and national forest lands. Hemingway (and Nick Adams) had hiked up the east side of the river and camped on the East Branch near the Lake Superior State Forest Campground, where the Michigan Outdoor Writers Association has installed a "Hemingway Fished Here" monument. I was on the west side of the river.

The Fox was running high and fast and cold, up into the alders and willows on both banks. There was a place to cast above a long deep run. In Hemingway's story, "the trout were rising, making circles all down the surface of the water, as though it were starting to

The Fox River was dimpled with raindrops rather than rising trout.

The Sturgeon River near Rondo has some very fishy-looking bends and pools.

rain." As I cast my fly, it actually started to rain, and large drips from the trees over the river looked like rise rings from trout, but I wasn't fooled. There were no trout rising. Instead, mosquitoes were attacking me in organized squadrons from the gray skies above.

During a futile hour of trying nymphs, dries, and streamers, not a single trout took a pass at my fly, nor did I catch 200 trout like Hemingway and his buddies. I found no live grasshoppers like Nick Adams had done to rescue my outing. I was sure there were trout in the river, but the conditions were not running in my favor. I chuckled to myself, thinking that perhaps I should write a Hemingway parody based on my failed outing called "The Trout Also Rises."

I'd rather remember the Big Two-Hearted version of the river, captured where Nick broke off the biggest trout he had ever seen:

His mouth dry, his heart down, Nick reeled in slowly. The thrill had been too much. He felt, vaguely, a little sick, as though it would be better to sit down.

The leader had broken where the hook was tied to it. Nick took it in his hand. He thought of the trout somewhere on the bottom. . . . By God, he was a big one.

That's the story that remains etched in my mind. Despite the high water, it was a thrill to experience the river Hemingway had fished and that later gave Nick Adams a new start on life after the Great War. I could feel the history as I trudged back up the trail to my car.

Leaving Seney behind, I crossed the 4,995-mile-long Mackinac Bridge to the Lower Peninsula and on to the lakeside town of Petoskey, where Hemingway's parents had a cottage when he was growing up. Young

Ernest fished local streams and did what young men do in this lakeside community until he married Hadley Richardson, his first of four wives, in nearby Horton Bay in 1921. In the run up to his wedding, Hemingway fished the Sturgeon River about thirty miles east of Petosky for three days with two friends in a "final bachelor's splurge," according to Baker, his biographer. I could imagine there was as much drinking as there was fishing, even for a twenty-year-old in the early days of Prohibition.

I had read that Hemingway may have frequented the historic City Park Grill in Petoskey, where there is a picture of him as a younger man over the bar. I sat below his handsome gaze and enjoyed a fine whitefish sandwich and a Founder's Centennial IPA. There is some question as to whether he actually sat at this bar, but I'll gladly go along with the local folklore that "Hemingway sat here," right where I was sitting. After another tasty ale, I retired to my hotel in Petoskey with plans to try the Sturgeon River in the morning before rolling on to the Au Sable River near Grayling.

Thursday morning, June 1

I knew that Hemingway had fished the Sturgeon, but not where. Had I known he had fished near the town of Vanderbilt, I would have gone there instead of trying my luck at a boat launch in Rondo, several miles north of where Ernest and his friends reportedly went.

Like all the rivers that I'd seen over the past two days, the Sturgeon was running vigorously, but this section was cold and clear. A promising pool and eddy above a huge gnarly tree leaning into the river looked like the perfect cover for trout. It was one of those places where you insist to yourself: *"If I were a trout, I would live here."*

Despite my enthusiasm, I managed only to get one trout to short-hit my fly a few times. Once again, I had no luck hauling in fish as young Ernest had done in these storied waters. While driving on I-75 toward Grayling, I could already hear my wife teasing me when I called her later that evening to tell her about my day: "Clearly, dear, you're no Hemingway."

- 17 -

The Auspicious Au Sable River in Michigan

Thursday afternoon, June 1

I had the Au Sable River in Michigan in my sights for the entire trip but somehow had managed to make no concrete plans about where, how, or with whom I would fish it. I knew that Trout Unlimited was founded on the Au Sable near Grayling in 1959 and that Henry Ford and Hemingway had both fished there, as did Jim Harrison and Jim Enger, who tells several vivid stories about the Au Sable in *The Incompleat Angler*. But I didn't have much specific to go on until I met Woody. We were driving up to the Yellow Dog when Woody took matters into his own hands.

"Well, no question, buddy," he said. "You have to go to Gates Lodge on the Au Sable. I go there a couple times a year. Let me see if I can help you out."

He punched some numbers into the screen on the console of his truck, and soon he was talking on his phone through the hands-free mic and speaker.

"Josh, hey, it's Woody! How the hell are ya? Are they catching any fish down your way?"

"Yeah, Woody, we're starting to see some Brown Drakes come off, and there are still a few Sulfurs around. The fishing is getting hot."

After a few minutes of good-natured banter, Woody had me booked into a room at Gates Au Sable Lodge smack in the middle of what's known as the Holy Water section of the main stem, which is world-class, flies-only, catch-and-release fishing. Josh Greenberg, the owner, is also author of *Rivers of Sand*, a beautiful and comprehensive blend of history, fishing, people, and reflection on fly fishing in Michigan, the Great Lakes Region, and, of course, the Au Sable (pronounced "oh-SAAB-l") in this neck of the woods, not to be confused with the Ausable River in New York, which most people pronounce "aw-SAY-bull").

"You and Josh will get along well," Woody assured me. "Maybe you can swap books with him. He runs a class outfit. But don't worry, it's not too fancy for you. He knows everything there is to know about fishing on the Au Sable. And the one thing you have to do is get down to the shop by 7 a.m. to catch up with some of the old-timers in there. They'll help you out. You'll love it!"

The Holy Water section of the Au Sable River is legendary among fly anglers everywhere.

Thanks to my growing network, I was set up for a visit to this famous river, so I decided I'd better do a bit more research on what to expect before I got there. The story of the founding of Trout Unlimited is worth relating.

This area of Michigan was heavily logged in the 1800s with massive log drives that disrupted the river ecosystems, including the Au Sable. Sadly, the abuses to the river, coupled with overfishing, wiped out the native population of Arctic grayling (*Thymallus arcticus*), a unique member of the salmon family with a huge, flowing dorsal fin. Today, the city of Grayling's name is a hollow reminder of the ecological disruption that had befallen the Au Sable and nearby rivers.

As the watersheds began to recover from the abuses of logging in the early part of the twentieth century, fisheries management in Michigan was for many years heavily slanted toward stocking hatchery-raised trout, including brown trout, brook trout, and rainbow trout, none of which were native to the Au Sable River. In 1959, Art Neumann and George Griffith (creator of Griffith's Gnat) organized a local group of sixteen fishermen at Griffith's home on the Au Sable to advocate for habitat management to protect water quality and support wild populations, which they believed would produce better results for less cost than "put and take" stocking with "cookie-cutter trout." And they were right. Their Trout Unlimited model has been replicated in TU chapters all across the United States and Canada.

While the wild (but non-native) trout populations in the Au Sable are now world-class, the native grayling are still absent. The Michigan Arctic Grayling Initiative, a partnership of more than forty agencies and organizations including the Michigan Department of Natural Resources, the Little River Band of Ottawa Indians, and TU, has recently developed a promising action plan to restore self-sustaining populations of Arctic grayling within its historical range in Michigan. Stay tuned.

The North Branch, South Branch, and main stem of the Au Sable flow through sandy jack-pine barrens, which are common in the northeastern part of the lower Michigan peninsula. Because of the immeasurable amounts of gravel that were deposited by the retreating Wisconsinan ice sheet, the rivers are spring-fed with plentiful clean groundwater flowing in the sandy river bottom. Much of the land in the Au Sable basin is now protected as federal or state forest land, including portions of the Huron National Forest, which ensures excellent water quality in the rivers.

This corner of the Michigan Lower Peninsula is also the primary breeding range for the Kirtland's warbler, a very rare and endangered songbird that nests only in small jack pines and open grasslands of this sandy plain. State and local landowners are trying hard to maintain suitable habitat for the bird's benefit in the Au Sable River watershed. Birders travel from all corners of the world to catch a glimpse of this blue-gray summer resident with its signature yellow breast, black streaks, and broken white eye ring. Unfortunately, I didn't see a Kirtland's warbler during my time on the river. When I realized I was in Kirtland country, I really wished I'd brought binoculars and had more time to go birding.

On the South Branch of the Au Sable, the Mason Tract was donated to the state by George Mason under the proviso that it must remain forever wild to protect the water quality and habitat in the region. George Mason made large piles of money as CEO of American Motors Corporation and used some of it to buy a large tract of land on the South Branch in the 1930s from another wealthy auto executive, Clifford Durant of the Durant Motor Car Company. Over a thousand acres of undeveloped woods and clean water became Mason's private wilderness retreat, where he fly-fished as an escape from the auto business in Detroit. When he died in 1954, Mason bequeathed the land to the State of Michigan as a permanent game reserve, never to be sold. Even camping was and still is prohibited. The original 1,500-acre gift was eventually enlarged to almost 4,500 acres on both sides of the South Branch, giving fly anglers access to eleven miles of blue-ribbon trout water.

In 1984, President Reagan signed legislation designating the Au Sable as a federal Wild and Scenic River, protecting it from any more dams and other major development. The wild trout—browns, rainbows, and brookies—have been the beneficiaries of all these protective policies, as have a myriad of other species . . . including humans carrying a fly rod, like me.

Thursday afternoon, June 1

I arrived at Gates Au Sable Lodge, just eight miles east of Grayling, late in the afternoon, hoping to settle in, get an early dinner, then fish through the evening until dark. The lodge, as Woody promised, was not overly fancy: simple motel-style rooms, an Orvis-endorsed fly shop, a top-notch (according to Woody and, later, me) BYOB restaurant with a view of the Au Sable's main stem, and friendly, very knowledgeable staff who quickly got me pointed in the right direction.

Alex Lafkas was tying flies when I came in to the shop. He greeted me and recommended I pick up a few different Brown Drake patterns. Brown Drakes are big mayflies about an inch

Jim Enger sought the ghost of Henry Ford here on the North Branch of the Au Sable near Dam Four in his book The Incompleat Angler.

long, which he said were starting to come off the North and South Branches, along with some lingering Sulfurs. I bought several in an emerger pattern (mimicking bugs in the process of emerging from nymph to adult in the surface film) that Alex suggested was one of his favorites. I also grabbed a handful of Mahogany Dun patterns (mimicking mature adults ready to fly off the water) and some spinners (spent adults that fall to the water after mating).

Kimberlie Yuhas, an energetic young woman who works in the shop, pulled out a map of the watershed and showed me where

and got ready for dinner. Gates Lodge reminded me vaguely of the fishing lodge that plays a supporting role in Keith McCafferty's *Cold Hearted River*, the sixth in the Sean Stranahan series, which was "inspired by a true story" (I love that phrase) about Ernest Hemingway's lost trunk full of fly-fishing gear. Stranahan is a Montana fishing guide and artist who is also a part-time private detective, an unlikely combination, but, heck, it's a murder-mystery fly-fishing novel. In trying to solve a pair of suspicious deaths in Montana, Stranahan flies back to Michigan to investigate a person of interest (an attractive woman, of course) who owns a fishing lodge on the Au Sable River, where Hemingway had purportedly fished. I won't spoil the mystery, but here's a short sample of McCafferty's description of the river and the woman he is investigating:

> The Au Sable seemed much more at peace with itself than the brawling Western rivers Sean had grown accustomed to, and he told her so. She was standing with her hands on her hips, and as he watched her watching the river, a trout made a quick circle on the surface.
>
> "He rose to a mahogany dun," Margarethe said, "All the mayflies are three weeks early this year."

As I walked up to the dining room for an early dinner, I called my own woman of interest to wish Cheryl a happy birthday. Indeed, this beautiful evening happened to be my ever-patient and tolerant wife's birthday. As I looked out at the shimmering water from my table, I silently toasted her in absentia, missing her radiant smile yet grateful that she understood and supported me in taking this unusual trip. We would celebrate together in about a week.

to park and fish on the North Branch. Some other folks within earshot insisted I bring a headlamp and fish until well after dark, as that was when the monster browns come out, especially during the Brown Drake hatch. I agreed I would stay out as late as I could. This was going to be interesting, to say the least.

Now that I was checked in and properly oriented, I plopped my luggage in my room

At 6:30, I rumbled down a dirt side road to a place on the North Branch called Dam Four. The logging-era dam, thank goodness, is long gone. So is Henry Ford's former camp, which once stood near the river here, as I learned from Jim Enger's story "The Ghost of Henry Ford." Several pickups and trailers were parked along the access road, triggering a sag of disappointment that I might have to share the water with other anglers within earshot. But when I got down onto the river, there was nobody in sight. I learned later that the vehicles parked there belonged to people who were floating the river in the narrow flat-bottomed Au Sable riverboats that are unique to this region.

The river was clear and wide, mostly knee-deep with a sandy bottom. I waded downstream a few hundred yards as quietly as I could and set up next to a deep glide sliding past a lichen-covered log along the bank. My fly of choice was Alex's big Brown Drake emerger, having seen a few drakes in the air, but none yet on the water.

A grackle hopped down onto the log, which I took as a good sign. When mayflies are hatching in great numbers, it's not just the trout that take notice. Swallows and bats often dive-bomb from above while the trout assault the bugs from below. Common grackles also feast on mayflies, hopping along the shore to pick the bugs off the vegetation, sometimes flitting out over the water to pluck an emerging mayfly right off the water, sometimes literally taking food out of a trout's mouth.

Grackles were my constant companions on nearly all the rivers that I had fished on this trip. I began to notice them working the shoreline on the Battenkill in Vermont, then again on the West Branch of the Delaware, on the spring creeks in Pennsylvania, and on virtually every stop in Wisconsin and Michigan. I started to think of grackles as my spirit animal, a sign of a healthy ecosystem. Grackles were working the river banks on the Au Sable everyday while I was there.

A splashy rise in the foam line near the log was another good sign. It took me two tries to get a proper drift line with my emerger, frantically mending my line to avoid drag. My effort was rewarded with a very fat, very energetic 12-inch brown trout. I'd call that an auspicious start.

I hooked another hefty brown just minutes later in the same run before I wandered downstream in search of new water to try. The drake hatch was steady but not heavy and, unfortunately, ended before dark. I stayed until 10:00 p.m. anyway, dreaming of a big ol' brown trout the size of a Clydesdale dragging me up and down the river until dawn.

Didn't happen. Even so, a half-dozen browns and one bright brookie made for a pretty good outing, especially after the almost fishless result the day before. Wading back to the car in the late dusk was a bit tricky, but a well-deserved victory march after a successful campaign.

Friday morning, June 2

I sauntered into the fly shop for coffee at seven sharp as instructed by Woody. Josh Greenberg greeted me from behind the counter. It was a pleasure to finally meet him and pass along greetings from Woody. I was looking forward to gleaning whatever wisdom I could from him and others in the room.

Josh is about fortyish and has been tying flies and guiding at Gates for most of his adult life. He bought the Lodge from his friend and mentor Rusty Gates, a Michigan icon who, sadly, died of cancer in 2009. Josh and his wife Katy have been working hard to maintain and improve Gates Lodge as Rusty would have done, while being careful not to upset the regulars, who like the throwback feel of the place.

The fly shop is outstanding, with the lion's share of the flies tied locally. Here is what Josh had to say about mornings in the fly shop in his book, *Rivers of Sand*:

The best time to work in the fly shop is the morning after a wonderful night on the river. Just after 7 a.m. the shop fills with coffee-hungry, bed-weary, bug-bitten anglers, and they all stand around and tell stories. There was the big fish on the South Branch that was swimming upstream with its mouth open, letting the spent flies pour in. And another fish on the main stem doing the same. There was the one that got away. And the one that got caught. Digital cameras make the rounds.

Josh confirmed that other anglers had experienced what I had seen the night before: bugs early but none after dark. Apparently, the holy grail is when Brown Drakes cover the water in the moonlight; that's when the big trout come out to play. "Well, I had a good evening," I reported. "I have nothing to complain about," which could have been the tagline for my entire trip so far.

After signing and swapping books with Josh, I mentioned that I wanted to go to Lovells Museum to see the monument to the TU founders. Josh and Colin, one of his guides, suggested I should start the morning near Twin Bridges, a few miles upstream from where I had fished the night before, on the North Branch, and fish until the museum opened at 11:00 a.m. I drove back north and followed their instructions to the letter. I was a little worried I'd run into crowded water near the easy river access at Twin Bridges but was again pleasantly surprised that I was the only one there.

Standing on the bridge, I could see, just as Colin had predicted, two fish rising regularly side by side in the smooth water under some huge trees. I waded quietly up from below and quickly took a sparkling brookie from the left side of the pool. The second one ignored my Brown Drake spinner pattern, but, as soon as I switched to an emerger, it slammed it on the first cast and ran all over the pool for twenty yards in every direction. Having now spooked every fish within shouting distance, I made a few half-hearted casts before heading to the museum, a few miles down the road.

Lovells Museum of Trout Fishing History is precisely in the middle of nowhere, on Twin Bridges Road in Lovell's Township with little around except a country store a short piece down the road. Front and center on the lawn near the walkway is an impressive stone monument and plaque commemorating the founding of Trout Unlimited. After reading the plaque, I stepped out of the bright sunshine into the museum to be greeted by Chase Lohr, a garrulous young volunteer who must have drawn the short straw to be working the museum on a warm Friday in June. Taking full advantage of his lone visitor, Chase was quick to extol the foresight of Art Neumann and other local TU founders, while also sharing his own stories of growing up nearby, fishing in the Au Sable and the kettle ponds that dot the local landscape. The museum is compact, making it easy to peruse the exhibits. It was a pleasant way to spend the brightest, sunniest part of the day when fishing can be futile. After bidding Chase goodbye and grabbing a sandwich at the lonely store nearby, I wound my way through the pine barrens to explore the South Branch of the Au Sable.

Friday afternoon, June 2

Josh and Colin had given me directions for exploring the scenic and unspoiled Mason

I suffered a bad case of buzzkill on the South Branch of the Au Sable in the Mason Tract.

Tract on the South Branch. Except for the soft, sandy roads (almost like driving on a dune), this area had the same remote feel as my home waters in the remote Dartmouth Grant in northern New Hampshire. Many of the turnouts for parking were empty on a Friday afternoon, so I chose one at random, pulled on my waders, and descended the steep bank to the river, which was visible through the understory about thirty feet below the road.

The South Branch itself reminded me of the Dead Diamond River in New Hampshire, as did the half-dozen six- to eight-inch native brook trout I took from small shady pools with crystal-clear water. Like the North Branch, the river was shallow and sandy-bottomed with rocks no bigger than cantaloupes, so the wading was easy. I tried various dry flies: a Quill Gordon, a Brown Drake spinner, and my trusty CDC Caddis

Emerger. Everything worked. I moved gradually downstream toward a promising pool at the next bend.

Location, location, location! If ever there were a perfect spot for trout, I had found it. The pool in front of me was deep and dark in a cutbank run with trees leaning out over the river. I cast my emerger out into the deep water and saw a sizeable flash at my fly, but couldn't get the fish to come back for another dry fly on the surface. This one seemed bigger, wiser, and more wary than any I'd seen so far—perhaps a big ol' brown trout unwilling to show itself, preferring the deeper water in the shade. I decided to tie on a big fluffy indicator fly with a weighted nymph dropper to dangle a delectable dining option down closer to the trout's nose. In *Rivers of Sand*, Josh likens this to bobber fishing, with the bigger indicator fly serving as the bobber while the nymph plays the role of the bait. He's right. But there's no shame in using this technique, as it isn't easy.

I had that lunker brown in my sights and was already playing the upcoming piscatorial battle in my head as I tied a nymph onto two feet of tippet that I had meticulously secured to the hook on my indicator fly. Suddenly, I thought I heard voices. I looked around but saw nobody upstream or down. So far that afternoon, I'd had the river to myself. Were the voices in my head? Had three weeks on the road, traveling alone, started to get to me?

Guided float trips are popular on all branches of the Au Sable River, so I suppose I shouldn't have been surprised when three drift boats came around the bend. My spirits sank when they floated noisily past me, one after another, right through my dark, deep pool over that finicky flashing fish that I had been working on for fifteen minutes, spoiling my chance for action in that pool for at least another fifteen minutes or more. Adding insult to my disappointment, the smell of their cigars and cigarettes lingered in the fresh forest air long after they were gone.

This was a total buzzkill. Glumly, I finished tying on the nymph dropper and threw a few perfunctory casts into the current, but my rod felt flaccid and my heart was no longer

Where & How— Au Sable River, Michigan

I'm going to describe something that I didn't do, but I wish I had: that is, fish with a guide from a flat-bottomed Au Sable riverboat at night, either during the Brown Drake, *Hexagenia* hatch, or mousin'.

Au Sable riverboats are unique to this region, having been developed in the late 1800s to move loggers and tools up and down the shallow, gravel-bottomed rivers. They are low profile, typically 24 feet long and 2½ feet wide, pointed in the bow and pointed or slightly square in the stern. The guide paddles or poles from the rear, and the one or two sports sit up front. Traditional boats are made of planks or plywood.

The biggest brown trout feed at night. They love big bugs or will take a Deerhair Mouse pattern swimming across the surface. An outing will begin at dusk and go until well after midnight. Check out the Gates Au Sable Lodge website for plenty of pictures of happy anglers with big browns lit up by headlamp.

What Works: It is important to have a guide who knows what night fishing on a river is all about. The fish are located by the sound of big mouths slurping flies during a night hatch, or by sight in the moonlight. They are very spooky so the boat has to be positioned to allow the angler to cast so the fly approaches the fish before the line. Casting in the dark is more about feeling the line and the rod than watching your loop. I'm told that when you hook one of these hogs, you are in for the time of your life trying to play it and land it in the dark.

I think it would be well worth another trip to the Au Sable for this unique fly-fishing experience. ■

into it. The mood had been spoiled. Hearing those voices around the bend was like hearing the baby crying in the next bedroom, just when things are getting warmed up for mom and dad.

My several hours of ecstasy amidst the scenery, smells, and sounds of this wild river had come to an abrupt end. It turns out I did have something to complain about after all! I trudged back up the hill to my car and said my goodbyes to the Au Sable and all the fine fishing of northern Michigan. It was time to head back east across southern Ontario to fish in the Adirondacks of upstate New York.

That evening I drove as far as Port Huron, Michigan, on Lake Huron near the border to Ontario, Canada. Staying in discounted hotels has its downside, as I found the lobby filled with an unhappy bunch of OUI offenders on a mandatory weekend alcohol education program. I lugged my cooler to my room and smugly enjoyed a cold Founders All Day IPA before bed to celebrate my successful experience on the Au Sable.

Saturday morning, June 3

I was up bright and early for the long, long, long, long drive across southern Ontario to Niagara, New York. I crossed the border near Niagara Falls (which I now knew was one hundred feet shorter than Kaaterskill Falls) and drove on through western New York toward the Adirondacks.

At 3:30 p.m., I entered the Adirondack Park. This was familiar country, as I grew up near the Adirondacks and spent many weeks in the summer enjoying the lakes and mountains in this 6-million-acre preserve. And, what do you think was the first bird I saw upon entering the park? Correct: a grackle flying low along a lake shore, looking for bugs. I took that as a good sign.

- 18 -

Stories Told & Untold in the Adirondacks

Saturday afternoon, June 3

Take a deep breath, we're in the Adirondacks. Mountain air, morning mist over a lake, a rushing stream, the spruce, hemlock and cedar forest . . . can you smell it?

Some places have a fragrance and a feel that never changes. The atmosphere, architecture, and general vibe of the Adirondack Park are like no other place I've been, a melding of the 1890s, 1930s, 1950s, 1990s, and beyond. As I set out through those rugged mountains that tower over scenic lakes and rivers in upstate New York, a deep-in-the-amygdala sensory deluge brought back a flood of memories.

I grew up just over an hour to the south and spent my formative years experiencing the outdoors in these lakes and mountains. My family vacationed on majestic Lake George on the eastern side of the Adirondack Park; we still do. A weeklong canoe adventure across Raquette Lake, Long Lake, and Blue Mountain Lake with my YMCA camp buddies was a highlight of my teenage years. My friends and I climbed Mount Marcy and several other high peaks in high school

and college. Shortly after my college graduation, a summer rugby tournament at Saranac Lake was a memorable weekend. Thirty years after that, the Herb Brooks Olympic Arena in Lake Placid provided a storybook location for my daughter's annual prep-school hockey tournament. Both physically and spiritually, I have never left the Adirondacks for long.

For all the time spent in the region, I'm chagrined to admit that I hadn't done much serious fly fishing in the most famous rivers in the Adirondacks, so I was anxious to rectify that shortcoming. I had several days planned for exploring the area while staying with my sister Nancy Van Wie and her husband Ed Mrozik at their farm near Elizabethtown on the eastern edge of the High Peaks area. I entered the park from the west near Old Forge, allowing me to fish my way across the park to get to their place.

Although I was familiar with the area and its history, I initially struggled to find authors and stories to guide my wanderings during my trip. James Fenimore Cooper (1789–1851) came immediately to mind, but Natty Bumppo—aka the Deerslayer, Hawkeye, or

Leatherstocking, depending on the book—wasn't noted for his fly-casting prowess.

I came across another classic, William H. H. Murray's *Adventures in the Wilderness; or, Camp-Life in the Adirondacks* (1870), which is credited with setting off a frenzy of interest in the region with his descriptions of the rugged north woods. This detailed guidebook covered every aspect of "camp life," including necessary gear and how to tolerate the black flies and mosquitoes. But Murray's breathless depiction of wilderness wonders, especially fly fishing for trout on remote ponds, was so over-the-top that it drew searing satire from contemporary Charles Dudley Warner, who laid bare the extravagancies of Murray's writing in his own book *In the Wilderness* (1878).

First, here's Murray:

No one knows what game there is in a trout, unless he has fought it out, matching such a rod against a three-pound fish, with forty feet of water underneath, and a clear, unimpeded sweep around him. Ah, then it is that one discovers what will and energy lie within the mottled skin of a trout, and what miracle of velocity he is when roused. . . . But if one should ask me what is my conception of pure physical happiness, I should assure him that the highest bodily beatitude I ever expect to reach is, on some future day, when the clear sun is occasionally veiled by clouds, to sit in a boat once more upon that little lake, with John at the paddle, and match again a Conroy rod against a three-pound trout. That's what I call *happiness!*

And here's Warner's snarky retort:

Trout-fishing in the Adirondacks would be a more attractive pastime than it is, but for the popular notion of danger. The trout is a retiring and harmless animal, except when he is aroused, and forced into a combat; and then his agility, fierceness, and vindictiveness become apparent. No one who has studied the excellent pictures representing men in an open boat, exposed to the assaults of a long, enraged trout flying at them through the open air with open mouth, ever ventures with his rod upon the lonely lakes of the forest without a certain terror, or ever reads of the exploits of daring fishermen without a feeling of admiration for their heroism.

Oddly, in spite of the world-class fishing opportunities, there is a paucity of more recent fishing stories set in this historic area. Ray Bergman (1891–1966), author of *Trout* (1938; rev. ed. 1952), shared timeless advice about fishing the west and east branches of the Ausable River (pronounced "aw-SAY-bull" by the locals), but he devoted just a few pages of his comprehensive masterpiece to fishing in the Adirondacks proper.

Fran Betters (1931–2009) penned *Fishing the Adirondacks* (1987) and an entertaining little book of stories and poems called *"Fish Are Smarter in the Adirondacks"* (1983). Here is the opening stanza from his poem "A Fisherman's Dream":

To share the melody of a stream
where rippling waters create dreams
of mayflies dancing in the air,
where fish abound in numbers fair.

Betters was born in Wilmington, New York, near the West Branch of the Ausable River and earned global reputation as owner of the Adirondack Sport Shop in his hometown. Best known as an innovative fly tier who developed the Ausable Wulff, Ausable Bomber, and Haystack patterns, he was a celebrated storyteller, guide, instructor, and rod builder. Today, Fran Betters is memorialized in the Fly Fishing Hall of Fame and with three giant steel sculptures of his famous flies in the town park near the Ausable River in Wilmington.

When searching for books set in the Adirondacks, I was quite surprised to learn that Ian Fleming's James Bond thriller *The Spy Who Loved Me*—the original book, not the movie—takes place at the fictional Dreamy Pines Motor Court on a small lake "10 miles west of Lake George." It turns out the movie producers bought the rights to the name but didn't use the story. Mercifully, as it turns out. In the book, Agent 007 shows up out of the blue to subdue the over-stereotyped bad guys and seduce the kidnapped heroine in cabin #3. I'm guessing this was meant to take place somewhere near Warrensburg, where the Schroon River meets the Hudson River. The book has absolutely nothing to do with fly fishing, but who can resist a good James Bond thriller, especially one set in the Adirondacks?

My sister Nancy had suggested that I read up on Follensby Pond near Tupper Lake, where the famous Philosophers' Camp brought together the likes of Ralph Waldo Emerson, naturalist Louis Agassiz, and artist William James Stillman in 1858. Journalist and historian James Schlett provides a detailed history of the gathering in *A Not Too Greatly Changed Eden* (2015). Emerson's poem "Adirondacs" told his firsthand story of the esteemed group's wilderness adventure at Camp Maple, as they called it. Stillman captured the scene with oil paint on canvas. Agassiz, the ichthyologist (and a 1984 inductee into the Fresh Water Fishing Hall of Fame), studied the trout caught by the group to support his creationist theories.

In 2008, Follensby Pond and the surrounding land was acquired from its private owners by the Nature Conservancy and the Adirondack Land Trust, with plans to transfer it to the State of New York as part of the Adirondack Preserve. That transfer had not been completed at the time of my trip, and access to Follensby Pond was tightly restricted, so I was not able to visit those storied waters to fish for its unique strain of heritage brook trout, genetically unchanged from the time of Emerson and Agassiz.

As with other stops of my trip, the stories told visually by painters in this region are as important as the words of famous writers. Artist Winslow Homer was a devoted fly angler who regularly visited the Adirondacks between 1870 and 1910. His dazzling watercolors feature the mountain scenery and grizzled Adirondack guides paddling and fly-fishing on ponds and rivers. Homer painted trout leaping from the water to catch mayflies from the air or taking a fisherman's fly. He captured the stunning colors of the native brook trout ("like tropical birds" said one reviewer) with breathtaking accuracy in *Jumping Trout* (1889) and *A Brook Trout* (1892). He also captured the dynamics of fly fishing in *Casting the Fly* (1894), *The North Woods (Playing Him)* (1894), *Waterfall, Adirondacks* (1889), and *Netting the Fish* (1889).

Homer stayed at a farm and lodging house near Minerva owned by Thomas and Eunice Baker. The Baker farm evolved into the North Woods Club, a private hunting and fishing preserve that still exists today. It's worth noting that the Adirondack Park was created at about this time, in 1894. The 6.5-million-acre park is over three times the size of Yellowstone National Park, with just over half the area in private land (under strict regulation) and 45 percent publicly owned forest preserve protected as "forever wild" by the state constitution, one of only two constitutionally protected landscapes in the

Winslow Homer's Jumping Trout *(1889) captures a brook trout in pursuit of a wet fly being cast in Adirondack waters.* WIKIMEDIA COMMONS, PUBLIC DOMAIN

world (according to the Adirondack Council.) Homer's paintings, Emerson's poem, and Warner's breathless descriptions helped generate the popular support for protecting the wild backcountry of the Adirondacks. Today, over a million acres are designated as wilderness.

While delving into Homer's career in the Adirondacks, I discovered an unexpected connection to my own personal story. My paternal grandfather, J. Allen Van Wie Sr., had belonged to the Gooley Club, also a private hunting and fishing club, right across the Hudson River from the North Woods Club. For a decade or more at the turn of the twentieth century, Winslow Homer and my grandfather frequented these remote accommodations just a mile or two apart, possibly hiking the same trails and fly-fishing the same waters.

Winslow Homer. INK WASH AND CHARCOAL DRAWING BY *JILL OSGOOD*

Born in 1875, Grampa Van Wie died in 1960, when I was three years old. My father was not much of a fisherman (I guess the fly-fishing thing skipped a generation), and his stories of his father and the Gooley Club were sketchy. But Grampa was also an amateur photographer who left a compelling collection of black-and-white photos and negatives from around 1900 through the 1940s and '50s. In preparing for my trip, I dug out an ancient family photo album and started looking through to see what I could find about my grandfather's time in the Adirondacks. Dozens of photos show him hunting, boating, and fly-fishing with companions in the Adirondacks over the span of several decades. His images, some fading and mottled with age, were captivating and, like Homer's paintings, full of stories untold.

I marveled at the details of rustic locations, the people, and their expressions. Grampa appears in some of the images, as does his older brother Fred and others unnamed. As I studied each image, the mysteries only grew deeper. Who were these people and exactly where were the pictures taken? I wish I could read their minds or have heard the stories that were never handed down.

The album was not in a clear order. I could only guess the time frame of each photo by the color of my grandfather's hair and the lines in his face. In some, he is obviously in his twenties with young men and women, usually near a lake or in boats. In others, he appears to be in his forties or fifties in the company of men with gray hair. It's hard to tell which pictures were taken at the Gooley Club and which were taken on hunting or fishing trips elsewhere, possibly Canada or Alaska.

One captivating shot is inside a hunting and fishing camp. My grandfather, wearing knee-high leather chaps and a necktie, is seated at a table with another studious-looking young man wearing a bowtie. They're both

My grandfather (right) with two companions in a camp in the Adirondacks, circa 1900. J. ALLEN VAN WIE

reading magazines, while a rough-looking character, probably a guide, peruses the label on a bottle. There's a revolver hanging on the wall and a pinup poster of a woman who looks like Rosie the Riveter, although this was likely from the World War I era, not World War II.

In another shot from the 1920s at Lake George, both my grandparents are dressed up in their finery in a pose much like Grant Wood's 1930 painting *American Gothic*, with my grandmother holding a long-handled fishing net while Grampa displays a stringer of a half-dozen fish that would probably be cooked for their dinner.

When I was growing up, Grampa's fly-fishing gear sat moldering in the basement. It's a shame we didn't take better care of his antique bamboo fly rods. When we cleaned out my parents' house after my mother's passing, the fly rods were in bad shape and either went to an estate sale or to the dumpster. All I have left is an antique Pfleuger 1494 Medalist single action fly reel, which desperately needs to be revived so it can once again throw line and a fly to a trout.

For almost a century, the Gooley Club leased 16,000 acres around the Essex Chain of Lakes from Finch, Pruyn, a paper company that operated a large mill in Glens Falls. The Finch, Pruyn land around the Gooley Club was acquired in 2007 by The Nature Conservancy as part of a larger transaction and donated to the State of New York as part of the Adirondack Forest Preserve, so these lands are now designated "forever wild" and open to the public. In a twist of intergenerational fate, my sister Nancy was involved in that land transaction as Director of Philanthropy at the Nature Conservancy and the Adirondack Land Trust. The Gooley Club's lease expired on September 30, 2018. According to news reports, the club relocated

its operations to other leased land a few miles away, while the fate of the buildings is yet to be determined. I wondered what Grampa would have to say about all that?

As I drove across Ontario, I couldn't stop thinking about these images and the historic buildings from my grandfather's day. I wanted to explore the area near the Gooley Club and Indian Lake to see what I could

A morning fog engulfs Nancy and Eddie's farm, a safe haven for rescued horses being rehabilitated while awaiting adoption and a forever home.

learn. Perhaps I'd be able to cast a line where Grampa fished with friends one hundred years ago and possibly crossed paths with Winslow Homer himself fishing or painting on a remote river or pond.

When I entered the Adirondack Park, my first stop was the impressive Adirondack Experience museum in Blue Mountain Lake to see their fishing exhibit. I found it disappointing compared to other exhibits there and to the several fly-fishing museums on my trip. The exhibit displayed old rods, reels, flies, images, and artifacts, but contained scant story development about local characters and places, so I picked up little new information.

Most impressive was Winslow Homer's painting, *The Two Guides* (ca. 1875), on display in the art gallery; this work, an oil, not a watercolor, has been described by notable critics as "the first of Homer's masterpieces." While I was exiting through the gift shop, I picked up a copy of David Tatham's informative book, *Winslow Homer in the Adirondacks* (1996) to guide me on this next part of my odyssey.

The museum was just a few miles from the Gooley Club Road. I ventured out to fish a little before dark and look for my grandfather's old stomping grounds. The bumpy dirt road followed the Indian River to where it enters the Hudson River, just upstream of Mink Brook, where Homer often painted. Just past a turnout with a trail to the Indian River, a vacant farmhouse with boarded windows and a broad covered porch sat at the edge of a clearing with a view of the Hudson River at the bottom of the hill. This was the Outer Gooley Club house, looking forlorn as if it knew it faced an uncertain future. The feral lilacs in the yard spoke of brighter days gone by, and still bloomed optimistically.

I climbed the stairs to the porch, tried the door, which was locked, and looked in the windows, peering into the past. I'm sure my grandfather once sat on this porch and passed through that door. I tried to imagine a group of men in 1920s fishing garb arriving in horse-drawn carriages after an arduous trip from Glens Falls or Troy, stomping across the porch, ready for a week of wilderness fly fishing.

From the porch, the view extended beyond the Hudson River to the hills where the North Woods Club is located. Homer's painting *The Rapids, Hudson River, Adirondacks (1894)* could have been painted on the rough-and-tumble stretch of water between the two clubs. Perhaps it is my grandfather casting the fly, but himself out of the picture, while the famous artist worked on the far bank.

There was still enough daylight left to try my luck fishing. I motored back to the turn-off and followed the trail to the confluence of the Hudson and the Indian Rivers. Both were running fast and strong, so wading was out of the question. But among the rocks along shore were a few quieter spots to put a fly. The occasional mayfly coasted gracefully over the water. They were vastly outnumbered by dozens of deer flies swarming around my head. While waving off the flies, I cast a streamer on my sinking line into the current across a slower glide. After a few unsuccessful sub-surface casts, I switched rods and bounced a Royal Wulff off a rock to drop lightly to the surface in the eddy behind it. I was poised for a trout, bright as a tropical bird, to leap clear of the water and take my fly on the way down, like in Homer's *Jumping Trout*. Wouldn't that have been perfect? Didn't happen.

After thirty or forty minutes, it was time to move on to get to my sister's farm in Westport at a reasonable hour. It was quite a thrill, though, to cast a line where my grandfather had fished and photographed, and where Homer had fished and painted. I tipped my hat to them both and headed north.

In addition to her fund-raising position with Adirondack Land Trust, Nancy, with her husband Ed, operates Crane Mountain Valley Horse Rescue, a nonprofit educational and humanitarian organization, where they rehabilitate abused or injured horses. Eddie works at the farm full-time. Nancy rises early to help feed the animals before driving to her office in Keene Valley. At the time of my visit, CMVHR had sixteen horses plus a full complement of pigs, chickens, dogs, and gardens that kept them very busy and well fed.

Their farm was my home base for four days as I explored the Adirondacks, starting with the Schroon River on Sunday morning. My brother, Doug, planned to drive up from Troy to meet me at the Bolton Landing exit of the Northway, a few miles west of Lake George. He and I had fished the Schroon River together maybe fifteen years ago. It was fun to know that this area was also 007 James Bond country.

Sunday, June 4

The Schroon River was running high from recent rains. Doug and I met a local fly fisher named Paul "Boze" Cummings at the parking area where we were putting on our waders. Boze generously recommended a few places upstream that would have some fishable water, including a place where a big eddy swirls below a roaring drop in the river.

Doug and I each staked out some precarious footholds near the eddy where I managed to fool a 10-inch brown trout with a dry fly. Doug, balanced on the rocks like the fisherman in Homer's *Casting* (1897), hooked a trout on a nymph before losing it when his line went slack for just a second or two. After an hour of challenging fast water conditions, I said goodbye to Doug and returned north on my own to explore the two branches of the Ausable River. Doug kept fishing and later called to gleefully let me know that he'd landed a plump rainbow trout on an Elk Hair Caddis.

The road took me through scenic Keene Valley, where Winslow Homer had met the two guides in his oil painting of the same name. In Upper Jay, I pulled over near the library to throw a line into the East Branch. There were no rises (and no grackles) on a sunny and breezy afternoon. Knowing from Fran Betters and Ray Bergman that this branch warms up more quickly than the West

Branch, I didn't spend too much time here. My destination for the evening was a place on the West Branch recommended by Nancy's friend Dirk Bryant.

Also on Dirk's advice, I made a stop at the Hungry Trout Fly Shop to stock up on Ausable Bombers and Ausable Wulffs, a mahogany-bodied version of a big fluffy Wulff-style mayfly. The shop was manned that afternoon by Jack Yanchitis, an effusive college student and certified guide who grew up near Saranac Lake. On wood-paneled walls hung waders, rods, reels, clothing, nets, and gadgets galore. Cabinets with rows and rows of small containers displayed thousands of flies in every shape, color, and size. Jack cheerfully gave me some pointers, picked out a few flies—including Bombers, Wulffs, and big stimulators—that he insisted would work and got me fully charged to get onto the West Branch.

I promised Dirk not to divulge his special spot, but I will say I enjoyed a long contemplative walk to the river through towering jack pines and white pines. Dirk had told me to "pick your water carefully," so I worked my way downstream to a long, deep run with big rocks beneath the surface, providing good cover for apprehensive trout. Mayflies and caddis fluttered that way and this over the water, but oddly there were no rise rings on some very fishy-looking stretches.

I tried the Ausable Bomber in several pools with no luck, then a big stimulator as suggested by Jack at the fly shop, but neither produced even a flash by a fish. Finally, I put a weighted nymph dropper on a huge size 10 Ausable Wulff.

On my first cast: SLAM! A big brown hit that big bad Wulff like a sledgehammer, and I had a howling joy ride on my hands with my wispy 3-weight rod and the heavy current. I had to work quickly to keep the fish from diving down into the rocks and move him into the slower current along the shore. My first Ausable River brown turned out to be "only" 14 inches, but it was as fat as a Central Park dachshund. I caught two more equally rotund 12-inch browns in short order, including one on the nymph dropper, before I worked my way back upstream to hike out in the oncoming dusk. Dirk's advice was right on all accounts, and I found myself smiling and singing "Many Rivers to Cross" all the way back through the pines to my car.

Monday, June 5

Nancy had arranged for me to meet her friend, conservationist and philanthropist Peter Paine, another avid fly fisherman, for lunch on Monday in nearby Willsboro. Peter serves on the Adirondack Land Trust Board of Directors and also played a role in the acquisitions of the Gooley Club and Follensby Pond parcels. After lunch, we drove to the site where his family had once owned a hundred-year-old paper mill on the lower Boquet River not far from Lake Champlain, proudly showing me where they had removed the old mill dam to allow landlocked salmon and other fish from the lake to swim freely upriver to spawn.

An Amish family, dressed in traditional clothes, was fishing in the big pool at the bottom of the thirty-foot cascading falls where the dam used to be. Father and son each wore wide-brimmed hats, and the mother and daughter wore long skirts and bonnets. When we asked, "Any luck?" the young boy offered that they'd caught a few fish for dinner, sounding pleased that their outing was worthwhile, which seemed to please Peter as well.

Back at the farm, Eddie was itching to take me to one of his favorite spots on the upper Boquet near Elizabethtown. "You're gonna love this place," he said in his gravelly voice and his downstate New York accent. "The water is gawgeous and the fishin' is usually pretty reliable."

We rumbled down the back roads, following the river much of the way. Eddie pulled his truck into a turnout and we geared up while the river gurgled pleasantly nearby. I worked my way downstream in the crystal clear water, while Eddie waded upstream with his light spinning rod to a pool he'd been thinking about all afternoon.

The sun plays on the rising mist on "Unknown Pond" in the Adirondacks.

My eye followed the river for several hundred yards downstream, and I was surprised to see no fish rising in several long, smooth glides on such a still and humid evening. A few minutes later, an osprey labored upriver along the treetops carrying a hefty trout in its talons. At least one of the locals was having some luck.

In the next hour, a variety of dries, streamers, and nymphs came up empty whether dead-drifted, swung slowly across the current, skittered across the surface, or retrieved fast and deep: everything in my bag of tricks. This sport can be so humbling when conditions appear so perfect but nothing seems to work. You know the fish are there, but there's just no magic in your wand.

Back at the truck, Eddie beamed with success having landed three 10- to 12-inch brown trout on wormy-looking weighted rubber lures that were obviously effective in the foamy plunge pools. He had the technique of the day, and I suspected he was quietly pleased to outfish the guy on the grand fly-fishing adventure. I was glad he was glad, despite my disappointing outing.

Tuesday, June 6

The next day was steady rain from the get-go. After a hearty breakfast at a greasy-spoon diner, I found my way to the historic Westport Library to do some writing. It was a quiet, peaceful day working in a beautiful old building with the rain steadily drumming on the roof. Good fortune again came my way, this time in the form of a Hemingway biography just waiting for me to pick it up to fill in some important details about Hemingway's early trout-fishing adventures in Michigan. Isn't it amazing when a library book practically leaps off the shelf at just the right time to help you

with your work? It's happened to me more times than you might imagine.

Wednesday morning, June 7

My final Adirondack outing on Wednesday morning was to another secret location; I'll call it Unknown Pond, after the one in Charles Dudley Warner's satirical story. Eddie wanted me to experience fishing on a remote, undeveloped pond with big wild brook trout, much like the rustic scenes in Homer's paintings. If we couldn't go to Follensby Pond or the North Woods Club, this was the next best thing. I chuckled, thinking of Charles Warner's biting satire, and teased Eddie: "I hope the trout up there aren't too big and dangerous. We'd better make it out alive."

We were up at dawn to drive a couple hours across the park, with me following Eddie in my own vehicle so I could go on my way after our morning excursion. We left my car

I carefully handle the heft of this heritage brook trout from Unknown Pond.

Where & How—
Ausable River, New York

Here's what Fran Betters has to say in his *Ausable River Guide*.

The West Branch is considered by many to be one of the best fly-fishing streams in the country. Its diversified water conditions allow each individual the ability to choose water to his or her liking, expertise, and wading ability. There is plenty of fast tumbling pocket water for the more adventurous, slow, easy wading water for the more timid; and lots of nice long runs, pools and riffles for those wishing to try their luck under all conditions.

The river offers almost twenty miles of quality fishing in some of the most scenic country you can imagine, starting near Mount Marcy, flowing past the Olympic ski jump near Lake Placid, over Flume Falls, and on to the rustic town of Ausable Forks. Two sections of catch-and-release water produce large, well-educated fish and are open all year. Beware that the faster, steeper sections can be very tricky wading.

What Works: In 1963, Fran Betters invented the Ausable Wulff fly, which he claimed, for decades, is the most productive fly on the river. Along with its cousins, the Ausable Bomber, Ausable Caddis, the Haystack, and Stonefly Stimulator, these dry flies float high and mighty in the fast water and will attract big fish from the depths of the deeper pools. Emergers, nymphs, and muddlers are also well regarded for when you get sick of catching big trout on dry flies. ∎

near the main road, as the last couple miles required some serious low-range four-wheel drive as we climbed a steep rocky pitch then crossed a beaver-flooded section with the water up to the hubs. I was nervous about whether the road was washed out under the water, but Eddie was characteristically confident as his truck had been through this before. And he was right.

The twenty-acre pond was surrounded by mature pines, spike-topped spruce, and alder-choked bogs. The morning mist rose in tall, dancing wisps illuminated against the dark shoreline by the sun, which had barely cleared the treetops on the surrounding hills. The water mirrored the dark trees, white wisps, and azure sky, broken only by a swimming loon calling out a warning as we carried our rods down to the shore. It was that perfect.

The only sign of human presence was a small floating dock and a sturdy rowboat standing ready to convey us around the perimeter. Eddie looked like a twenty-first-century version of Homer's watercolor *The Adirondack Guide* (1894), rowing while I cast a dry fly toward shore.

On our first lap, Eddie laughed when I caught a small chub, then a tiny, iridescent bluegill, both on my nymph dropper. Clearly the dropper tactic was a poor choice. On our second pass, Eddie trolled his line in deeper water and caught the first brook trout—14½ hefty inches—on his spinning rig. I switched rods to retrieve a Mickey Finn on my sinking line and soon hooked a small horse—a brawny brook trout about 18 inches long—that hit hard on the gaudy red-and-yellow streamer. I relished the contest and the "will and energy . . . within the mottled skin" as I worked for several minutes to bring the feisty trout to the boat for Eddie to net. I unhooked the fly and cradled it underwater while it caught its breath before darting into the deep. I always enjoy watching them swim away as much as I enjoy catching them. And I was relieved that neither of us was harmed in the heroic combat.

Ed caught one more leviathan about that same size before we had to call it a day. I was anxious to move on across Vermont to meet my darling wife for our first reunion after four weeks on the road. As we loaded our gear in the truck, Eddie was pleased that we had hooked into some heritage trout that are direct descendants of the trout that swam in these remote waters in Louis Agassiz's day. And I was grateful to Eddie and Nancy for being my hosts, and to Ed for being a most competent guide in the grand Adirondack tradition.

- 19 -

Vermont Rivers

Wednesday evening, June 7

Tucked into the hills west of Norwich, Vermont, Lake Mitchell is hardly a lake. It's all of twenty-eight acres, with Mitchell Brook flowing in and out over a small dam with a burbling sound you can hear almost everywhere on a quiet evening. Loons, ospreys, ducks of all types, and eagles frequent the private pond, owned by the Lake Mitchell Trout Club (LMTC). Great blue herons look down from a rookery near the shore. Stocked rainbows and brown trout swim beneath the glassy surface.

Entering LMTC's historic lodge is to travel back in time, as little has been changed from the turn of the century (1900, not 2000), when the lodge was built. It's an exquisite example of period architecture and ambience, full of antique furniture and old-school taxidermy. I don't know the full story of the LMTC, but according to a framed letter in the large living room, "Silent Cal" Coolidge fished here in 1929 (silently, I would guess) and was made an honorary member.

Rhona Dallison, the superintendent/caretaker/chef and a talented fly fisher, keeps the building and grounds and flowers in meticulous shape. She makes everyone feel welcome and well-taken care of. And so do her dogs.

After a four-hour drive from the Adirondacks, I checked in as a guest of my good friend Bob Chamberlin, who is a member there. LMTC is only twenty minutes from Dartmouth College in Hanover, New Hampshire, where I had met my then future wife, while Bob and I were in graduate school. Cheryl, also a Dartmouth alum, and I had stayed at the LMTC lodge once before on a homecoming weekend. I was now four weeks into my trip, so I had asked Bob if Cheryl and I could get a room at the Trout Club for a brief reunion of our own before I continued for another two weeks across northern New England.

After cleaning up, I met Cheryl in Hanover for a romantic dinner. We sipped good wine while catching up on both my adventures and hers over the past few weeks before we returned to the lodge for a nightcap by the fire. We had the quiet lodge all to ourselves.

Rhona served us a delicious breakfast the next morning, then Cheryl and I took a walk in the woods before she returned to Maine while I stayed on for another couple days to enjoy the quiet environs of Lake Mitchell while writing about my Au Sable and Ausable experiences.

I'm not much of a pond fisherman. It seems pretty random: You have 360 degrees to cast, so you pick one point on the compass, cast in that direction, and hope. In my weaker, less charitable moments, I whine that pond fishing is like Cow-Flop Bingo, a rural fund-raising event in which they grid off a pasture with numbered squares. People buy chances on each square, they turn a cow loose to graze, and if the cow drops a pie in your square, you win the prize. The sponsoring organization earns some cash. The cow gets nothing, except some green grass for dinner.

In Trout Pond Bingo, you flip your fly out there and hope you put it in the correct "square," where a trout is waiting. When the trout are rising, the squares are actually rings, so you usually aim your fly at a ring, hoping the trout will see it drop gently onto the water. But rarely do the trout stay in one place, so you often find yourself chasing rings around the pond while fish cruise in random directions sipping mayflies and spinners and who knows what other bugs you usually can't see.

This is what happened on Thursday evening when I fished the pond. I had rowed out from the dock toward an area that had several fish rising steadily, dimpling the smooth water here and there with expanding circles. I tried casting at a ring, then did my best to determine which direction the fish was moving. I'd cast ahead into its path, or so I hoped, but after an hour of this, frustration was getting the best of me. Bob Chamberlin rowed out to join me as the sun was setting, but he had no more success than I did. There

were mayfly spinners on the water which my fly mimicked well, but the fish were ignoring our offerings. But on a gorgeous evening it was still a pleasant way to enjoy the sunset.

As dusk settled into dark, we put away our boats and walked up the hill to the lodge. I told Bob I was anticipating a trip the next day to the White River. On my drive over from New York, I had followed Route 100 through

A glorious June sunset at Lake Mitchell Trout Club in Sharon, Vermont.

the Green Mountains of central Vermont and met up with the White River at Stockbridge and followed it all the way to Sharon. As I passed through scenic Vermont towns, the venerable river had looked very enticing with a full range of pools, runs, and cascades amidst dairy farms and woodlands. River fishing is always more to my liking.

W. D. Wetherell never gave away which river was the primary subject of his acclaimed book, *Vermont River* (1984). "If I have left it nameless, it is not for protective secrecy, but because to me it stands for the dozen New England rivers I have come to know," he says in the preface. He mentions the White River and the Battenkill separately, so these bigger rivers are clearly not "the Vermont river I love." No matter.

Wetherell does a fine job describing the personal journey that is a life of fly fishing. His descriptions express what scores of fishermen wish they could express themselves. It doesn't really matter which covered bridge spans the pool you are casting into, nor which ledge the water cascades over to churn into foam before swirling around the next boulder. The river is your friend, your lover, and your companion. What matters is that you are there, smelling the sweet ferns as you walk the bank and cursing the no-see-ums as you tie on the fly you are convinced will fool the fish that flashed briefly at your prior prospect. In "Take a Writer Fishing," Wetherell pays tribute to many of the writers mentioned in this book and their skill in capturing the love affair many of us have with rivers and fly fishing.

Many Vermont rivers were recently changed dramatically by an unusual climatic event. In August 2011, Hurricane Irene dumped so much water in central Vermont that mountain streams small and large, including the White River, became raging monsters, taking out scores of bridges and houses, washing away roads, isolating entire towns, scouring the river beds, and devouring shoreline vegetation like no other storm since the Hurricane of 1938. River channels and pools were altered drastically, while logs, boulders, and debris were stacked in enormous mounds along river bends and flats. The White River that I was planning to fish was quite different from the White River that Wetherell wrote about in 1984.

Biologists estimated that trout populations dropped by 30 to 60 percent in the years after the storm. The US Fish and Wildlife National Fish Hatchery on the White River near Bethel, Vermont, was nearly destroyed and remained closed for five years. Today, more than six years after Irene, riverine habitat has stabilized, and trout fishing in the White River has finally started to come back. Trout Unlimited has been working hard to restore habitat in high priority areas, although it is debatable whether fishing in the White River will ever be what it was before the storm. Certainly, the scars from Irene will not go away for decades, even as the trout are still making the best of the situation, as trout will do.

Friday morning, June 9

Back at the trout club, I asked Rhona, who had been fishing the White River earlier in the week with some success, if she had any tips on where I should go. She pointed on the map to the section above Bethel, which is special regulation water—fly fishing only. She said that some of the pools and runs there hold decent fish, including stocked rainbows and brown trout, plus some wild rainbows and brook trout. Yes, the river had changed, she said, but the fishing was well worth the effort.

River Road above Bethel indeed had some promising water. After two false starts, I found a fast run powering into a deep pool on the outside of a big bend with slower water on the inside. I waded carefully across below the pool and walked up the pebble beach on the inside of the bend. Near the fastest part of the run, I started by dead-drifting a weighted nymph down the main current into the slack water using the Ausable Wulff as my strike indicator. After a few dozen casts, I started to mutter to myself about a Vermont curse. I'd had no luck on the Battenkill earlier in the trip, and the same result on Vermont Creek in Wisconsin. After a fishless night on Lake Mitchell, here I was in danger of getting skunked yet again.

Bob Chamberlin contemplates his next play in Trout Pond Bingo.

I switched flies to a Brown Owl, a big buggy-looking streamer tied with mallard feathers and deer hair to look like a stonefly. With sinking line on my 6-weight rod, I let the fly dead-drift like a nymph deep in the current, then swung it out in the dark depths of the eddy below me. This is an excellent way to snag the bottom and lose your fly. But I wanted to get the fly down as far as I could.

As the line swung to the right, my rod bent as if the fly had snagged on a log or stick. But then I felt a tug. My rod moved and moved some more. A big stick might wobble in the current, but the movement I felt seemed more active. With a smaller trout, the rod quivers as the panicked fish darts about with rapid jerks. This movement felt slow and heavy and lazy. A bigger fish moves to a different, more deliberate rhythm. This was a large fish for sure.

I eased up on the pressure, not wanting to break my leader, but was careful to keep the line tight while I let the trout decide what it wanted to do. It moved first into the slower water on my side, then headed back out into the faster current, so I steered it again into the eddy.

Ten minutes (and six seconds of video) later, I had a 20-inch rainbow trout at my feet. As I reached with my net, it flopped and spit the hook and swam back to its lair, saving me the trouble of holding it down to achieve the same result. Luckily, I had enough time to marvel at its girth and compare it to the opening of my net. It was easily my biggest fish of the trip. Thank you, Rhona! My Vermont curse had been broken. And my Brown Owl survived to fish another day.

Friday evening was a celebratory dinner at the LMTC, not because of my big fish, but because my good friend Bill Conway (another Dartmouth classmate and a coauthor of *The Confluence*) and his family were there to mark the occasion of his older daughter Catherine's graduation from Dartmouth. After so much solitude and fishing with just one or two companions, it was a nice change of pace to feel the energy of Bill's extended family enjoying cocktails at sunset and a delectable dinner. After they departed for town, I had the quiet clubhouse to myself again—it now felt eerily empty—before turning in for an early start on Saturday.

Saturday morning, June 10

Rhona sat with me at breakfast to hear about my big rainbow on the White River and my plans for the next leg of my trip to the Northeast Kingdom of Vermont, often abbreviated as NEK. I said goodbye to Rhona and her friendly pooches and drove up I-91 with Eva Cassidy's angelic voice singing "Wade in the Water" on my car stereo. My next goal was as much spiritual as it was lyrical or geographical: to wade in the waters of the Kingdom River.

There is no real river in Vermont called the Kingdom River, but to fans of the late Howard Frank Mosher, the Kingdom River is vivid in the mind's eye. Mosher, who died in January 2017, is mourned by thousands of readers who loved his fictional version of the NEK, which he called Kingdom County. All of his novels have some tie to Kingdom County in various time periods, from the Civil War (*Walking to Gatlinburg*, 2010) to the present (*Points North*, 2018), and all have at least a few passing references to fly fishing. Mosher loved fly fishing and wove fishing stories and references into the rural culture and characters of his novels. My favorites, from a fishing standpoint, are *A Stranger in the Kingdom* (1989) and *God's Kingdom* (2015), which both follow young Jim Kinneson and his family through tumultuous events in the small town of Kingdom Common in the 1950s. Mosher brings the Kinneson family saga up to the present day in *Points North* (2018), the third in that series, which he finished just before he died. All three books are an impressive

Howard Frank Mosher. INK WASH AND CHARCOAL DRAWING BY JILL OSGOOD

combination of rich storytelling and insightful social commentary.

The Kinnesons all fly-fish in the Kingdom River, which flows through town and also past their family's camp deep in the craggy hills near the Canadian border. Mosher's Kingdom River is some combination of the Black River, which flows through Irasburg where he lived, the Willoughby River near Orleans, the Clyde River near Newport, and perhaps a few others. He borrowed features from each and brought his own version alive in his writing for the reader to imagine.

In *A Stranger in the Kingdom*, Jim tries to teach his new friend Nat how to fly-fish. Nat is the son of a black minister who had recently moved to Kingdom Common from Montreal to become a pastor in one of the local churches. Father and son are struggling to settle in to their new home amidst numerous expressions of racism from many of the townsfolk. Young Jim tries hard to find common ground and help Nat feel at home, while Nat finds it difficult to appreciate the joys of rural living while fending off taunts and physical attacks from other boys. Jim hopes that some quiet fishing will be a respite from the stress. Nat is skeptical:

"Come on, Kinneson. Let's get this fly fishing business over with. I've at least two hours of chemistry problems left to do tonight."

I had a lot of questions I wanted to ask Nat, but his impatient manner and condescending way of calling me by my last name put me off. So we trudged on in silence to the river.

There I simply couldn't contain my excitement. Over the long pool hovered the largest hatch I'd ever seen: thousands upon thousands of gigantic pale yellow mayflies I called spinners because of the way they twisted down onto the water.

Better yet, the entire surface was boiling with rising trout, feeding voraciously on everything that floated by. Everything, that is, but the flies I had tied on to the end of Nathan Andrews' leader. Try as he might, with wet flies and dry flies, with big brightly colored traditional patterns and dun-toned sinking nymphs and garish streams as long as trout fingerlings—flailing upstream and down, leaving several of my flies in the high limbs of a bankside soft maple tree behind us, several more in the jaws of a hungry trout, and one in the visor of my Red Sox baseball cap, Nathan Andrews did not, under my frustrated tutelage, land a single fish.

Later, when Nat and Jim are attacked by rock-throwing farm boys, Jim realizes the magnitude of the struggle Nat and his father are facing:

But I was amazed to see that Nathan Andrews was nearly crying.

I wanted to console him, but what could I say? I was beginning to see that being a Negro was different and harder than being white, whether you lived in Canada or Europe or Kingdom County, Vermont.

Mosher continued these themes through both *God's Kingdom* and *Points North*. Beneath the top layer of storytelling runs a strong undercurrent of today's most pressing social issues: racism, intolerance, and fear of immigrants and outsiders. Mosher crafted a sweeping allegory in which the "trouble in the family" that threads through the all three books is not just trouble in the Kinneson family but in the entire family of man—in all of God's kingdom. Heavy stuff sometimes, but skillfully woven into an entertaining narrative that pulls you along like a canoe through a rocky set of rapids.

I never had the pleasure of meeting Howard Mosher face to face, but I did correspond with him by email. When we were looking for advance reviewers for *The Confluence*, another writer I knew suggested I contact Howard, who was always willing to help and encourage new authors. Howard agreed to read our book and promptly sent along a positive review to use as a blurb for our cover. I invited him to join me fishing during the summer of 2016, but he declined due to a tight publisher's deadline. I was shocked and saddened just a few months later to hear that he was seriously ill, and soon after, that he'd succumbed to the cancer he had been battling for years.

While deeply saddened by the passing of a great writer and a loving husband to Phillis, who inspired several strong characters in his books, I was selfishly disappointed that we never had the chance to cast a line together

This covered bridge on the Black River near Irasburg, Vermont, inspired Howard Frank Mosher's vivid writing about his fictional Kingdom County.

on the rivers that he loved. As the hills of the NEK came into view, I wanted more than ever to experience fly fishing in the "Kingdom River."

As luck would have it, a friend of a friend, Kathy White, knew Howard and Phillis well, and she connected me with David Smith, the former proprietor of the Irasburg General Store and a retired guide, who had fished with Howard. David agreed to take me out on the Clyde River, which flows into Lake Memphremagog, and share a few memories of Howard. The big lake, which straddles the border with Quebec, and the rivers flowing

into it feature prominently in many of his stories. A 1993 movie by Jay Craven based on Mosher's 1978 novella *Where the Rivers Flow North*, starring Rip Torn and Michael J. Fox, was filmed on location near these storied waters.

On my way to meet David, I drove through Irasburg, where Howard and Phillis had lived, and cast a line for a few minutes into

the Black River (which also flows north into Lake Memphremagog) below the Lord's Creek covered bridge just downstream from the village. I'm sure Howard used this spot as inspiration for more than one Kingdom River scene. I wish I could report that I caught a trout that magically revealed all of Howard's secrets of Kingdom County, but that was not to be.

Up the hill from the bridge was the town square with its baseball diamond surrounded by the library, town hall, and a "brick block" like the one described in *Waiting for Teddy Williams* (2005). It's a testament to Howard's skill as a writer that the town and landscape looked familiar, because he'd captured perfectly the visual details as well as the spirit of the region, giving his readers a clear sense of place.

Saturday afternoon, June 10

After Irasburg, the back roads meandered past family farms (and a herd of several dozen American bison) through Newport to Derby, Vermont. The afternoon was sunny and very warm. David Smith met me for a late lunch, then took me to the nearby Clyde River, where he was hoping to hook me up with one of the very large landlocked salmon, rainbows, or brown trout that move up into the river from the lake. When I asked David, "How large is large?" he replied, "Oh, maybe five or six pounds. Some are bigger."

"Okay," I said, "I guess that's large enough!" I quickly swapped my light 6X leader for a more robust 4X number, while wondering if my recent luck with Vermont rivers would continue.

We hiked up a steep dirt road toward the site of the old dam. A few years my senior, David stopped a few times to catch his breath in the heat and humidity. I was a bit nervous he wouldn't make it, but the rest stops

Where & How—
Northeast Kingdom, Vermont

The Willoughby River is best known for the spring spawning run of rainbow trout (steelhead) that draws crowds to watch these big (several pounds) trout leaping up the falls near the village of Orleans. Steelhead migrating up from Lake Memphremagog can also be seen leaping up Coventry Falls on the Black River in Coventry. The spawning run begins at ice out on the lake and lasts through April and May, but the peak time for leaping fish is usually ten days in early May.

Spring steelhead runs in the Willoughby, Black, Clyde, and Barton Rivers attract anglers from all over Vermont and New England who aspire to hooking a 2- to 4-pound rainbow trout. Fishing is allowed in these rivers during the spawning run, but Willoughby Falls and Coventry Falls, and a section upstream of Willoughby Falls, are closed until June 1 to protect the spawning fish. Fall landlocked salmon runs are also popular on these same rivers.

The leaping fish at Willoughby and Coventry Falls provided inspiration for Howard Frank Mosher's descriptions of similar events on the Kingdom River. Here's a reference in *God's Kingdom*:

Jim and Prof walked down the lane through the field behind the manse to watch the rainbow trout jumping the High Falls on their way upriver to spawn. The run was at its peak this weekend. Several fish a minute fought their way up through the rapids, arcing out of the water to clear the falls, their crimson sides flashing in the spring sunshine.

What Works: In *Flyfisher's Guide to New England* (2016), Lou Zambello says that the post-spawn period in June is the best time to catch big rainbows returning to the lake. Flies of choice, says Lou, include streamers dead-drifted in the current, a weighted nymph pattern such as a Michigan Wiggler, or an egg pattern with a little sparkle. I found a local attractor pattern streamer called the Willoughby Willie, which looks like a cross between a Mickey Finn and a Gray Ghost, available online from Squaretail Flies and Guide Service. ∎

gave us time to admire a stand of tamarack trees with bright green needles and young magenta cones. The road soon leveled off and we scrambled down to a series of cascades and pools where a small dam had recently been removed, thanks to the efforts of David and his Trout Unlimited chapter. The dam had once blocked prime habitat just downstream of a larger hydropower dam on Clyde Pond. In one of the deeper pools, we caught two energetic smallmouth bass on streamers and a third on a weighted nymph, but saw no signs of trout or salmon. David said he had caught several salmon there a week or so earlier, but the water had warmed up some. Fortunately, he didn't say those dreaded words, "You should have been here last week!"

At about 6:00 p.m., we hiked back down to our vehicles, then drove downriver to a long glide right in the village of Newport, where public access is maintained for anglers along a grassy field. There were no rises visible, so we started casting streamers. I was using sinking line and the same Brown Owl fly that I had used on the White River to catch that big rainbow.

Thanks to the Brown Owl, I had a chance to see how big those salmon are. Three times a huge fish slashed and splashed at my fly but didn't take it. The dorsal fin that poked through the surface was the size of dollar bill folded in half. I couldn't get that big fish to take my fly, nor the next one, nor the next one. I had riled a behemoth, but it appeared to be onto my game.

My fixation on the fish was interrupted when my stomach began rumbling around 7:00 p.m., making me realize that David might want to get home for dinner. He had generously given me, a total stranger in the Kingdom, his entire afternoon and some of his evening. I had made a new friend who, like Jim Kinneson, helped an outsider fish his favorite river. While I didn't catch a single trout or salmon under his tutelage—more of my Vermont luck—at least we caught a few bass in the "Kingdom River."

We shook hands warmly and David turned toward home while I moved on to Lancaster, New Hampshire, to stay with my daughter Rosa before my next adventure on the upper Connecticut River.

- 20 -

Delightful Days on the Upper Connecticut River

Saturday evening, June 10

Lancaster, New Hampshire, is a delightful little town. At the time of my visit, the per capita level of delight in that North Country village of 3,500 souls was at an all-time high because our daughter, Rosa, was living there. She pulled the average way up with her zestful personality and love for life. As a kindergarten teacher, she spread additional delight to the next generation, their families, and community members, thus amplifying her overall contribution. She was indeed the motherlode of delight tucked in the hills north of Mount Washington. Not that I'm biased.

Crossing the Connecticut River from Lunenburg, Vermont, into Lancaster at dusk, I cruised down Main Street. There is not all that much to this place, the county seat of Coos County, the largest and northernmost county in the Granite State—just the main drag plus one or two back streets and a dozen or so side streets. Downtown is only a few blocks long, with more churches than there are stores. Surprisingly, this small town is blessed with two superb bakeries/coffee shops within a block of Rosa's apartment.

Main Street also boasts a second major source of delight in town, which was visible from afar on that early summer evening: the Rialto Theater, a two-screen, nicely renovated movie house dating to the 1930s with its landmark neon marquee. They serve beer, wine, and food with their first-run films. On that weekend, they were showing *Wonder Woman*, which seemed a fitting metaphor for my four-night stay with Rosa and her friendly cat, Amy, who both greeted me when I climbed two long flights of stairs to stay in her spare bedroom.

Sunday, June 11

Sunday was forecast to be very hot and sunny, so I passed on fishing and spent the day with Rosa, swimming at a nearby state park beach. After we returned, and in dire need of aerobic exercise, I hopped on Rosa's mountain bike for a ride along the Connecticut River south of town. The section near Lancaster is a wide swath of flatwater above the Moore Dam several miles downstream near Littleton. After joining a couple of her friends for dinner, Rosa and I capped off the evening by watching the Pittsburgh Penguins win the final game of the Stanley Cup playoffs at J. L. Sullivan's, an Irish pub just two blocks from Rosa's place. Two bakeries, a neighborhood pub, and a funky movie theater—yes, delightful.

Monday morning, June 12

My plan for Monday was to fish the upper Connecticut River near the Connecticut Lakes. Corey Ford's comment on the Connecticut Lakes region in an article from the 1950s entitled "Headwaters of the Connecticut" could have been written today: "Progress hasn't changed it much; there is still the same pioneer feeling about it, the unostentatious hospitality, the primitive beauty."

The two and a half miles of river below First Connecticut Lake is known as the Trophy Stretch, which is fly fishing only for brook trout, rainbows, brown trout, and landlocked salmon. Other sections of river in the Connecticut Lakes area are also superb coldwater fishing, including the bigger water below Murphy Dam and Lake Francis, where a drift boat is the way to go.

My informal guide for the day would be Ron Ouellette, president of the Ammonoosuc Chapter of Trout Unlimited. He was returning from a weekend on the Magalloway River in Maine via the back roads, so we had arranged to meet at noon at the Magalloway Road bridge across the Connecticut River between Second Connecticut Lake and First Connecticut Lake. I was expecting Ron to be accompanied by Art Greene and Joe Homer, all three of whom I had met when I spoke at the Ammo TU meeting the prior fall.

At about 10:00 a.m., I started the ninety-minute drive north from Lancaster through Groveton, Colebrook, and Stewartstown toward Pittsburg, the northernmost town at the tip of New Hampshire. Again, Corey Ford described it well:

As you drive north through New Hampshire on Route 10 [and Route 3], the water gets clearer and the river grows narrower and somehow younger with each successive mile, leaping playfully over boulders and wandering here and there across the

The Rialto Theater lights up Main Street in Lancaster, New Hampshire, a delightful little town.

meadows like an active child until, around Colebrook, it is back in its own childhood again, an ebullient trout stream with shallow riffles and sandbars and deep, lovely pools—as much it was a century ago, when the Atlantic salmon came all the way up to these headwaters to spawn. The salmon are gone forever, but there are still rainbows and squaretails and canny browns to fill the creel of a cannier angler.

Today, the upper Connecticut watershed is home to (non-native) landlocked salmon, so the Atlantic salmon's distant freshwater relative, at least, is still swimming these waters. This area along the upper Connecticut River has quite a rich and unique history—it was once an independent country known as the Indian Stream Republic. Corey Ford recounted the story in his essay, and Howard Frank Mosher worked permutations of the remarkable history of this area into several of his novels, including one tale in which the green flag of the independent Kingdom Republic features a leaping brook trout.

Daniel Doan published a more fact-based history in his book 1997 *Indian Stream Republic.* During the colonial years, there were competing land claims being granted by New York and New Hampshire in the upper Connecticut River valley. From 1777 until 1791, Vermont declared itself an independent republic with its own constitution until it was admitted into the Union as the fourteenth state. However, the land between Hall's Stream, which flows into the Connecticut from the north near Canaan, Vermont, and the Connecticut Lakes above Pittsburg, New Hampshire, was once literally no-man's-land between Canada and the United States because of confusion about the border between the two young countries. The 1783 Treaty of Paris set the US-Canada boundary as "the northwesternmost

head of the Connecticut River." But it was unclear which tributary was northwesternmost: Hall's Stream, Indian Stream, or Perry Stream near Pittsburg? Or the main stem of the Connecticut above Third Connecticut Lake? The United States and Canada submitted the ambiguity to the king of Holland for arbitration in 1827, but that led to further dispute when the United States didn't like his ruling.

In the confusion, and facing double taxation from both countries, the local settlers near Pittsburg decided to take matters into their own hands, declaring themselves an independent nation, the Indian Stream Republic, in 1832. They wrote a constitution and mustered a militia of a few dozen men. There were several disputes and skirmishes with Canadian and US law enforcement, resulting in a few prisoners who were jailed. Four years later, the short-lived republic decided to rejoin the United States. This news apparently was a surprise to many folks in our nation's capital, who were not aware that the "Streamers" had left. The disputed border was ultimately resolved in 1842 with the Webster-Ashburton Treaty, setting the boundary as Hall's Stream as far south as the 45th parallel, which created a small panhandle of Vermont that extends from Hall's Stream east to the Connecticut.

What is not disputed is that the scenery north of the 45th parallel is spectacular. Today, the lakes and rivers are clean and undeveloped, and people drive many miles to come here for the fishing and snowmobiling. I was here, of course, for the fishing.

Pittsburg is reputed to be the largest township in the Lower 48. There's no letter *h* on this Pittsburg, but with the Penguins' win the night before, I half expected to see a Stanley Cup celebration on Daniel Webster Highway as I drove through town. The only commotion while I pumped gas from the old-fashioned pump at the Pittsburg Trading Post came from a couple guys who filled up their ATVs before roaring down the road, a common site on roads throughout the North Country.

Monday afternoon, June 12

Looking down from the Magalloway Road bridge, the Connecticut River—here a modest stream just a dozen yards wide—looked like it was begging me to throw in a fly and catch some fish. But my watch said straight-up noon, so I decided to wait for Ron and company in a comfy patch of shade next to the burbling stream and tie some flies streamside, something I had always wanted to do. As my friend Phil Odence once quipped, "Tie flies when you're having fun!" I pulled out my kit, opened a cold Stoneface IPA, and munched on a sandwich while I set up my vise on a rock.

The mosquitoes were tolerable and I must have brought along some surplus delight from Lancaster, because I was enjoying myself immensely, winding feathers, fur, yarn, and tinsel onto tiny hooks, when Ron and Joe pulled in. Art Greene wasn't feeling well, so it was just the two of them. Ron and Joe are both soft-spoken, personable guys about my age, with many years of fly-fishing experience between them. They admired the two Wood Specials I had tied and asked about my trip while I put away my fly-tying kit and pulled out my waders and rods.

We all rigged up and Joe went downstream while Ron and I fished near the bridge. The water coming over the dam from Second Connecticut Lake was fairly warm—about 65 degrees—after several days with afternoon highs well into the 80s, so we didn't expect too much action from bigger fish. A couple smaller trout splashed unconvincingly at my Hornberg on the surface but wouldn't

Ron Ouellette nets a small landlocked salmon on the Trophy Stretch of the upper Connecticut River below First Connecticut Lake.

come back for two different patterns. After thirty minutes, Ron suggested we move down below the First Lake Dam to the Trophy Stretch, which is a bottom-release tailwater. The water would be much colder, closer to 50 degrees. Cold water holds more oxygen than warm water, so the trout and salmon literally breathe easier and have more energy to feed.

Ron was right. In short order he and Joe combined for an Upper Connecticut Grand Slam: Joe caught a brown trout and a rainbow on nymphs above Bridge Pool, and Ron caught a landlocked salmon and a brook trout below the Bridge. Nothing real big, but at least they had some action. The most I can say for my time there is that the wading was very cool and pleasant. My feet felt comfortably numb after an hour in the cold stream. But I remained fishless.

On our way upstream back to the car, we met a guy in flashy-looking gear and a straw hat, smoking a cigar while nymphing. As he landed a fish, he smugly announced his successful fly: "Black stonefly!" We said something polite like "Nice!" And then with an even smugger shrug and smile he said, "I've caught five on five casts." It wasn't so much *what* he said, but *how* he said it. Maybe I was just jealous, but he sure seemed over the top. What a smug asshole. Did I mention how smug he was? Asshole. I'm sure my bad attitude was more about my own fishing than his. Anyway.

Ron and Joe needed to get home after their long weekend of fishing, but I wanted to stay on to fish a bit more, hoping to avoid being skunked. Ron suggested going downstream a short distance near the covered bridge, but it was filled with cars and fishermen, so instead I drove back upstream and parked near the dam, where there were only two cars. On my way down the trail, two women walking up the hill with fly rods in hand told me cheerfully,

"We left plenty for you!" I wasn't sure how to interpret that. Were they skunked? Or were they leaving because they were sick of catching so many fish? At least they weren't smug, so I smiled and said, "Thanks, I appreciate it!"

Fifty yards farther down the path was Ledge Pool, where the river drops about ten feet in three stairstep falls. The cold water

Ledge Pool is one of the famous named holes on the Trophy Stretch of the upper Connecticut River.

and mist from the falls chilled the warm afternoon air by about 20 degrees. The temperature change was energizing, and I was confident that a big rainbow or brookie was waiting for me.

I fished a streamer below the falls with no success, then walked farther downstream to a deep glide under an overhanging tree. It was *verrrrrry* fishy looking. I tried my trusty Brown Owl and reliable Wood Special in the deep water and at the tail of the run. Nothing.

I sat on a rock to build a double nymph dropper rig and proceeded to drift a half-dozen nymph patterns through the run,

Where & How—
Upper Connecticut River

The Trophy Stretch of the Connecti-cut River is fly fishing only from First Connecticut Lake Dam to the inlet of Lake St. Francis. There is a spring run of landlocked salmon and rainbows chasing smelt out of Lake St. Francis and a fall spawning run of landlocked salmon and brook trout. This section is heavily stocked but also has wild fish and holdovers of reputable size. Lake St. Francis State Park offers local camping.

There are eleven named pools in this stretch, plus the so-called In Between Section between Ledge Pool and Boulder Bend Pool. Tall Timber Lodge provides a printable map of the area on their website that shows roads and parking areas along this heavily fished area and a list of recommended flies to match the hatch chart for the areas.

The section of the Connecticut below Murphy Dam and Lake St. Francis is a high quality tailwater fishery with cold bottom-release water. Guided float trips are popular for chasing big brown trout, rainbows, and brook trout.

What Works: I can't tell you what worked for me, because nothing did, but that smug guy in the straw hat was doing well with black stoneflies in mid-June. The Tall Timbers Lodge chart recommends that same fly along with a Brown Owl or a dry fly with a bead-head nymph dropper like I was using. I probably wasn't getting the nymph deep enough, which is critical for wary fish sitting on the bottom among the rocks. Ron and Joe caught all their fish on nymphs, so absent an obvious hatch, this seemed to be the way to go for midday early June fishing. ■

including black and yellow stoneflies, green bead-head caddis, and a Prince Nymph, certain that a hungry trout would find one of them irresistible. Each one was a whiff, one after another.

Like the Mighty Casey, I struck out swinging nearly every fly I could think of through that strike zone. There were fish there, I was certain, but my mojo was definitely not working. Finally, I called it a day and trudged back up the trail, grumbling in my slump. I vowed to come back on another day to avenge myself.

On my drive back down Route 3, I was tempted to stop near Colebrook to make a few casts in a section where Lou Zambello

and I had fished a few years earlier by canoe. He and I both caught several vivacious rainbows on a placid evening. I noticed a rise or two on the smooth surface of the river but didn't stop because I wanted to see Rosa before her bedtime—yes, teachers go to bed early on a school night, too.

Soon I turned down Main Street in Lancaster toward another reminder that progress hadn't much changed this part of the north country: the cheerful neon glow of the Rialto's sign. My spirits lifted, despite having struck out on the upper Connecticut that afternoon. There was still joy in Mudville. In fact, my entire day had been a delight.

- 21 -

The Twisted Rivers of Northern New Hampshire

The young Canadian, who could not have been more than fifteen, had hesitated too long. For a frozen moment, his feet had stopped moving on the floating logs in the basin above the river bend; he'd slipped entirely underwater before anyone could grab his outstretched hand. One of the loggers had reached for the youth's long hair; the older man's fingers groped around in the frigid water, which was thick, almost soupy, with sloughed-off bark. Then two logs collided hard on the would-be rescuer's arm, breaking his wrist. The carpet of moving logs had completely closed over the young Canadian, who never surfaced. . . .

—*John Irving*, Last Night in Twisted River *(2009)*

Tuesday and Wednesday, June 13 & 14

The ghosts of the log-drive era are everywhere in the north woods of New England. I'm not talking about ghostly spirits, although there may be some of those, but more the physical evidence left in the woods and along the streams and rivers: remnants of old dams; stone-filled cribs from abandoned log booms; cellar holes, stoves, and junk piles from logging camps; holes drilled into rock ledge and steel pins that once held log booms. The woods of northern New Hampshire were for many years filled with logging camps and thousands of rugged men who manhandled the logs to mills in Berlin and Gorham from the 1800s through the 1960s.

The grim opening to John Irving's novel *Last Night in Twisted River* evokes the last years of those mighty log drives in the upper Androscoggin River basin. Starting in 1954 in Coos County, New Hampshire, near Milan and Errol in the fictional town of Twisted River, Irving's story follows the life of Danny Baciagalupo, a twelve-year-old boy whose father was a logging-camp cook. After opening with the tragic demise of young Angel, the book is a meandering tale of Danny's life through "a world of accidents," ultimately ending back at Twisted River some fifty years later.

The deaths of Angel Pope and other memorable characters in the book symbolize the passing of an era. Danny's guardian angel, veteran river driver Ketchum, evolves through the story from a wild, unrefined yet big-hearted character during Danny's youth to a tamer, more civilized old-timer living outside of Errol until 2001. In much the same way that Ketchum slowly and reluctantly changes, life in the north woods has softened with the encroachment of cell phones, satellite dishes, and ATVs, while still clinging to its wild spirit.

The next destination of my own meandering trip was the Second College Grant, a 27,000-acre forest reserve owned by Dartmouth College, where I have been fishing with six classmates from Dartmouth (class of 1979) each June for twenty-five years. On my way to the Grant, I would drive through Milan and Errol, crossing over the fictional Twisted River (somewhere) to get there. I would be meeting close friends for several days in a remote cabin at the confluence of the Swift and Dead Diamond Rivers, either of which could very well be the Twisted River in Irving's tale.

Last Night in Twisted River is by no means a fishing story. The only part that comes close is when Danny fishes Angel's waterlogged body out of the river, covered with leeches. And yet, Irving's novel captures much of what I have sensed while fishing the Swift Diamond and Dead Diamond Rivers over the decades. Standing up to my knees, casting peacefully in the quiet of a June evening, I conjure images of the river hogs who lived and often died during the spring log drives when the water was a raging torrent, well up over my head and the steep banks behind me.

I won't go into too much detail about my annual gatherings with "the Boys of the Grant" as we call ourselves, as there is an entire book about our fly-fishing adventures cowritten by all seven of us. If you've read *The Confluence*, you know our stories set among these beautiful hills and waters. You also

know the history of the Dartmouth Grant—how the land was granted to Dartmouth College in 1809 to provide income for the fledgling college and scholarships for New Hampshire residents.

The first roads were built in the Grant during the 1940s, and a few cabins were constructed in the 1950s and '60s to allow better access for timber management, hunting, and fishing. Today, the college manages the Grant

The Diamond River is fast and free after exiting the gorge below the confluence of the Swift and Dead Diamond Rivers.

for timber, recreation, wildlife, and scientific research. Eleven cabins, scattered across the ten-mile-by-six-mile tract, are available for rent by students, alumni, and employees of the college.

In one chapter in *The Confluence*, I describe the Grant as "An Eddy in Time": "From the first, I relished the Grant's timelessness and was fascinated by its history, from ancient time when native peoples inhabited this area to the days of log drives and the camps that supported them."

During the late 1800s and first half of the twentieth century, a sizeable community of men and women lived in logging camps in the Grant along the Swift and Dead Diamond

Rivers, but the forest has largely reclaimed the land where those camps used to be. "Time and the trees have wiped away most of the impact on the landscape," except for some foundations, rough roads, and rusting relics hidden here and there in the woods. When we come back to the Grant year after year, I love that the wild rivers and the weather and the fishing are never the same. And I love that there is always a new experience when we visit.

Wednesday afternoon, June 14

L. L. Cote in Errol is a sporting goods store and much, much more. As a last outpost before the border with Quebec, this rural retailer nonpareil appears in both *Twisted River* (near the end, in the 2001 time frame) and *The Confluence* (in the beginning and in several stories). After leaving Lancaster on Wednesday morning, I planned to meet up there with two friends—Kevyn Fowler and Chris Ricardi—from my home in New Gloucester, Maine. Kevyn and Chris were excited to join me for fishing on Wednesday and Thursday prior to the arrival of the rest of the Boys. Our rendezvous was timed perfectly, and we quickly picked up a few flies, including a few more Brown Owls, stocked up on bug dope, and drove north a dozen miles to the Grant, anxious to hit the water.

At six-feet-many-inches tall and fifty-some years old, Kevyn remains an overgrown kid, seeing the world every minute with wonder, amusement, and good nature. He's a professional videographer for a TV news station and a talented photographer with a keen eye. He focuses on the pleasant. Chris is an environmental chemist and a musician. He and I worked together for eleven years at an engineering firm and also spent many hours watching our sons play soccer together. Both men are accomplished fly fishers who are at home in brook trout country.

David "Klingon" Klinges, one of my college roommates, was arriving at the Grant a day earlier than the rest of our regular crew so he could connect with his son "Nature Dave" Klinges, who was staying in one of the student cabins with seven of *his* classmates to celebrate their graduation from Dartmouth earlier in the week. Thus, we would have a brief overlap of two generations of Dartmouth alumni enjoying fellowship in the north country.

Kevyn, Chris, Klingon, and I were staying in Sam's Cabin, which was the year-round home for Sam Brungot, fire warden and caretaker of the Dartmouth Grant from 1951 until his retirement in 1961—coincidentally the same time frame as the first few chapters of Irving's story in nearby Twisted River. Like Ketchum in the novel, Sam was a legendary character who personified an entire era of life in the north country. Sam famously presented flies he had tied to President Eisenhower when Ike visited the Dartmouth Grant in 1955 at the invitation of Dartmouth president John Sloan Dickey. Sam's spirit clearly lives on in his cabin, and a painted portrait of Sam on the wall is a constant reminder that we will always be guests in his home.

The four of us tossed our bags onto our bunks, loaded food and beer into the propane-power fridge, and hightailed it out onto the Dead Diamond for an afternoon and evening of fishing. Despite the low, clear water, blue sky, and bright sunshine, we all managed to catch a few of the wild and wily native brook trout. This watershed is one of the last undammed rivers in New Hampshire with wild brook trout. The fish here aren't known for their size ("set your Thrill-o-Meter at 8 inches" is a favorite mantra), but they are always enchanting.

Klingon put his rod away early so he could track down his son, while the rest of us stayed out until daylight faded after 9:00 p.m. Kevyn, Chris, and I got back to the cabin in the dark, where we found Klingon, Nature Dave, and his buddies finishing a boisterous dinner under the gaslights. The cabin was rocking with youthful exuberance.

The beer flowed and the chili satisfied our mountainous appetites. As we mopped up our plates, we heard boots clomping on the porch and a knock on the screen door. We were pleased to see Dave Bradley (Dartmouth class of '58), a member of the "Old Dean's Group" who have been fishing in the Grant for over forty years. Sadly, his usual companion, our good friend and mentor, Ralph Manuel, '58, was ill and couldn't make the trip this year but had sent along a bottle of Famous Grouse scotch whisky so he would be with us all "in spirit." Dave raised a glass to toast *three* generations of alumni enjoying the Dartmouth Grant, especially the newest

generation who would carry the torch well into its third century. And, of course, we toasted to Ralph.

Thursday morning, June 15

The next morning the four of us fished Diamond Gorge, accessible only in low water. Starting at the huge boulder we call Gateway Rock, we worked our way down between the steep walls, around deep pools and rushing falls. The morning light, sparkling water, and long shadows made for a magical setting. It was not so magical, however, that we might fear an encounter with the giant "Hag Trout" rumored to lurk deep in Diamond Gorge, waiting to prey on unsuspecting fisherman, devour circling ospreys, and even attack bears. The story of the mythical Hag Trout of Coos County, "a Trout of no earthly provenance," was written by Norm Richter as one of the tall tales in *The Confluence*, riffing

A typical wild brook trout from the Dartmouth Grant is modestly magnificent.

Chris Ricardi and Kevyn Fowler found good fortune in the Diamond River gorge.

on Robert Frost's 1922 surreal poem "The Witch of Coos."

Our sights were set on some sizeable trout in the 12- to 14-inch range. The gorge was filled with warm air and a morning swarm of big mayflies, probably March Browns or Brown Drakes, dancing in small clouds. Rarely do we see such concentrated hatches in the Grant. The prospects for success were as bright as the morning sun.

Kevyn had quick success at the pool below Gateway Rock with a small streamer that fooled a 7-inch brookie. Chris and Klingon locked onto the next two deep pools, which had submerged rocks that looked like great cover for wary trout. Chris was drifting nymphs, and Klingon went with his standard Hornberg fished dry and wet. Mostly wet. I moved down farther into the gorge.

Partway down the gorge, the north wall of sheer rock rises fifteen feet up and out over the river. I found a place to wade across to the south side and sat quietly for a moment, observing the pool with water rushing over a drop from the pool above. Near the edge of the slack water, a fish rose, making small splashes in the foam. Using a fluffy March Brown imitation, I bounced the fly off the rock wall so it fell gently onto the smooth dark water below. On the second cast, the fly disappeared under a quick splash, and suddenly I was tethered to a fat 10-inch trout as it raced around the pool. Soon it was in my net, where the speckled brook trout lit up in the morning sun. I quickly removed the hook and slid the fish back into the water where it darted back into the depths.

We all caught fish that morning—on dries, streamers, and nymphs, even Klingon who, by his own admission, often trails in the fish count but always keeps a positive attitude about his time in the Grant. I caught one

12-incher on the Brown Owl, which now had a solid streak of attracting big fish. None of our fish were Hag Trout size, but Chris and Kevyn were thrilled to have experienced a memorable morning in the gorge. Kevyn and Chris returned to Maine around noon, just before the rest of the Boys arrived on Thursday afternoon.

Thursday afternoon, June 15

By 2:00 p.m., we had our usual gang together. The Boys of the Grant: Phil Odence, Norm Richter, Bob Chamberlin, Ed Baldrige, Bill Conway, Klingon, and me. Everyone was anxious to get out on the water. We split into two groups, hoping to find shady water where the trout might be hanging out on such a bright afternoon. Ed, Phil, and I found just such a place.

We stopped first at one of the more heavily fished ledge pools which was partially shaded. There wasn't room for all three of us, so I bushwhacked a few hundred yards upstream toward a shady run. There, a ledge outcrop formed a pool with smooth but moving water above a deep, dark hole and a cutbank shaded by tall hemlocks on the far shore. Even after twenty-plus years of fishing this river, this was a new spot for me. It looked propitious.

On my first five casts, I caught two chubby 8-inch brookies on an Elk Hair Caddis fished both dry and wet. A couple more fish were rising just inside the shady edge of the run. I put down my rod and walked back to summon my colleagues, who were having little luck at the first ledge. They soon joined me, and Ed was quick to land two rambunctious trout of his own. Phil was frustrated at first by a series of short hits but finally was able to bring a colorful and chunky brookie to hand.

After an hour of side-by-side entertainment, we headed back to the cabin for a snack and a cold Harpoon IPA, then joined the other Boys to fish the lower river below the gorge until dusk. Again, there was a variety of mayflies and caddisflies fluttering upstream and down. The mosquitoes and no-see-ums made it hard to concentrate as they swarmed our hands and faces, even when we swabbed ourselves with generous amounts of bug dope. Amidst all that insect life, most of us caught several fish, or had plenty of opportunities. Once again, the Brown Owl came through for me.

Friday June 16

No bugs, no glory. Thanks to an abundance of flying insects of all types, the fishing was good but the sleeping was not. With the combination of a cool, wet spring and the warm muggy weather during our stay, the biting bugs were especially numerous and ferocious all weekend, with legions of mosquitoes swarming us nonstop on the stream and invading the cabin night and day. The leaky screens seemed to serve no function, especially during the rainy day on Friday, when I stayed in the cabin to tie flies. Even fully loaded up with bug dope, I was swatting mosquitoes every few seconds.

None of us could recall this level of torment. It was especially bad at first light, when the high-pitched whine of five or six skeeters around my head shattered the silence like an air-raid siren. Only Norm snored through the onslaught, while the rest of us were up earlier than usual to fight off the piercing proboscises. For four days, we had all four types of the biting bastards in full force: mosquitoes, black flies, deerflies, and no-see-ums, sometimes all at once.

Bugs dominated the conversation, as you might imagine. We marveled at how the Native Americans, loggers, and early sportsmen could inhabit these woods during the

Where & How—
Upper Androscoggin River

The upper Androscoggin River offers excellent fishing from Errol Dam down through the 13-Mile Woods section with plenty of access from Route 16.

The Dartmouth Grant is open to the public for nonmotorized use. Parking is available near the gate just in from Route 16 in Wentworths Location. The Diamond River below the gorge is an easy walk in, about a mile, and the lower portions of the Swift Diamond and Dead Diamond can be reached by mountain bike. The upper reaches of the Dead and the Swift outside the Grant can be reached by the public over well-maintained logging roads.

What Works: The Brown Owl is a classic fly pattern that imitates a large adult stonefly that hatches in late June and July in the upper Androscoggin and Connecticut River watersheds. This pattern was born nearby, originated by Bob Broad, the owner of the Brown Owl Camps and Tackle Shop, which used to be one of the few businesses in Wentworths Location near the entrance to the Dartmouth Grant. The former shop is now one of the buildings housing the US Fish and Wildlife Service at Umbagog National Wildlife Refuge.

The stonefly hatch occurs right at dark and beyond, but the fly can be used almost anytime, especially in the morning. These stoneflies are huge and tend to attract bigger fish. Brown Owls can be tied from size 8 up to size 4 on a heavy streamer hook. On the first cast, try floating the Brown Owl like a dry fly, then let it dead-drift under the surface and be ready for a strike any time, especially on the swing.

Brown Owls are available in the L. L. Cote fly shop in Errol, and there are several instructional videos and fly recipes available online if you want to tie the pattern yourself. ■

buggiest months before the days of DEET and other insect repellents. Natural aromatic oils—cedar, lemon eucalyptus, lemongrass, and peppermint—or simple grease and tar can only be so effective, but nothing stops the buzzing around your ears and the bugs' amazing ability to find unprotected skin. Head nets help, but they're annoying and hamper your vision.

I recalled reading about a fisherman who visited the sporting camp on the Dead Diamond River built by Amasa Ward in the early 1880s. In his well-researched book *Wintering with Amasa Ward*, Jack Noon (Dartmouth '68) relates a passage from an August 1888 issue of *Forest and Stream* in which J. W. Barney described fly fishing in the lower Diamond River below the Gorge:

My waders went on, and with rod, reel and creel adjusted, in an incredibly short time I had introduced an Orvis white-winged coachman to a pound-and-a-half trout. . . . In my eagerness, I neglected to coat my face and hands with "fly medicine." Consequently, though we fished only about an hour, [the bugs] got in their work on me in great shape, and blood was running from a score of places on my face and neck. However, I did not mind that much; we had taken fourteen trout averaging nearly a pound and a quarter a piece and later on four tired and hungry men sat down to a trout supper at Bennett's.

Bennett's was located near the confluence of the Dead Diamond and the Magalloway Rivers at a time when trout in these rivers were larger and more numerous than we find today.

Amasa Ward operated his own sporting camp just below Hellgate Gorge, where we would fish the next day. It took us thirty minutes to drive up there over ten miles of dirt-logging road, which was nothing compared to how Ward and his guides would transport their sports upriver by boat, poling them over fifteen miles (if you include all the meanders) upstream to the falls and big pool at the mouth of Hellgate Gorge. It took them a full day to get from the Magalloway River to Hellgate.

Ward died in 1891 of "chronic diffuse nephritis," which roughly translates into too much drinking. Sporting camps continued to operate in the Hellgate area until the 1940s, the last by Arthur Muise, who later became a New Hampshire Fish and Game officer, according to Jack Noon. Muise used the old Fish & Game Cabin that dated back to around 1900. The historic Fish & Game Cabin was moved back from the river and renovated in 2002; it's now called Pete Blodgett Cabin.

Saturday, June 17

At this point in my eventful odyssey, I was not at all surprised by the chance meeting that occurred on Saturday afternoon near the bridge above Hellgate. Phil, Bob, Norm, and I met a man named Clark Corson, who, with a lifelong friend, had just spread his father's ashes in "Buck's Pool" above the bridge. Clark's father, Buck Corson, was once New Hampshire's director of Fish and Game and a regular visitor to the Dartmouth Grant, where he sometimes stayed at the Hellgate cabins with Arthur Muise. Jack Noon dedicated *Amasa Ward* to Buck Corson and Arthur Muise, who helped him with his research about the fishing history of the Grant. It's amazing how stories intertwine in unexpected ways.

Another story from the Grant eerily parallels John Irving's telling of Angel Pope's tragic death in *Last Night in Twisted River*. It involves one of the enduring mysteries in the Dartmouth Grant: Hand on the Rock, a lichen-covered boulder along the bank of the Swift Diamond River where someone carved a crude bas-relief image of a left hand with the index finger pointing upward and the

The curious carving of a left hand pointing up or toward the Swift Diamond River has kept people wondering for decades.

initials *WMDOW* above a heart. No one knows who made this carving, when, or why. The weathering and lichens covering the hand and letters suggest that it was done long ago.

John Harrigan, longtime writer for New Hampshire newspapers, offered two theories in a 2002 article in *North Country Notebook*: (1) that it's a memorial to a river hog who died in a log drive near where the finger is pointing, or (2) that it was carved by a Dartmouth graduate and minister named William Dow (class of 1861) to mark a spot that was important to his spiritual development. There is no evidence to confirm either alternative. According to Harrigan, caretaker Sam Brungot used to tell people a story about how Vikings had carved it while exploring the river. Hmmm.

We may never know the true story of Hand on the Rock, which I visited on Saturday evening while fishing the Swift Diamond. I prefer the lost logger story, as it (coincidentally?) aligns with John Irving's novel, in which Ketchum was obsessed by the thought of chopping off his left hand and throwing it into the river. But mostly, the Hand on the Rock reminds me that these valleys, and these waters, are filled with stories long forgotten. Up here, along the twisted rivers of northern New Hampshire, the thunder in the hills comes not from Henry Hudson's men bowling tenpins as in Rip Van Winkle's Catskills, but from the eternal spirits of river hogs blasting log jams and stomping on the plank floor of the music hall in an everlasting Saturday night.

- 22 -

Louise Dickinson Rich's Forest Lodge on the Rapid River

I'm not sure what I expected, but certainly not this.

When I was planning the Storied Waters trip, I included the Rapid River in Maine, where Louise Dickinson Rich lived and wrote her 1942 memoir, *We Took to the Woods*. This Book of the Month Club bestseller is still in print and has a strong fan base today because of Rich's humor, humanity, and ability to relate in detail a sense of place and time about life on a remote river, which remains a world-class fly-fishing destination. Louise loved fly fishing and tying flies, and her voice is a compelling part of fly-fishing history.

I was at the Western Maine Fly fishing Expo in Bethel in March, telling some people about my planned adventure and my desire to fish the Rapid. I think it was Jeff Reardon, conservation director for the Maine Council of Trout Unlimited, who said, "You should talk to Aldro French. He lives in the house where Louise used to live on the Rapid."

"Okay, good idea. I don't know him, but I'll see if I can figure out how to reach him."

"That should be easy. He's right over there. I'll introduce you."

Aldro had been a fixture in Maine fly fishing for more than fifty years. He looked the part: flowing white hair and white beard, and the weathered face of someone who has guided for years. He eyed me warily as I told him about my plans and desire to visit Forest Lodge near the end of my trip. Aldro wrote down his email address, asking me to confirm the date with him and arrange a time to meet. I was sure both of us felt this was all rather tentative.

I had fished the Rapid once years ago with my longtime fishing buddy, Lou Zambello, mountain biking in on the private logging roads from the gate. Knowing how difficult the access was, I was hoping just to get in for an afternoon to see the place where Louise Rich had lived, interview Aldro, take some photos, and maybe cast a line in the river for an hour. I didn't want to be a bother.

Aldro ran Forest Lodge, Rich's former home, as a sporting camp (part-time for thirty-eight years and full-time for twenty years) but had recently wound down operations, taking no new clients, just a few of his long-time regulars who returned to fish and socialize. As "keeper of the lodge," he faith-fully preserved the history and spirit of Lou-ise Dickinson Rich and her husband Ralph Rich, maintaining the Summer House, the Winter House, and the Guide Camp essen-tially as a living museum, entered on the National Register of Historic Places in 2008.

In late May, I got an email with a map to the gate (more than fourteen miles across rough dirt logging roads) and instructions to meet Aldro there at noon on June 18. "Bring good coffee," he added. With no phone and sketchy email and texting at the lodge, our communications were cryptic.

Sunday morning, June 18

Leaving the Dartmouth Grant Sunday morn-ing, I stopped to pick up a few things in Errol, where I found a text on my phone from Aldro: "I'll be at the gate at 2 p.m. on Sunday. Please confirm."

Hmm, I thought, *meet at 2. This will be an abbreviated visit!* But I was glad to have the chance to get in there at all. I sent a text to confirm my arrival, but I was unconvinced he would get it in time.

With an extra two hours, I had time to fish for a short while on the lower Magalloway River in Wilson's Mills, Maine, below Azis-cohos Dam. I had no luck in some sweet-looking runs below the Route 16 bridge, nor in the popular Mailbox Pool, which I had to myself. I didn't have enough time to really work it and figure out where fish might be holding, but I made a few casts before mov-ing on. My focus for the day was the Rapid River and Forest Lodge.

I'd fished many times with Lou on the upper Magalloway above Aziscohos Lake and Parmachenee Lake, including Little Boy Falls, where President Eisenhower fished in 1955. A photo of Ike landing a trout there was on the front page of newspapers all over the world. I was surprised to learn from Alice Arlen's biography of Louise Dick-inson Rich (*She Took to the Woods*, 2000) that Little Boy Falls was also where Louise started a guided canoe trip with her sister Alice in August 1933. They traversed Parmachenee Lake, Azicoshos Lake, and Umbagog Lake with a portage up the Carry Road along the Rapid River past Forest Lodge. "After an interval in hell you discover that your aches and cricks have vanished and you are pad-dling automatically," Louise noted.

Louise learned to fly-fish on that eventful and impressive trip. Not only did she fall in love with fly fishing ("hooked, as they say," she quipped) and the backwoods of Maine, she also met her soon-to-be husband, Ralph, a Harvard-educated engineer who had moved to Forest Lodge on the Rapid River to escape the corporate rat race. I guess there was a corporate rat race even back in the 1930s.

For both Louise and Ralph, each married before, it was love at first sight. They both

Louise Dickinson Rich. INK WASH AND CHARCOAL DRAWING BY JILL OSGOOD

The Winter House, where Louise Dickinson Rich lived and wrote We Took to the Woods, *is perched above the Rapid River just below Pond in the River.*

realized quickly that they shared many interests and values. He wrote to her constantly over the next few months, and at Christmastime, Louise left her teaching job in Massachusetts and took to the woods with Ralph. To supplement their meager income, she began writing stories set in "these parts" for national magazines and published her first book, *We Took to the Woods*, in 1942. The book is a warm, vivid, and personal account of rustic living, raising children, surviving frigid winters, and appreciating the hardships and wonders of a life among loggers and sportsmen, far from "civilized" society. There is plenty of fly fishing, of course.

The Riches lived at Forest Lodge from 1933 until Ralph died suddenly in 1944. Louise continued to spend summers there until 1955, when she sold the property to a close family friend. She went on to publish more than twenty books in her career. Louise died

in 1991 at her daughter Dinah's home in Massachusetts. Her son, Rufus, scattered her ashes in the Rapid River below Forest Lodge.

Sunday afternoon, June 18

I pulled up to the gate as Aldro had instructed at precisely 2:00. I'm used to driving on rough roads, so I made good time in my 4WD Nissan Rogue. There, also waiting for Aldro, was a couple from Vermont, Dr. Jack "Doc" Beecham and Allie Stickney, in their Prius. *Wow*, I thought, *it must have taken them hours to pick their way around the rocks and puddles with that low ground clearance.*

Jack introduced himself, noting that he had retired from Dartmouth's Norris Cotton Cancer Center, and said he'd been coming up to Forest Lodge for many years. He and Allie had recently been married. Before I could learn much about Allie, Aldro pulled up in his pickup.

Aldro suggested that I go ahead to the lodge, as it would take longer with the Prius, and they would need to unload their gear to the truck for the last mile, where the road gets too rough for smaller cars.

"You'll be staying in the Winter House, first building on the left," he said. To me.

Okay . . . what? Staying in the Winter House? The one in the book?

I hadn't planned to spend the night, but I'd been thinking about asking if there was a room available, given that I really wanted to fish the river on what promised to be a perfect evening. At that point, I still had no idea what to expect at the lodge, as I regretfully hadn't done much research, other than read the book and arrange the date for a visit. I went ahead while the others trailed behind slowly.

I pulled up to the Winter House and stepped onto the porch, which has a spectacular view of the river and what is left of Pond in the River Dam. It certainly looked like the pictures I had seen. The Riches had lived in this building in the winter because it was smaller and easier to keep warm. I noticed a sign on the outside wall about the Friends of Forest Lodge, a nonprofit Aldro had set up, dedicated to preserving Louise Rich's legacy and the historic buildings on site. The larger Summer House was only fifty yards away, much closer than I had thought.

Inside, the three-room Winter House looked like it hadn't changed since the 1940s. The wallpaper on one wall was a collection of faded original magazine covers, comics, ads, and articles from the 1930s and '40s, including *Saturday Evening Post, Liberty,* and *Cosmopolitan*, probably issues that ran Louise's articles.

I put my bag on the bed in the bedroom, where Louise and Ralph had slept. The furnishings and books on the shelf were probably there when Louise left. The propane

lights were "new," but an original oil lamp was still mounted on the wall. I imagined Louise and their hired hand, Gerrish, tying flies at the table by lamplight, as she described it:

About two years ago Gerrish and I took up fly tying. We thought it would be nice to have a hobby for our evenings for one thing. For another, flies are expensive to buy if you fish as much as we do. We're always losing flies, or having them ruined by a big fish, and it's always the fifty-cent types that meet with grief.

I thought I'd just dabble but it didn't work out that way. . . . We thought at first that we'd be satisfied if we could make a few streamers and some of the simpler stock patterns of wet flies. . . . We weren't even going to consider tying dry flies. . . . That state of mind lasted about a month. . . . Then we faced the truth. The bug had gotten us. . . .

And there's no feeling quite like the lift you get when eventually you hit on the right combination, and a walloping big trout comes surging up out of the shadows and grabs your very own fly, the fly you conceived and executed all by yourself.

Aldro still hadn't pulled in, so I wandered down toward the Summer House and a small cabin next to it, where I met Richard Hegeman, a jeweler from Rhode Island, tying flies on the porch that overlooked the roaring river below. Richard showed me the tiny brown Rapid River caddisfly pattern he had tied, and said he'd been coming here since the 1990s, about as long as Doc Beecham. The two of them had a few misadventures over the years. According to Richard, Doc was good at falling in the river.

I told Richard I wanted to make a few casts in the river below while waiting for Aldro, Doc,

Louise Dickinson Rich and her hired man, Gerrish, tied flies at the kitchen table in the Winter House at Forest Lodge.

and Allie to arrive. I grabbed my two rods, one rigged with sinking line and one with floating line, and descended the steep wooden steps to the pool below the porch where Richard was working. As the name implies, the Rapid River was powerful and loud. I found a foothold on the rocks at the edge of a strong current and a swirling back eddy.

I flipped a white marabou soft-hackle Black Ghost out into the water and pulled some more line off the reel. The weighted fly disappeared into the foam. As the fly came back into view, a large silvery shadow rose and disappeared near the fly. I threw the fly out again, a little farther.

On the second strip, I knew I'd hooked a big fish. I could feel the individual shakes of its head—whump whump whump—rather than the quiver you feel from a small fish. I kept the line tight and tried to determine what the fish would do.

It ran . . . across the pool into the heavy current, taking in all my slack line and a bunch more off the reel. When it stopped, I started to work it back into the slower water near shore.

"Richard! Can you bring me a net!" I shouted above the roar of the river. I felt like an idiot. I had just met the guy. All I had was my rod. And this felt like the biggest trout I'd ever had on the line.

Richard hurried down the stairs with a net as I moved the big fish up toward my feet. Suddenly it ran again, this time upstream for the rocks and the deep water under a small drop, back in the heavy current. As it disappeared into the rocks . . . snap!

F-bomb. From me, not the trout.

I sheepishly looked up at Richard who was standing there, net in hand at the bottom of the stairs. Now I really felt bad. He had come running for naught. I reeled in my broken leader—a brand-new 5X, which was a poor choice for this river—and saw that the line had broken cleanly.

"Well, if someone ever catches that trout, they'll get the fly I tied yesterday as a bonus."

I thanked Richard for his help and went up to grab my vest and net and returned to the same place, deciding to try nymphs to see if I could entice that beast again with something different. I switched to a 4X tippet and tied on big Yellow Stonefly. No luck. I moved down the pool a ways and drifted a big Royal Wulff on top with a small red nymph dropper down a couple feet in the slower water. On the first cast, a landlocked salmon took the nymph and immediately leaped clear out of the water and across the pool. This time I landed the fish, a 15-inch fistful, before heading back up the stairs.

At the top near the Summer House, I met Aldro and reported my misfortune with the big trout. His nonresponse indicated he had seen fools like me lose big fish plenty of times.

"Why don't you go down into the kitchen and meet Ginny. She's making dinner. She can tell you what time we'll be eating."

Ginny Sislane, whose four dogs were lounging in a portable pen near the house, was making a scrumptious-looking dessert with fresh strawberries and rhubarb from the garden. She was planning an early dinner so we could all fish afterward until dark. I learned later that Ginny worked as a controller for a seafood company near Boston when she wasn't up here fishing.

At about six o'clock, the six of us sat down for dinner in the basement of the Summer House. Aldro reminded me to remove my hat and said grace. We enjoyed the venison meat loaf and dessert as I listened to some good-natured ribbing and storytelling among old friends. I felt privileged to be part of this interesting family of conservation-minded

folks who clearly loved the setting and its history.

After dinner, Aldro and Ginny walked up to Pond in the River to fish from a canoe. I waded into the river below the footings of the old Lower Dam and found a nice seam where two currents joined in a deep pool. While stripping a streamer through the run, I saw a salmon jump clear out of the water across

The Rapid River near Forest Lodge is a rollicking run of sharp drops and deep pools.

the river. There were a few more splashy rises within casting distance, so I switched to my dry-fly rig.

The salmon were probably taking caddis-flies, so a Hornberg worked, as did a caddis emerger. I landed four, all 12 to 15 inches of quicksilver energy, each one leaping into the twilight. Quite a way to end an unexpected day!

Monday morning, June 19

At 7:00 a.m. I went down to the kitchen, where Richard poured me some of the coffee I had brought, as instructed—Kickapoo brand from Wisconsin—and graciously cooked a couple soft-boiled eggs and toast for me as well. We chatted as the others rolled in. After coffee, Aldro invited me on a guided tour of the buildings, some original and others newer. He told me that his father had bought the place in the late 1950s but died several years later, passing it to Aldro.

"My family, we're all Bowdoin folks," he said with a wry smile, ribbing me about my connection to Dartmouth. And he told me about the time when John Gierach and friends stayed in the Guide Camp and partied with his friends on the porch under the stars. Gierach wrote a tamer version of the story called "Fireproof" in *A Fly Rod of Your Own* (2017).

Aldro worried aloud about what would become of Louise and Ralph's physical legacy (and his own, I suspect) on the Rapid River. He admitted that he was finding it harder and harder to maintain the dozen buildings and had been looking for the right buyer for several years. Meanwhile, he was doing his best to preserve the signature structures and artifacts. (The following summer, I learned

that Forest Lodge had been acquired by a new owner who reportedly plans to preserve the historic value of the property.)

Later that June morning, Aldro said I had time for one more fishing excursion before he would escort me and Ginny to the gate. He suggested I take one of his four-wheel ATVs downstream about a mile to Cold Spring Pool and Smooth Ledge, one of Louise's favorite places. I loaded my rods and gear onto the red Honda FourTrax and headed slowly down the rough Carry Road, maneuvering carefully around rocks and across small streams. It was another muggy and buggy day, so the slight breeze on the ATV was a relief. In this remote part of western Maine, it appeared I had the entire river to myself.

At Cold Spring, I stood on a ledge at the head of the deep emerald-green pool; it had a fast current down the middle but some smooth, slower water on each side. There was no need for wading and, indeed, no place to

Fly fishing offers fewer rewards better than a Rapid River brook trout from Cold Spring pool.

Where & How—Rapid River

The good news is that the shoreline along both sides of the Rapid River is held in conservation easement by the Rangeley Lakes Heritage Trust. So the river, its legendary whitewater, and the epic fly-fishing-only water are protected from development.

The bad news is that the Rapid River is very tough to get to, either by land or by water. I guess that doubles as good news, because it means the fishing pressure is relatively low. By land, the access is across many miles of rough logging road to a gate several miles from the river, so unless you have a guide, it comes down to hoofing it for two to five miles. Mountain bikes are no longer allowed.

By water, there is a choice between crossing Umbagog Lake from the New Hampshire side or Lower Richardson Lake from the Maine side to Lakewood Camps. Having someone who knows where they are going is essential, as the weather up here can be rough and change rapidly. Cedar Stump campsite at the mouth of the river is a popular spot, part of the Lake Umbagog National Wildlife Refuge, but campsites are first-come, first-served. Lakewood Camps at Middle Dam on Lower Richardson Lake was founded in 1853 and calls itself (rightly so) "the quintessential Maine sporting camp."

What Works: If you've never been to this area, find a Registered Maine Guide to show you the ropes and tell you whether a Gray Ghost, a Royal Coachman, a CDC Caddis Emerger, or a Parmachenee Belle is the fly of the day. In the heavy current of the Rapid, you will need to get the fly down quickly, so use weighted nymphs with extra split shot, or a weighted streamer on fast sinking line or sinking tip line with 4X or 3X tippet.

Oh, and the landlocked salmon often prefer the tail of the pool. ■

wade here among the large rocks and ledge that sloped steeply into the deep pool. A pileated woodpecker repeated its short calls as I tied on a heavier leader, knowing from experience that a larger fish would break me off in the heavy flow.

I started by drifting a weighted nymph below an Ausable Wulff functioning as my strike indicator. On just the second cast, I hooked a burly Rapid River brook trout: 14 inches of green and gold with bright red spots like bull's-eyes inside larger pale-blue circles. In short order I caught two more of its cousins, all over 14 inches, one on an emerger and one on a smelt pattern streamer.

Monday afternoon, June 19

After forty minutes or so, I scrambled back up to the ATV and motored down to Smooth Ledge, where one could fish all day and never tire of the amazing rock formations. I could see why this was a favorite spot for Louise and Ralph—a great spot for a picnic and plenty of water for several people along one hundred yards of gently sloping ledge on one side. I caught another broad-shouldered, barrel-chested brookie on my emerger in the foam of a swirling eddy. While removing the hook, I declared to the river, *Okay, this is my last cast.*

Twenty-five casts later, I finally tucked the fly into an eyelet on my rod and padded my way through the scented spruce needles up the hill to the road, smiling to myself that I had such an unexpected and delightful twenty-four hours at Forest Lodge.

I can't express my thanks enough to Aldro, Ginny, Richard, Doc, and Allie for welcoming me and making me feel at home at Forest Lodge on the bank of the Rapid River. What an indulgence for my soul as I started the final week of my trip!

After my visit to her storied home, I fully appreciated Louise's words from the closing chapter of *We Took to the Woods*:

Why did we come to live here in the first place? We thought it was because we liked the woods, because we wanted to find a simple, leisurely way of life. Now, looking back, I think that we were unconsciously seeking to find a lost sense of our identity. . . . Living here has changed me. I hope it has changed me for the better. Certainly I am happier. . . . Certainly I am more at home in this world that we have created than ever I was in that vast and confusing maelstrom that we call civilization. —L.D.R.

I couldn't agree more.

- 23 -

Kennebago to Katahdin: Back in Thoreau Country

Start with Thoreau, end with Thoreau. That was the plan.

My Storied Waters excursion began at Walden Pond in recognition of Thoreau's influential role as a writer, naturalist, and philosopher. Thoreau vigorously explored the frontiers of human society and nature with his own excursions, seeking to understand where the boundary lies and why. He was fascinated by all species of fish and argued strongly—over 150 years ago—for removing dams, a physical and metaphorical boundary between human enterprise and nature that hindered runs of anadromous fish like Atlantic salmon and American shad.

I would end my journey in the Maine woods, coming full circle to where Thoreau immersed himself in the rugged wilderness of "Chaos and Old Night," as he put it. Thoreau made three major excursions in Maine: in 1846 to Mount Katahdin; in 1853 from Moosehead Lake to Chesuncook Lake; and in 1857 by canoe from Moosehead Lake to Allagash and Eagle Lakes and down the East Branch of the Penobscot River back to Bangor. Some critics disparage Thoreau as being

a little soft, emphasizing that he had guides on his trips to Maine to help with gear, provisions, and portages. One wag called him "Maine's first tourist." But I happen to think Henry was pretty badass. Thoreau's three trips to Maine were each in their own way impressive feats of fortitude and endurance. This was definitely not what is now called glamping.

Thoreau first trip to Maine occurred, ironically, during the two years, two months, and two days he was supposedly reveling in the solitude of Walden. He began his famous retreat to Walden Pond in July 1845, but by August 1846 he was restless enough to take a break from all that inspiring solitude to make his first excursion to the wilds of Maine. Leaving on August 31, Henry traveled by boat, buggy, and boot from Boston to Bangor to what is now Baxter State Park to attempt an ascent of Mount Katahdin, at 5,269 feet the tallest peak in the state.

Thoreau traveled with his guides up the wild West Branch of the Penobscot, camping and fishing at its confluence with Abol Stream on September 6, before climbing the mountain from the south. With no trails up Katahdin, Henry and his party bushwhacked up to 3,800 feet, where they camped. He twice scrambled along the summit ridge but unfortunately never reached the highest point. He watched as clouds and mist enshrouded the summit, knowing that it was unlikely he could reach it safely. "But at length, fearing that my companions would be anxious to reach the river before night, and knowing that the clouds might rest on the mountain for days, I was compelled to descend."

In spite of his disappointment, Henry realized he was engulfed in true wilderness. It was an epiphany for Captain Epiphany himself.

Perhaps I most fully realized that this was primeval, untamed, and forever untameable Nature, or whatever else men call it, while coming down this part of the mountain. This was that Earth of which we have heard, made out of Chaos and Old Night. Here was no man's garden. . . . It was the fresh and natural surface of the planet Earth, as it was made for ever and ever.

He caught a steamer back to Boston in Bangor after ten days in the wilderness, which certainly had as much impact on his writing of *Walden* as his time actually spent in Walden Woods.

In 1853, Thoreau made a two-week excursion to Moosehead Lake, traversing the lake by steamer (okay, that was a little soft), then paddling to Chesuncook Lake and back with guide Joe Aitteon and several companions in birch-bark canoes. He participated in a moose hunt on that trip and reflected on the morality of hunting in his essay "Chesuncook." And he fished for trout in the upper West Branch at the mouth of Raggmuff Stream but made no mention of how they fished or whether they caught anything.

In 1857, Thoreau, his friend Ed Hoar, and guide Joe Polis completed his most ambitious trip. They canoed from Greenville in late July and paddled roughly thirty-five miles to North East Carry, paddled and portaged to Eagle Lake and Chamberlain Lake, down the East Branch of the Penobscot River from Grand Lake Mattagamon to Medway, continuing all the way to Old Town on the main stem. They completed the almost 300-mile trip from Greenville to Bangor in eleven days. That was a badass trip.

Thoreau doesn't dwell much on the hardships, although he sometimes marvels at what his guides were capable of doing without a second thought. Most of his descriptions are matter-of-fact: weather, water, mud, bogs, and bugs. They came with the territory.

Well, okay, he did complain now and then about the bugs. Who wouldn't? On the night of July 31, on the East Branch of the Penobscot, he wrote,

It turned out the mosquitoes were more numerous here than we had found them before. . . . I noticed, as I had done before, that there was a lull among the mosquitoes about midnight, and that they began again in the morning. Nature is thus merciful. But apparently, they need rest as well as we.

Things haven't changed much in 250 years. We'd been tormented by mosquitoes and biting flies for several days in the Dartmouth Grant. The bugs were more tolerable at Forest Lodge on the Rapid River. But the next night, at the camp where I stayed on Kennebago Lake, the mosquitoes came down the chimney to invade the living room and eat me alive. Lou Zambello and Lindsey Rustad were kind enough to let me stay in their comfortable camp, but on that muggy, drizzly night I was there alone and had to retreat to a small bedroom, close the door, and battle several relentless mosquitoes that had followed me in and kept me awake half the night.

Tuesday morning, June 20

After a fitful night's sleep, I was rewarded for my suffering with a glittering silver sunrise across a quiet Kennebago Lake as rain clouds gave way to morning light. I was up early to do some fishing before driving several hours across the great state of Maine to visit the brand-new Katahdin Woods and Waters National Monument, which straddles the East Branch of the Penobscot where Thoreau had paddled during his final excursion to Maine. Roxanne Quimby, cofounder of a very successful natural skin-care company called Burt's Bees, had purchased 87,500 acres of timberland on both sides of the East Branch of the Penobscot River and donated it to the people of the United States to enjoy. In 2016, President Obama accepted her generous gift of land and designated it a national monument, which later became a political target when President Trump took office. I was looking forward to seeing the KWWNM for myself.

After that, only two more stops remained on my journey: the West Branch of the Penobscot on Wednesday, where Thoreau had fished on his first trip to Mount Katahdin, and the Kennebec River on Thursday and Friday. Suddenly, I realized that my trip would come to an end in just a few days. After forty days and forty nights, it was hard to believe my Storied Waters adventure would be over soon.

The Kennebago region is near the top of my list of favorite places to fish anywhere. Kennebago Lake, the Little Kennebago River, and the big Kennebago River are all world-class waters for catching big brook trout and landlocked salmon on a fly. In the fall during the spawning run, Lou and I are usually up and out before first light, so this wasn't my first sunrise, so to speak. For more information about fishing in this neck of the woods, you can read Lou's noteworthy book *Fly-fishing Northern New England's Seasons* (2nd ed. 2018) and his latest book, *In Pursuit of Trophy Brook Trout* (2019). Local author Bob Romano has written a series of trout-fishing novels set in the Kennebago and Rangeley Lakes region, including his latest, *The River King* (2017).

On this morning, however, I was on my own and destined first to the Little Kennebago River. With rain overnight, the river was high but still clear. There were no other footprints on the path down the steep gravel bank, so I knew I was the first to this pool, where the river makes a hard right. This spot was known for big trout freshly up from the lake that often slam a Black Ghost streamer on the first cast.

No such luck this time, although a curious trout, maybe 10 or 11 inches, chased my fly to my feet. I couldn't convince him or her to give that fly, nor several others, a good chomp.

With no immediate success on the Little Kennebago, I drove back across the causeway and down to the dam where the big Kennebago River begins its ten-mile journey to Cupsuptic Lake. Here I imagined a big landlocked salmon rushing up to my fly from the pool beneath the tailrace. I didn't have any luck on a streamer, but I did manage to take a sneaker-size salmon on a Prince Nymph drifted beneath a Yellow Humpy as the indicator fly. It was good to feel some real fish flesh in one of my favorite rivers before stowing my rods and moving on to Thoreau country. But first I wanted to make another quick museum stop.

Tiny Oquossoc, Maine, the closest town to Kennebago Lake, is the home of the Outdoor

Sporting Heritage Museum (OSHM). I grabbed a coffee at the country store across the street, then wandered over to where Bill Pierce, the director, was wrapping up an on-camera interview with a local TV crew about the upcoming Lupine Festival and Carrie Stevens Weekend. The museum was not officially open on a Tuesday, but Bill, whom I have known for years, invited me in to see the new exhibits they had added since I was there the previous summer.

The OSHM is an absolute gem. After visiting five other fly-fishing and outdoor-sports museums in the last six weeks, it's easy to say that the OSHM is a world-class experience. In their spacious spruce log building, they showcase the rich and diverse history of the western Maine region, including some of the biggest names in fly-fishing history, featuring several women. Here are a few:

♦ Carrie Stevens, the fly-tying legend who developed the Gray Ghost streamer fly; she also caught a 6-pound, 13-ounce brook trout in 1924 at nearby Upper Dam.

♦ Cornelia "Fly Rod" Crosby, the first official Maine Guide (License #1) and as big a personality in her day as Buffalo Bill Cody and Annie Oakley, who visited Crosby in Rangeley in 1905. My college classmate Julia Hunter published a fascinating biography: *Fly Rod Crosby: The Woman Who Marketed Maine* (2003).

♦ Herb Welch, the renowned taxidermist and fly tier, who developed the Black Ghost streamer pattern.

♦ President Dwight D. Eisenhower, a lifelong fly fisher who stayed at the Parmachenee Club in 1955 and fished the Magalloway River with local guide Don Cameron.

The Outdoor Sporting Heritage Museum in Oquossoc, Maine, featured an exhibit of Louise Dickinson Rich's typewriter and papers.

Bill proudly showed me the new exhibit on Louise Dickinson Rich and Forest Lodge, featuring her old typewriter and other artifacts donated by Aldro French and the Rich family. I wish I'd had another hour to enjoy all the exhibits, but the East Branch of the Penobscot was a long haul before dinner.

Tuesday afternoon, June 20

Four hours later, I turned north from Medway toward Grindstone, following the East Branch on my left, just as a huge, menacing thunderhead darkened the sky south of Mount Katahdin. Minutes later, rain pounded my windshield so hard that driving was dangerous. I pulled into the Maine DOT rest area at Grindstone Falls.

While waiting for the rain to subside, I thumbed through *Upriver & Down: Stories from the Maine Woods* (1965) by Edmund Ware Smith. Ed Smith owned a camp at the headwaters of the East Branch on Grand Lake Matagamon. He was a "master yarn spinner," according to an editor of *Field & Stream*, who wrote stories for *Outdoor Life*, *Atlantic Monthly*, and other national magazines. Smith was on hand to cover President Eisenhower's visit to the Dartmouth Grant for *Sports Illustrated*, writing about it in "Mr. Smith Meets the President." Other tales feature his group of friends, known as Jake's Rangers, gallivanting in the backcountry from Baxter Park to Grand Lake Stream down east.

At some point, Smith learned that Thoreau had camped on an island visible from his camp porch. Ed was pleased to learn that each time he traveled to his or from his camp, upriver and down, he followed Thoreau's path on his final Maine excursion. In his story, "Along Thoreau's Canoe Trail," Smith imagined a conversation with the great man:

"Edmund, tell me. Have men spoiled my Maine country?"

"Some of it—but not this part. These upper reaches of the East Branch remain just as you saw them. I wish you'd come back for another look. I'd be glad to drive you up from Bangor."

On their imaginary drive, Thoreau got excited when he saw Grindstone Falls, and Smith asked:

"Mr. Thoreau, did you run these rapids in your canoe, or lug around?"

"We thought it wise to carry."

As I sat at Grindstone Falls reading Ed Smith's words, Thoreau's ghost suddenly appeared in the seat beside me. I had surely felt a connection with the spirits of many writers at various times on my trip, but here now was a full-scale apparition. Maybe I was feeling woozy from a short night of mosquito-interrupted sleep and too much caffeine. Mr. Smith called him Mr. Thoreau. I felt more comfortable calling him Henry. [Note: In this chapter, Thoreau's imaginary words to me and my responses are in italics; non-italicized quotes are real qotes from Henry's writings.]

"August 1, 1857," Henry's ghost said to me while peering out the foggy window, *"Actually, Joe Polis proposed a race over the carry during our portage around these falls. I won."*

I considered for a moment how to reply. *"You know, not to be disrespectful,"* I said, *"but I've been doing lots of research. In* The Maine Woods, *you said you two raced at* 'what are probably called Whetstone Falls.' *But J. Parker Huber points out in his book* The Wildest Country *that, based on your mileage and description, you were likely here at Grindstone Falls."*

"Yes, I was in error. It was right here." Henry admitted. "'One cannot too soon

A fierce thunderstorm aroused Thoreau's spirit at Grindstone Falls on the East Branch of the Penobscot River, where Henry had raced his guide Joe Polis along the portage in 1857.

forget his errors and misdemeanors. To dwell long upon them is to add to the offense,' *as I once said.*"

"Yes, but didn't you also say, 'To forget all about your mistakes adds to them perhaps'?" I smiled, knowing that there are so many Thoreau quotes it's hard to keep them straight, even for Henry's ghost, apparently.

He ignored my comment. *"And,"* he added, *"I didn't have the benefit of GPS back then to double check my bearings."*

"Touché, Henry."

It was still raining catfish and dogfish, so I reached into my back seat and pulled out my copy of *The Maine Woods*, turning to Henry's account of that part of his trip in "The Allegash and East Branch." I reread aloud how Polis carried the canoe while Henry lugged the gear: frying pan, plates, paddles,

and a sooty kettle. Even after dropping his load once and having to repack his bundle, Henry arrived downstream ahead of Polis, who had purposely handicapped himself by going barefoot over the rocks. Still, Polis got a laugh out of it: "O, me love to play sometimes," Henry had quoted him as saying.

Henry's ghost smiled wistfully at the memory.

After the rain subsided, Henry and I continued upstream toward the entrance to Katahdin Woods and Waters. I was happy to have some company after six weeks of driving alone.

"You like music, don't you, Henry?"

"Yes," he replied. "When I hear music, I fear no danger. I am invulnerable. I see no foe. I am related to the earliest times, and to the latest."

"Okay, good." I cranked up a tune on my playlist.

"I like this composition!" Henry beamed, and soon he was singing along at the top of his lungs: *"Lord I was born a ramblin' ma-han!"*

Really.

We passed several "National Park No" signs in people's yards and along the logging road. Many of the locals, as well as our own governor, showed no appreciation for the generosity of Ms. Quimby, who had even agreed to allow hunting and snowmobiling on large parts of her donated land and provided $20 million for improvements. Somehow, the specter of federal ownership blinded these folks to the fact that giving her land to the National Park Service (with an endowment, no less) was fully within Quimby's rights as a private property owner. She could have put a fence around it and told everyone to stay the hell out. But instead she chose to add to Governor Percival Baxter's legacy by expanding the ecological and recreational importance of the 200,000-acre Baxter State Park, which abuts the national monument to the west.

Henry looked at the signs and repeated his own words, "If a man walks in the woods for love of them half of each day, he is in danger of being regarded as a loafer; but if he spends his whole day as a speculator, shearing off those woods and making the earth bald before her time, he is esteemed an industrious and enterprising citizen."

He paused, then said, half under his breath, "In wildness is the preservation of the World."

"Yup," I replied, with all the wisdom and eloquence I could muster.

We drove west down a long dirt access road from Route 11, and I felt a curious sense of relief when we crossed the boundary into the national monument itself. I stopped, got out, and walked around, feeling the actual dirt beneath my feet before driving on. At a dusty junction, the entrance road turned left, back onto private timberland, and down toward the East Branch. The main section of the monument continued for miles on the west side of the river. Henry and I stopped at the bridge over the East Branch at the Whetstone Falls picnic area.

"Yes, you are right, I confused the names," said Henry as we pulled up, *"but I did say 'probably called Whetstone Falls.'"* He winked at me. *"We traversed this section in the canoes."*

I was impressed to think Thoreau's party had paddled through these rapids in birchbark canoes. I climbed down onto the rocks and cast a streamer along the edge of the big rapids as the sun began to sink behind the hills. The water temperature was 68 degrees—fine for swimming, but too warm for trout. I mumbled that I'd probably hook a chub, which Henry also called chivin or roach. He had caught, and eaten, chivin from the Concord and Merrimack Rivers and on various excursions to Maine. "The chub is a soft fish, and tastes like boiled brown paper salted," he said. I tried a couple different flies with no action. After thirty minutes, I stowed my fly rod, ignoring Henry's suggestion that I try a worm.

I sorely wanted to explore the new national monument, but it would take days to canoe all the beautiful rivers and streams and hike the mountains. I drove down to the next entrance and turned around, confident that I'd come back another time for a longer visit, but I was glad to have made its acquaintance.

My next mission was to find Jim Lepage's cabin before dark. Henry and I returned to the main road the way we came in and turned right at Medway to follow the West Branch of the Penobscot through Millinocket and onto the Golden Road, a ninety-six-mile private dirt logging road from Millinocket to the Canadian border.

Tuesday evening, July 20

Recall that when I visited Orvis headquarters in Vermont at the start of my trip, Jim Lepage had offered me the use of his rustic camp on Caribou Lake, along the Golden Road west of Millinocket, for the final leg of my journey. "You're welcome to use it. I can tell you where to find the key," he said. Jim was head of manufacturing for the esteemed fishing and hunting retailer, and used his camp for, well, hunting and fishing with his family. Caribou Lake is now connected to Chesuncook Lake, thanks to the construction in 1920 of Ripogenus Dam at the outlet, which raised the water level and thus joined the two lakes.

Jim's offer was beyond generous. I jumped at the chance, especially when he mentioned the spectacular view across the lake to Mount Katahdin. Somewhere during my stay in the Adirondacks, I had confirmed the arrangements with Jim and got directions.

Nineteen miles west of Millinocket, the Golden Road crossed the West Branch at Abol Bridge, just below where Abol Stream joins the river. Thoreau's party had camped at this spot during his first trip to Katahdin in 1846.

I stopped on the bridge to get a photo of Mount Katahdin not far off in the distance. As is typical, the tall plateau was making its own weather on a clear evening with clouds streaming across the peak, lit up by the setting sun. At first, Henry didn't recognize the spot, now a popular campground, but it didn't take long before he figured out where we were. He was excited to tell me that he and his party had caught so many "speckled trout" and "silvery roaches" here that he had dreamed about it that night. In his essay "Ktaadn" (1846), he wrote:

> In the night I dreamed of trout-fishing; and, when at length I awoke, it seemed a fable that this painted fish swam there so near my couch, and rose to our hooks the last evening, and I doubted if I had not dreamed it all. So I arose before dawn to test its truth, while my companions were still sleeping. There stood Ktaadn with distinct and cloudless outline in the moonlight; and the rippling of the rapids was the only sound to break the stillness. Standing

Thoreau had paddled through these rapids at Whetstone Falls on the East Branch of the Penobscot.

on the shore I once more cast my line into the stream, and found the dream to be real and fable true. The speckled trout and silvery roach, like flying-fish, sped swiftly through the moonlight air, describing bright arcs on the dark side of Ktaadn, until moonlight, now fading into daylight, brought satiety to my mind, and the minds of my companions, who had joined me. [Ktaadn, 6 September 1846]

We climbed back into my vehicle and continued down the Golden Road. It was not lost on me that we were traveling comfortably on four wheels. I tried to imagine what it was like for Henry's party traveling upstream on

Mount Katahdin towers over Abol Stream Campground when viewed from Abol Bridge over the West Branch of the Penobscot River.

the West Branch by bateau with the guides poling deftly among the rocks and everyone scrambling out to lift the boats over the steeper drops. I have to admit that, even as a passenger, Henry had to be a resourceful and resilient traveler.

We drove right by Jim's camp at first but backed up to the steep driveway that led down to the lake and unlocked the gate chain in the headlights of my car. Henry asked if he could drive the car through the gate, but I said no, I'd do it. At the bottom of the hill,

digs were luxurious compared to Henry's house at Walden Pond.

Henry couldn't help himself: "Most of the luxuries, and many of the so-called comforts of life, are not only not indispensable, but positive hindrances to the elevation of mankind," he lectured.

"Yeah, but at least there are no mosquitoes in here," I replied.

"Touché, David," I heard faintly, as Henry's aura faded into the darkness.

"Good night, Henry," I said, as I sat making notes in my journal. *"Will I see you tomorrow?"* No reply.

During the night in Jim Lepage's camp on Caribou Lake, I dreamed of trout fishing, just as Henry had at Abol Stream. This was no surprise, considering I was almost six weeks into my Storied Waters fly-fishing adventure. I'd love to tell of a fantastical dream about a huge enchanted trout that dragged me down into Ripogenus Gorge, or silvery roaches leaping over Katahdin in the moonlight, but like many dreams, nothing specific happened. Just a strange and disorderly mishmash of me wading in a river and trout jumping to take my fly. When I awoke, I shook out the cobwebs, made coffee, and admired the sun rising across the lake over Mount Katahdin as I planned my day, hoping to turn my fishy dream into reality. There was no sign of Henry's ghost on that fine morning.

The West Branch of the Penobscot is a powerful river noted for big trout and landlocked salmon, as well as Class IV and V rapids for whitewater rafting. My one time on the West Branch was thirty years ago on a whitewater rafting trip with Cheryl and our friend Steve Richardson. Oddly, I had never fished the famous river, so I had to do some exploring to find a good spot.

Driving east from camp, my first stop was the spectacular Ripogenus Gorge, where a

we parked under towering pines and maples. The cabin's key was right where Jim had said it would be, and the propane lights lit the cabin warmly. Henry looked around while I pulled out my sleeping bag, threw it on the futon couch, and opened a Frye's Leap IPA. I offered one to Henry, but he declined. Even without running water or electricity, these

A landlocked salmon put up a spirited battle on the scenic West Branch of the Penobscot between Little and Big Ambejackmockamus Falls.

fisherman worked the big water from the far shore near the mouth. I found no good places to wade on my side and continued driving downstream.

Chris Ricardi had suggested fishing above Telos Bridge just below the Gorge, but there were a couple cars parked there, so I kept going, past Big Eddy Campground, looking for an unoccupied access point. Not far from

Big Eddy, there was a rough boat launch between Little and Big Ambejackmockamus Falls without a soul in sight. A slim back channel of the river reenters the main flow there, creating a seam with a small eddy. A perfect spot to wade safely.

I'll take a moment here to note that, had the "Big A Dam" been built at Big Ambejackmockamus Falls as proposed by Great

and other members of the coalition of environmental groups fought so hard to save the river. They argued that investments in electric efficiency and demand reduction should take precedence over blindly building more power plants, especially when public resources like the West Branch and the environment were at stake.

Ultimately, the staff at Maine Department of Environmental Protection refused to issue a water-quality certification for the dam. And fortunately, despite concerted efforts by the governor and the legislature to weaken Maine's water-quality standards to allow the project, the damned dam was canceled. Thank heavens.

The sky was mostly clear with steady passing clouds. The air was warm and calm and a bit humid. Perfect for hatching bugs. I waded out in waist-deep water to a convenient rock near the eddy and climbed up onto it. This allowed a full circle for casting with no need to worry about my backcast. Now if the fish would just cooperate.

Starting with a Black Ghost streamer, my rod bent with a couple hearty tugs by a fish of decent size, but no solid take. At least the fish were where they were supposed to be. Soon, a trout rose right on the edge of the eddy. Then, a salmon leaped clear out of the water "describing a bright arc," to use Thoreau's words, against the dark spruce shadows across the smooth fast-flowing water. Mayflies and caddis swarmed in small clouds here and there.

The next four hours were a dream come true. Just a few miles from where Henry had his midsummer-night's dream, I caught more than a dozen salmon and brook trout of various sizes, while a dozen more slashed at my flies as if they were playing a game, simply to test my reflexes. Henry's ghost was nowhere

Northern Paper Company in the early 1980s, the place where I was putting on my waders would be under *fifty feet* of water. Four and a half miles of this spectacular wild river—a world-class fishery and whitewater destination—would have drowned under the impoundment.

I was working at Maine Audubon at the time that the fierce legal battle raged over the Big A Dam, although I played no direct role in it. I am grateful, however, that my colleagues

Where & How—
West Branch of the Penobscot

The Maine North Woods around Baxter State Park is an embarrassment of riches when it comes to fishing for native brook trout and landlocked salmon. The maze of logging roads around the park provides access to rivers, streams, lakes, and ponds that have ample cold, clean water to support trout and salmon. The Golden Road provides access to eleven miles of prime fishing on the West Branch between Ripogenus Dam and Abol Stream. This is big water that is worth floating with a guide in a drift boat. The famous salmon pool at Big Eddy gets hit heavily, what many of us call combat fishing, but many other wadable sections can be accessed from pullouts or short side roads. It takes some exploring, but there is plenty of water to go around.

What Works: Smelt are a major food source for both brook trout and landlocked salmon, so smelt patterns like a Black Ghost or a Conehead Marabou Soft-Hackle (see any of Lou Zambello's books for this fly pattern). When bugs are hatching, any caddis pattern does well up here, especially an Elk Hair Caddis.

But my favorite fly for brook trout and salmon is the Wood Special. Its orange and tinsel body, mallard down-wing, and grizzly hackle make it look like a stonefly when dead-drifted in the current, and it fishes well in various sizes when stripped like a streamer. There are plenty of theories about why this fly works, but none of them really matter. What matters is it works almost any time of year. ∎

to be seen, but I felt his spirit in the river and in the trees. Once again, I was in heaven.

The bright afternoon softened to evening. The light on the clouds and reflections on the river became more scintillating by the hour, while the fish continued to rise and splash across the entire width of the river. By 8:00 p.m., after almost four hours on the river, I was content to pass on the last hour of daylight and retreat to camp for dinner and a cold brew.

Yes, bigger fish feed later, and it was probably foolish for me to leave, but I was smiling all the way back to the car, looking forward to the next day on the Kennebec. On the drive back to the cabin, my playlist cued up "Catch & Release" by Matt Simons.

I stopped briefly to see what was happening at Big Eddy, the most famous pool in the river, notorious for big salmon. A license plate in the parking lot read HEX FLY, or something like that. A dozen boats and two or three wading anglers were wedged into an area not much bigger than a rugby pitch. I guessed they were waiting for the *Hexagenia* hatch. That kind of combat fishing is not my cup of tea at all. I'd had the river all to myself for the afternoon. Smaller fish, perhaps, but as Thoreau said, "Ah! I need solitude. I have come forth to this hill at sunset to see the forms of the mountains in the horizon—to behold and commune with something grander than man."

- 24 -

Dud Dean's Kennebec River

Thursday morning, June 22

I didn't dream of trout again that night. Instead, I dreamed of home. With just one more night left on this remarkable trip, I was looking forward to seeing my beautiful bride and sleeping in our own bed after six weeks on the road. But I had one more important stop first: the Kennebec River, where I would be fishing in the fictional footsteps of Dud Dean.

I was up and out of Jim's Caribou Lake cabin quite early, with a long drive to The Forks, a small village where the Kennebec and the Dead River converge, to meet Jeff Reardon, the conservation director for Maine Trout Unlimited. Jeff loves fishing the Kennebec region and had several options for us to explore, depending on the conditions. My original plan was to meet Jeff here on my way to the Penobscot, but he had a schedule conflict and couldn't meet me until Thursday afternoon, so I pushed through to the Penobscot region and instead fished the Kennebec on my way home.

Several months before my trip, Jeff had introduced me to the Dud Dean stories by Arthur Macdougall Jr., published in *Field &*

Stream in the 1930s and later collected in several books: *The Sun Stood Still* (1939), *Where Flows the Kennebec* (1947), and *Dud Dean and the Enchanted* (1954). These books are out of print and hard to find. Fortunately, Macdougall's son Walter published a collection of his father's stories called *Remembering Dud Dean* (2001), which is still available in print and e-book form.

Arthur Macdougall (1896–1983) was a fly-fishing minister from Bingham, Maine, who created one of the most colorful characters in fly-fishing fiction. Dud Dean was full of native wit, wisdom, and insightful observation about people of all types. Most of the stories were written in the first person as a conversation between Macdougall, or "Mak," and his fictional friend Dud, who together spun fabulous yarns about guiding on the Kennebec River and the surrounding rivers and ponds. Some of the places in the stories are literally gone beneath Wyman Lake now, after the Wyman Dam was built by Central Maine Power in 1930.

The genius of the Dud Dean stories is Macdougall's brilliant rendition of a Maine vernacular that hypnotizes the reader, transporting us to a time when automobiles were scarce and the trout were as big as we imagined them to be. Some readers were convinced Dud was real and would call Bingham town hall, trying to find out how to reach him to arrange a trip.

Macdougall could sketch out his characters and related entire scenes in a single sentence. Here are a few examples from different stories:

- ♦ "Henry Gates was the mildest spoken man that ever took anythin' to pieces with his bare hands."
- ♦ "Dud, it has been revealed to me that youth passed me some time back, and it wasn't going my way, either."
- ♦ "Of course, the black flies was thar to remind a man that life is no bed of nursery rhymes."
- ♦ "When I remember sech times, I feel it'll be all right if they don't let me inter heaven. I know what it's like."
- ♦ "A fish like that knows more'n some folks that wanted to run fer president."
- ♦ "This leader I've got on is as thin as a guess an' a maybe."
- ♦ "I saw Dud struggle to smooth out his own face, which, of course, was of a mind to laugh."

As Macdougall's son notes, Mak's and Dud's memorable one-liners are "not occasional, but omnipresent." Sadly, Dud, Mak, and their friends, much like the eccentric gang in Corey Ford's Lower Forty Club, are sliding from our collective consciousness. These stories and characters are an important part of American fly-fishing culture and deserve the same immortality that Paul Bunyan and John Henry enjoy. We owe it to them.

It was a bright, blue-sky day as I drove west on the Greenville Road toward Kokadjo and Moosehead Lake. In Greenville, at the southern end of Moosehead Lake, I stopped for coffee and a muffin, and enjoyed a steaming cup in the morning sun on the shore while watching the crew load supplies onto the restored steamer *Katahdin*, which still cruises up and down the lake, now under diesel power.

Between Greenville and the town of Monson I again crossed paths in the space-time

Jeff Reardon works the small pools on Cold Stream, a tributary to the Kennebec River and nursery water for native brook trout.

continuum with Henry David Thoreau. Henry had visited Greenville twice—in 1853, when he steamed from Greenville to North East Carry, and in 1857, when he paddled the length of the lake with his guide Joe Aitteon. There was no sign of Henry's ghost at the lake as I might expect that he resides for eternity in the wilderness near Mount Katahdin. I continued south on Route 6 to Monson, following roughly the same route Thoreau had traveled in an open wagon both from and back to Bangor. At Monson, I turned west onto Route 16 toward Bingham.

Jeff and I had a peaceful evening canoeing and casting on remote Durgin Pond near Jackman, Maine.

At the height of land on Route 16 in Kingsbury Plantation, a long string of wind turbines turned majestically in the morning breeze before the road descended the steep ridge to Macdougall's hometown on the Kennebec River. Bingham surely has seen better days, and perhaps it did when it was also home base for Roscoe Vernon "Gadabout" Gaddis of the 1960s TV show *The Flying Fisherman*. Macdougall and Gaddis were the same age, so I wouldn't be surprised if they knew each other and perhaps cast a fly together now and then. Main Street in Bingham continues north as Route 201 along Wyman Lake to Caratunk and The Forks, where I had arranged to meet Jeff Reardon at Berry's General Store.

adage that "a man must come to love his own river."

On such a sunny and breezy day, Jeff suggested we forego the main stem of the Kennebec and instead fish a tributary, Cold Stream, where TU had purchased land and improved the in-stream habitat as nursery water and summer refuge for brook trout moving up from the Kennebec. Come evening, he said, he'd take me to one of the remote "heritage" ponds (never stocked) up at the headwaters of Cold Stream where TU was instrumental in protecting 8,000 acres around the ponds and along the entire length of Cold Stream. He also promised to show me a good place to camp for my last night at Durgin Pond not far from Lone Jack Pond, which appears in one of Macdougall's Dud Dean stories. Jeff had to be home that evening, so I'd be on my own to fish the Kennebec in the morning.

We left my vehicle near the main road, hopped into Jeff's pickup, and soon we were bouncing down some very rough and rutted two-track roads. I doubt I could find the spot where we parked, but if I didn't know better, I would say we were in Montana or Wyoming. Cold Stream flows through a steep valley that has a distinct Rocky Mountain feel. This was small water fishing at its best, with wild brookies in every plunge pool and hiding along undercut banks.

In the next two hours, Jeff and I caught well over twenty fish combined, none over 9 inches, mostly on Elk Hair Caddis dry flies or Hornbergs fished both dry and wet. If this is nursery and refuge water, then the Kennebec fishery has a rosy future. Plenty of fun on a gorgeous sunny day.

As the shadows lengthened in the afternoon, we headed back to Route 201 and north toward Jackman. This time I followed Jeff down the logging road to the pond in my own vehicle, as I planned to camp there

A lover of dark beers and the Red Sox, Jeff is a character himself, though not quite as colorful as Dud Dean, but just as knowledgeable about all things Kennebec and trout. I had met Jeff twenty-some years earlier when Trout Unlimited was negotiating with Central Maine Power and other parties to relicense hydroelectric dams across the state. Jeff is the embodiment of Dud Dean's for the night—the last chance of the trip! I had brought a tent, a folding cot (yes, soft, I know), and sleeping bag but had not had occasion to camp out. Every time I found a good place to camp, either it rained or I found a cheap hotel that tipped the equation toward a hot shower and electric power to run my laptop.

The tent site was a grassy area with a picnic table at the edge of the pond, which was about a quarter mile long and 200 yards wide. Jeff even brought dinner—a couple steaks, peppers, mushrooms, and potatoes. While I pitched my tent, Jeff cooked the steaks and vegetables on his portable gas grill.

Soon Jeff called out, "These steaks are just about perfect. You drinking beer? Or do you want some of this wine?" He held out a bottle of Zinfandel and two wine glasses. The glasses were plastic, but they had stems. Clearly, he had done this before. We sat down to a delicious dinner pondside as the sun was setting. Several trout splashed across the pond, rising for their own dinner, while others sipped mayflies quietly nearby. We tried hard not to hurry through our meal.

Finally, we packed up the dishes and climbed into Jeff's canoe just in time for the rises to abate, from steady to occasional. We had the entire pond to ourselves and spent the next hour chasing rises from one end to the other as the water reflected the peach and powder blue of the sky. Jeff did a masterful job of steering us toward the nearest rise rings, each of us casting to either side of the ring to hedge on which way the fish was moving. "We're creating a virtual hatch," Jeff chuckled.

Despite all the rises, I managed to land just one fat brook trout, although I hooked and lost a couple more. Jeff fared better at Trout Pond Bingo, landing four, all about 12 inches or larger. These were healthy and vigorous

wild fish. A sublime way to spend the twilight of my six-week adventure.

As Jupiter rose into the darkening sky, the mosquitoes attacked in small squadrons. We loaded the canoe onto the truck with flashlights, shook hands, and soon Jeff's tail lights disappeared into the darkening forest. Alone deep in the Maine woods, I retreated to my tent to escape the bugs and enjoy the sounds

I caught my last fish of the trip—a brook trout—here in the Kennebec River in a subtle seam behind a submerged rock.

of the frogs and a hooting owl serenading me to sleep.

Friday morning, June 23

The next morning, a soft rain on the tent awoke me at first light—about 4:30 a.m. Not wanting to get thoroughly drenched on the final day of my trip, I quickly packed up my soggy tent just as the rain shower passed and the sun peaked out, lighting up the tops of the tall pines across the pond in a golden blaze. Rather than fuss with a stove and coffeepot among the mosquitoes, I opted to get coffee in The Forks, then fish for an hour or so in the Kennebec and be home by noonish. But I couldn't leave without making a least one cast, thinking of Dud's story on Lone Jack Pond:

It was early mornin' and the ferever was all eround Lone Jack. I mean, it's good fer the saint er the sinner to go fishin' in the early light; good fer the genius er the dullard to be fishin' afre the sun comes up over the beloved near-at-hand.

Jeff had suggested that I fish the Kennebec just below The Forks near the ramp where whitewater rafts land and launch. It was early in the season, so the ramp would be quiet on a Friday morning. As long as I was off the river by noon, I wouldn't have to worry about the river rising from a release at Harris Dam several miles upstream. As I drove into town, I felt a little self-imposed pressure to end the Storied Waters tour on a good note; I didn't want to get skunked on the last day.

There's a public boat launch just a short distance above the former (actual) site of the Gilroy Boom, where (fictional) Dud Dean guided Olivet Bumpus, an English professor at Durum College, and her successful soap-salesman beau, Atterly Dumstead, in "The Way of an Old Maid." In his telling of the story to Mak, Dud found himself in a competition with the city-slicker, know-it-all boyfriend. Olivet mooned over her man: "Have you noticed his flawless technique?" she gushed, and issued a challenge Dud didn't expect: "I dare say you cannot match Mr. Dumstead's art?"

Damnation if she warn't laughin' at me. I put on a Cow Dung, thinkin' erbout salmon. But that was a bad mistake, as Dumstead soon demonstrated 'ith three nice trout. Thar didn't seem to be any salmon in thar at all.

We-eel, who don't like the Kennebec when she's in a trout mood? I switched to a nice, slim Parm Belle. An' I hooked a trout

How sweet it was to catch the final fish of my Storied Waters journey, a Kennebec River brook trout.

Where & How—
Upper Kennebec River

The Kennebec is a big river with multiple dams that control the flow,
so it is important to know the timing of
releases, which affect fishing conditions
significantly. Wading is possible in the tail-
waters and shallower sections when flows
are favorable. Float trips with guides are
also a popular way to access the river. The
East and West Outlets below Moosehead
Lake and the section below Harris Dam
hold both wild and stocked fish, including
brook trout, rainbows, brown trout, and
landlocked salmon.

What Works: When fishing bigger
water, a productive but underused tactic
is to carry two rods right into the river:
one rigged with floating line and a dry fly
or nymph dropper setup, and the other
with sinking line or sinking-tip line and
a streamer. Start by prospecting with the
streamer while watching for rises or a fish
chasing your fly. The second rod can be
fastened to your vest, with the bottom
loop and Velcro tab on the chest pointing up over the opposite shoulder out of
the way. If you see a rise or flash, or if a
fish tugs the streamer, switch to the dry fly
and work the specific spot where the fish
is located.

Another way to prospect with a dry fly is
to "paint the water" by skittering an attractor pattern like a Royal Wulff, a stimulator,
or a Hornberg in arcs across the surface.
This will often induce a fish to make a
slash at the fly, giving away its location.
And now you are in business. ■

that was a half pound bigger'n any Dumstead had found, but the Bumpus paid no
attention to that. Instead, everytime he remembered to look in her direction, she
waved at him as if he was a fust class descen-
dant of old Izaak Walton hisself.

Dumstead then moved out onto the log
boom to cast to a fish he had seen rising.
Bumpus joined him as he hooked a huge
salmon while standing on logs "as slippery
as cheap soap in a bathtub." You can guess
where this is going. The story is all in the telling, of course, and nobody did it better than
Macdougall's Dud Dean "hisself."

As I waded out above the boat launch, the
drizzle stopped and started several times. The
water was a perfect 58 degrees. The first spot
I tried showed no signs of life, so I moved
downstream, looking as always for a seam in
the current. I found a big rock just beneath
the surface and waded out thigh-deep slightly
downstream of its wake, barely within casting
distance. Now it was I who needed to match
Dumstead's art.

I was relieved to see a salmon leap at my
fly at the end of a long drift. It was clearly
stimulated by my stimulator, sailing clear out
of the water but missing my fly on the way
down. But "now I knew that I knew where a
fish was," to quote my friend Phil Odence.

A few caddis fluttered clumsily by in the
drizzle. After a few more unsuccessful casts, I
switched flies to a Hornberg, but couldn't get
a good drift across or downstream, so I threw

the fly up behind the rock. This allowed a longer drift—one, two, three—before the fly disappeared with a lazy slurp. I could tell right away that it was a brook trout, not a salmon, by how it moved, heavy and slow in the current.

Now I had to bring this baby in. Far worse than being skunked would be to hook a good fish and lose it and then get skunked. And I didn't want to lose my footing and get soaked, as Dumstead and Bumpus had.

I held my rod high and kept pressure on the fish in the current while patiently reeling in the slack line in front of me. Slowly, the trout moved toward me, then downstream, then up to my feet and into the net: a fat 'n' happy 14-inch wild Kennebec squaretail, perhaps a former resident of Cold Stream. Another dream come true.

I danced one of those little victory jigs right there in the river as I released the fish, watching it swim away in the clear water. I had my final fish, and yet I couldn't resist making a few more greedy casts—I was thinking a big salmon like Dumstead's—before deciding to end the trip on the high note I had just hit. The spots on that particular brook trout served as the punctuation marks at the end of my Storied Waters story.

It seemed like a long wade to shore. I stoically stowed my waders and rods for the last time and pointed the car south toward New Gloucester, punching up "Rivers and Roads" by The Head and the Heart from my playlist.

In our yard, the daylilies were bursting their buds. My odyssey had ended. Our dog April remembered me, as faithful Argos recognized Odysseus in Homer's epic tale. I was encouraged to see that Cheryl, thankfully, hadn't changed the locks while I was gone. And, no, I didn't have to kill any suitors.

Epilogue:
The Storied Waters
Chronicle

"Fishing is at once an endless source of delight and an act of small rebellion. . . ."
—*John Voelker (Robert Traver), "Testament of a Fisherman"*

As one would expect after getting home from such an unusual adventure, people have asked me many questions:

"How was your trip? Was it anything like what you expected?"

"How was the fishing? Did you catch many fish?"

"How have these famous rivers and ponds held up to development and pollution?"

"What was the best part of the trip overall?"

Let's take each question separately.

How was your trip?

Fabulous! Pretty mind-blowing, really.

First, on the practical side, I had no major mishaps: no flat tires, no speeding tickets, no broken rods, no barroom brawls. I didn't fall in a river while wading, nor did I hook myself with a fly. I never got lost. There were no crossed wires or miscommunications with people I had planned to meet, nor major disappointments about my destinations. Okay, I stayed in a few cheesy hotels, but that was my own choice because I'm cheap. Overall, the lack of negatives equals a big positive!

Second, I got to do something that perhaps no one else has done before. And in doing so, I visited spectacular fishing destinations, waded up to my knees almost daily in beautiful water, and experienced nature in all her glory. I befriended delightful people who went out of their way to welcome me to their towns, their favorite fishing holes, and sometimes into their homes. And, most importantly, I got to cast a fly with some excellent fly fishers who pointed me toward plenty of fish.

Yes, I did miss my darling wife and was glad to get home after six weeks! For me, the weeks flew by, as I was busy every minute driving, fishing, writing, editing photos, making new friends, tying flies, and sleeping like a rock pretty much every night.

Here's a quick recap of my six-week odyssey:

The Storied Waters excursion was forty-three days: I left home on May 12 and returned home on June 23. My odometer logged 5,700 miles through eleven states from Maine to Wisconsin and back. This was a surprise, as my original mapped itinerary showed my expected distance as about 3,000 miles, but with all the side trips and

Home at last.

backroads, the mileage was almost double the most direct route.

I fished on thirty-eight out of forty-three days in eight different states: Massachusetts, Vermont, New York, Pennsylvania, Wisconsin, Michigan, (New York and Vermont again), New Hampshire, and Maine, in that order, hitting one fabled fly-fishing destination per day, on average. When I wasn't fishing, I was usually taking photos, writing, driving, eating, or sleeping. I only took one day totally "off" to hang out and swim with my daughter, Rosa.

Meals included a lot of pub fare, but not too much fast food. I wish I'd kept a complete log of all the local microbrews I enjoyed along the route. Thanks to friends (new and old) or family and inexpensive hotels, I camped out just one night—the last night of the trip.

> "A trout is purty in any light."
> —*Dud Dean*

How was the fishing?

It was entirely possible that I could run into persistently lousy conditions, either washouts from too much rain, or hot days and warm, low water like we had in 2016. Fortunately, none of that happened. Overall, the fishing conditions were excellent for the entire six weeks. A few days were a bit too warm, and a few were pretty chilly. But overall, peak conditions prevailed all along the route. There were just two days of steady rain on the entire trip, but I was happy to take those days off to write or tie flies.

As I've said, "no bugs, no glory," and I certainly ran into plenty of bugs. Mayflies and caddisflies were hatching almost everywhere I went. I ran into impressive Hendrickson hatches in the Catskills, Sulfur hatches in Pennsylvania and Wisconsin, flying ants in Wisconsin, caddis and Brown Drakes in Michigan, caddis and Hendricksons in the Adirondacks, and plenty of caddisflies and a few mayflies in New Hampshire and Maine. For the first time ever, I caught a trout on a crane fly pattern in Wisconsin and again in Maine.

I was nervous at the start that I would sheepishly be reporting time and again that I'd been skunked, flogging the water with no success in any number of locations. On the contrary, I had very steady action, including a few very memorable days. I caught fish on well over half of the days or outings, no matter how you count them. When I didn't catch something, I usually had strikes or interested fish to keep me entertained. I can't be anything but thrilled with those results.

Some people want numbers, but I rarely keep careful count. Going back through my notes and my blog posts, I estimate somewhere around 200 fish landed and released. Most were brown trout and brook trout, pretty evenly split, with several rainbows, smallmouth bass, a few landlocked salmon, and a couple chubs (Thoreau says chivin!) in the mix. Oh, and one teeny, tiny bluegill.

> "What a piece of wonder a river is."
> —*Henry David Thoreau*

How have the rivers and streams held up?

In short, the water quality in these blue-ribbon streams is generally excellent. Thanks to the Clean Water Act and diligent efforts of Trout Unlimited and state fish-and-wildlife agencies, the famous waters I visited are in pretty good shape. Not always pristine, but if they can support trout, then they are better than many other waters. This trip was testament to how important our environmental laws have been in restoring and maintaining good water quality and trout habitat.

This tiny bluegill took a nymph dropper on that unknown pond in the Adirondacks.

The White River near Bethel, Vermont, is slowly recovering from the devastation from the floods from Hurricane Irene in 2011.

Development, limited access, and crowding can be problems, especially in New York, Pennsylvania, and Wisconsin. But I was pleasantly surprised by how much quality trout water is out there and easily accessible. Looking to the future, my biggest worry is warming temperatures and extreme weather events from climate change. We are already seeing changes in seasonal migrations, behavior, spawning, and fish populations because of warmer water and earlier springs and later falls. I hope the trout and our fisheries agencies can adapt to the new reality.

What was the best part of the adventure overall?

You mean other than that little bluegill I caught in the Adirondacks?

The Storied Waters journey was better than I ever imagined it would be. Going to all these different places, one after another, in a single journey tested my fly-fishing skills every day. Great fishing, great people, some unexpected adventures, plenty of personal and professional challenges, and so many precious memories. And yet, the totality was so much more than the words and pictures in this book.

When I conceived this trip, I wanted to see these extraordinary places through the eyes of the great writers who had a special attachment to them and who brought them alive in their stories. I wanted to rekindle interest in those writers who have fallen from our collective consciousness over the years and bring them to life for a new generation of readers.

The author swings a wet fly/nymph combo in a pool in the Diamond River gorge in New Hampshire.

And the best part? Easily all the warm and wonderful people who welcomed me into their world and helped me along the way. I was overwhelmed with generosity and good-will at every turn. I made wonderful new friends who share my interest in fly fishing, literature, nature, good ale, and protecting our environment. I raise my glass to every-one who helped make the Storied Waters tour such a memorable adventure!

A few words from the closing of *The Philosophical Fisherman* (1969) by Vermont's own Harold Blaisdell sum up my own feelings about this journey:

> After the day is over he'll go back to . . . kidding himself as usual that whenever he raises a trout to his fly he has done something noteworthy. At the same time, he will know the truth: he is mortal, ephemeral and of little consequence unto all but himself. And, no matter how puny and contrived, he will not be ashamed of his efforts to make something of his nothingness.

Bibliography

Arlen, Alice. *She Took to the Woods- Biography of Louise Dickinson Rich.* Rockport, ME: Down East Books, 2000.

Atherton, John. *The Fly and the Fish.* Mineola, NY: Dover Publications, 1951.

Baker, Carlos. *Ernest Hemingway: A Life Story.* New York: Charles Scribner's Sons, 1969.

Baughman, Michael. *A River Seen Right.* New York: Lyons & Burford, 1995.

Bergman, Ray. *Trout.* 1938; reprints, New York: Alfred A. Knopf, 1945, 1952; New York: Derrydale Press, 2000.

Berners, Dame Juliana. *A Treatyse of Fysshynge Wyth an Angle,* Book of St. Albans, 1496; reprint, North River Press, 1979.

Betters, Fran. *Ausable River Guide.* Wilmington, NY: Adirondack Sport Publications, 1999.

———. "Fish Are Smarter in the Adirondacks." Wilmington, NY: Adirondack Sports Publications, 1983.

———. *Fishing the Adirondacks.* Wilmington, NY: Adirondack Sports Publications, 1983.

Blaisdell, Harold F. *The Philosophical Fisherman.* Boston: Houghton Mifflin, 1969.

Burroughs, John. *In the Catskills,* 1910; reprint, Project Gutenberg EBook #14108, 2004.

———. *Pepacton,* 1881; reprint, Project Gutenberg EBook #7441, 2005.

Carter, Jimmy. *An Outdoor Journal.* New York: Bantam Books, 1988. New Edition: Fayetteville: University of Arkansas Press, 1994.

Doan, Daniel. *Indian Stream Republic.* Lebanon, NH: University Press of New England, 1997.

Duncan, David James. *The River Why.* New York: Bantam (Sierra Club Books), 1983.

Emerson, Ralph Waldo. "The Adirondacs," 1858. *The Complete Works of Ralph Waldo Emerson,* With a Biographical Introduction and Notes by Edward Waldo Emerson. Boston and New York: Houghton Mifflin, 1904; reprint, New York: Bartleby.com, 2015.

Enger, Jim. *The Incompleat Angler, A Fly Fishing Odyssey.* New Albany, OH: Countrysport Press, 1996.

Fleming, Ian. *The Spy Who Loved Me.* New York: Viking Press, 1962.

Flick, Art. *New Streamside Guide to Naturals and Their Imitations.* New York: Crown Publishers, 1969.

———. *Streamside Guide to Naturals and Their Imitations.* New York: G.P. Putnam's Sons, 1947.

Ford, Corey. *The Best of Corey Ford.* Edited by Jack Sampson. New York: Holt, Rinehart and Winston, 1975.

———. *The Corey Ford Sporting Treasury,* Compiled and Edited by Chuck Petrie. Wautoma, WI: Willow Creek Press, 1987.

———. *Minutes of the Lower Forty.* New York: Holt, Rinehart and Winston, 1962.

———. *Trout Tales & Other Angling Stories,* Compiled and Edited by Laurie Morrow. Gallatin Gateway, Montana: Wilderness Adventures Press, 1995.

———. *Uncle Perk's Jug.* New York: Holt, Rinehart and Winston, 1964.

———. *You Can Always Tell a Fisherman (But You Can't Tell Him Much).* New York: Henry Holt and Company, 1958.

Gierach, John. *A Fly Rod of Your Own.* New York: Simon and Schuster, 2017.

Gilmore, Tom. *Flyfisher's Guide to Pennsylvania.* Belgrade, MT: Wilderness Adventures Press, 2016.

Greenberg, Josh. *Rivers of Sand.* Guilford, CT: Lyons Press, 2014.

Harrison, Jim. *True North.* New York: Grove Press, 2004.

Hemingway, Ernest. "Big Two-Hearted River." *The Complete Short Stories of Ernest Hemingway.* New York: Scribner, 1987.

Hemingway, Ernest. *The Nick Adams Stories.* New York: Scribner, 1972.

Huber, J. Parker. *The Wildest Country, A Guide to Thoreau's Maine.* Boston: Appalachian Mountain Club, 1981; Second edition, 2008.

Humphreys, Joe. *On the Trout Stream with Joe Humphreys.* Harrisburg, PA: Stackpole Books, 1989.

Hunter, Julia and Earl Shettleworth. *Fly Rod Crosby: The Woman Who Marketed Maine.* Thomaston, ME: Tilbury House Publishers, 2003.

Irving, John. *Last Night in Twisted River.* New York: Random House, 2009.

Irving, Washington. "The Angler" and "Rip Van Winkle." *The Sketch-book of Geoffrey Crayon, Gent.,* Paris: A & W Galignani, 1825.

Knickerbocker, Deidrich [Washington Irving]. *A History of New York from the beginning of the world to the end of the Dutch dynasty.* New York: Inskeep & Bradford, 1809.

Leopold, Aldo. *A Sand County Almanac.* New York: Oxford University Press, 1949.

———. "Mixing Trout in Western Waters." *Transactions of the American Fisheries Society,* 47:3, pages 101-102, 1918.

Macdougall, Arthur. *Dud Dean and the Enchanted.* Falmouth, MA: Falmouth Publishing House, 1954.

———. *Remembering Dud Dean.* Compiled and introduced by Walter Macdougall. Camden, ME: Countrysport Press/Down East Books, 2001.

———. *The Sun Stood Still.* Bingham, ME: A.R. Macdougall, Jr., 1939.

———. *Where Flows the Kennebec.* New York: Coward McCann, 1947.

Maclean, Norman. *A River Runs Through It.* Chicago: University of Chicago Press, 1976.

MacQuarrie, Gordon. "Now, In June" *The Gordon MacQuarrie Sporting Treasury.* Compiled and Edited by Zack Taylor. Minocqua, WI: Willow Creek Press, 1998.

———. *Last Stories of the Old Duck Hunters Association.* Minocqua, WI: Willow Creek Press, 1990.

Marbury, Mary Orvis. *Favorite Flies and Their Histories.* 1892; reprint, Boston: Charles T. Branford Co., 1955.

Marinaro, Vincent C. *A Modern Dry-Fly Code.* New York: Crown Publishing, 1950.

McCafferty, Keith. *Cold Hearted River- A Sean Stranahan Mystery.* New York: Penguin Books, 2017.

Merwin, John. *The Battenkill.* New York: Lyons and Burford, 1993.

Mosher, Howard Frank. *A Stranger in the Kingdom.* New York: Doubleday, 1989.

———. *God's Kingdom.* New York: St. Martin's Press, 2015.

———. *Points North.* New York: St. Martin's Press, 2018.

———. *Waiting for Teddy Williams.* Boston: Houghton Mifflin, 2005.

———. *Walking to Gatlinburg.* New York: Crown Publishing, 2010.

———. *Where the Rivers Flow North.* New York, Viking Press, 1978.

Murray, William H.H. *Adventures in the Wilderness; or, Camp-Life in the Adirondacks.* Boston: Fields, Osgood and Company, 1869.

Noon, Jack. *Wintering with Amasa Ward.* Warner, NH: Moose Country Press, 2009.

Norris, Thaddeus. *The American Angler's Book.* Philadelphia: Porter & Coates, 1864.

Page, Margot. *Little Rivers: Tales of a Woman Angler.* New York, NY: Avon Books, 1995; New edition, Pawlet, VT: Three Winds Media, 2015.

Peterson, Harry. "Aldo Leopold's Contribution to Fly Fishing" (contains "Sick Trout Streams"). *The American Fly Fisher- Journal of the American Museum of Fly Fishing.* Vol. 29, Number 4, June 2003.

Rich, Louise Dickinson. *We Took to the Woods.* Philadelphia: J.P. Lippincot Company, 1942.

Romano, Robert. *The River King.* West River Media, 2017.

Rosenbauer, Tom. *The Orvis Guide to Hatch Strategies,* New York: Universe Publishing, 2017.

Schlett, James. *A Not Too Greatly Changed Eden.* Ithaca, NY: Cornell University Press, 2015.

Schwiebert, Ernest. *The Compleat Schwiebert.* Edited and with an introduction by John Merwin. New York: Truman Talley Books/Dutton, 1990.

———. *Trout.* New York: E.P. Dutton, 1978.

Shields, Daniel. *Fly Fishing Pennsylvania's Spring Creek.* Lemont, PA: DLS Enterprises, 2003.

Smith, Corinne Hosfeld. *Westward I Go Free: Tracing Thoreau's Last Journey.* Sheffield, VT: Green Frigate Books, 2012.

Smith, Edward Ware. *Upriver & Down: Stories from the Maine Woods.* New York: Holt, Rinehart and Winston, 1965.

Smith, O.W. *Trout Lore.* New York: Frederick A. Stokes Company, 1917.

Sparse Grey Hackle [Alfred Miller]. *Fishless Days, Angling Nights.* New York: Crown Publishers, 1971.

Tatham, David. *Winslow Homer in the Adirondacks.* Syracuse, NY: Syracuse University Press, 1996.

Thoreau, Henry David. *A Week on the Concord and Merrimack Rivers.* Boston: James Munroe and Company, 1849; reprints, Boston/Cambridge: Houghton Mifflin, 1906 and New York: Literary Classics of the United States, 1985.

———. *Excursions.* With Biographical Sketch by Ralph Waldo Emerson. Boston: Ticknor and Fields, 1863; reprint, Project Gutenberg E-Book #9846, 2006.

————. *The Maine Woods*. Boston, Ticknor and Fields, 1864; reprint, New York: Literary Classics of the United States, 1985.

————. *Walden; or, Life in the Woods*. Boston: Ticknor and Fields, 1864.

Traver, Robert [John D. Voelker]. *Anatomy of a Fisherman*. New York: McGraw-Hill, 1964.

————. *Anatomy of a Murder*. New York: St. Martin's Press, 1958.

————. *Danny and the Boys*. Cleveland and New York: The World Publishing Co.; reprint, Detroit: Wayne State University, 1987.

————. "Testament of a Fisherman." *Anatomy of a Fisherman*. New York: McGraw-Hill, 1964.

————. *Trout Madness*. New York: St. Martin's Press, 1960.

————. *Trout Magic*. New York: Crown Publishing, 1974.

Valla, Mike. *The Founding Flies*. Mechanicsburg, PA: Stackpole Books, 2013.

Van Wie, David, Philip Odence, Norm Richter, Bob Chamberlin, Ed Baldrige, David Klinges, and Bill Conway. *The Confluence- A Collection of Essays, Art & Tall Tales about Fly-fishing & Friendship*. Portsmouth, NH: Peter E. Randall Publisher, 2016.

Walton, Izaak, and Charles Cotton. *The Compleat Angler*, 1676; reprint, Major's Edition. New York: Thomas Y. Crowell & Co., not dated, 1880s.

Warner, Charles Dudley. *In the Wilderness*. Boston: Houghton Mifflin, 1878.

Wetherell, W.D. *Vermont River*. New York: Lyons & Burford, Publishers, 1984.

Zambello, Lou. *In Pursuit of Trophy Brook Trout*. Belgrade, MT: Wilderness Adventures Press, 2018.

————. *Fly Fishing Northern New England's Seasons*. Belgrade, MT: Wilderness Adventures Press, 2013.

————. *Flyfisher's Guide to New England*. Belgrade, MT: Wilderness Adventures Press, 2016.

Index